Health Alert Notice

For International Travelers Arriving in the United States

To The Traveler

Keep this card in your wallet or purse 6 weeks. If you become ill during this period, give this card to your physician and advise him of your recent travel outside the United States.

You may have been exposed to a communicable disease before arriving in the United States. If so, a knowledge of the possibility of exposure abroad will help your physician arrive more quickly at a diagnosis.

U.S. DEPARTMENT OF HEALTH, EDUCATION, AND WELFARE
PUBLIC HEALTH SERVICE
HEALTH SERVICES AND MENTAL HEALTH ADMINISTRATION
CENTER FOR DISEASE CONTROL
FOREIGN QUARANTINE PROGRAM
ATLANTA GEORGIA 30333

HSM 13.22 (CDC) Rev. 3-72

FEVER!

Other Books by John G. Fuller

The Gentlemen Conspirators

The Money Changers

Incident at Exeter

Interrupted Journey

The Day of St. Anthony's Fire

The Great Soul Trail

200,000,000 Guinea Pigs

FEVER!

The Hunt for a New Killer Virus

by

JOHN G. FULLER

READER'S DIGEST PRESS · NEW YORK · 1974
DISTRIBUTED BY E. P. DUTTON & CO., INC.

Library of Congress Cataloging in Publication Data

Fuller, John Grant, 1913–
    Fever! The hunt for a new killer virus.

    Bibliography: p.
    1. Virus diseases. 2. Medical geography—Nigeria.
I. Title. [DNLM: 1. Fever—Popular works. 2. Virology—
Popular works. WC195 F966f 1974]
RC114.5.F84   616.9'2   73-21818

Published simultaneously in Canada
by Clarke, Irwin & Company
Limited, Toronto and Vancouver
ISBN: 0-88349-012-9

"But things are now under control," Stone said. "We have the organism, and can continue to study it . . . we understand what's happening now in terms of mutations. That's the important thing. That we understand."

—From *The Andromeda Strain,* by Michael Crichton

FEVER!

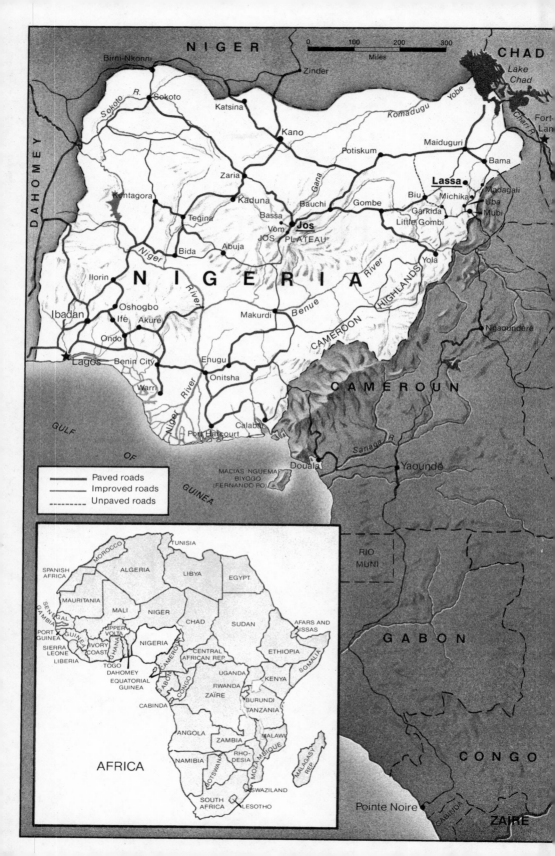

Author's Note

The hardest job in researching this story was to keep reminding myself that everything about it is true, documented, verified. The events are so strange, so shocking, so tragic that in
traveling by Land Rover to lonely mission stations from one
end of Nigeria to the other, to the maximum-security laboratory of the Center for Disease Control in Atlanta, to the virus
laboratories at Yale, and to scattered locations elsewhere to
interview the principals of the chronicle, I had the feeling
that this was some kind of science-fiction story unfolding, and
not reality.

Yet the virologists, the physicians, the missionaries, the
Nigerian tribesmen, the scientists, and all the others are very
real people of considerable courage and dedication, many of
whom died in the bizarre course of events. Their experiences
are actual, and they have not been decorated or elaborated
upon.

All the details in the story are carefully reconstructed from
long, painstaking interviews with those still living. In many
scenes the juxtaposition of several interviews made it possible
to create a rounded picture that could not have been achieved
with a single interview. In cases of minor differences of recall,
the information of the person most intimately connected with

the incident has been used. Reconstruction of dialog has purposely been kept to a minimum, unless vividly recalled.

Other information has been gathered from original medical and hospital records, medical journals, United Nations and government bulletins, and from correspondence, notes, and diaries of the people involved.

Detailed acknowledgments, of which there are many, will be found in the Bibliography at the end of the book.

John G. Fuller
Peterborough, New Hampshire
February 1973

Chapter One

Although she was used to being wakened at any time of night, the rap on the door shortly after three in the morning on Sunday, January 19, 1969, brought Laura Wine to the realization that the pain in her back was worse. With some effort she fumbled for her flashlight and shined it through the thick canopy of mosquito netting. Assured there were no African vipers lurking on the cement floor, she parted the netting, tapped her slippers upside down to dislodge any scorpions that might be inside, and put them on.

She called out that she would be at the hospital directly, then went about lighting the kerosene lantern on the table by the door. Her nurse's uniform was resting neatly on the chair by her bed, and she hurried into it. Upstairs in the attic the bats fluttered restively between the eaves and the corrugated tin roof.

Laura Wine was on the threshold of seventy, but most of her acquaintances thought she was barely out of her fifties. Smallish, with a broad motherly face framed by sandy hair, she moved with a sprightliness that belied her age, and the nagging pain in her lower back.

Picking up the lantern, she took her walking stick from against the door and stepped cautiously out on the stoop. The

African night was still and hot, and there were always vipers to contend with. They were afraid of light, however, afraid of the sound of the walking stick swishing through the grass, and would scurry quickly out of the way. Although she had spent more than sixty-five years of her life in Chicago and its suburbs, her four years in the Nigerian bush had removed her fear of these deadly snakes. But she had treated enough cases of snakebite to respect them, often plunging the antivenom directly into the vein of a swollen patient while blood was oozing from the victim's nose.

The small bush hospital was several hundred yards away, and a wheezing gasoline generator kept a few bare electric bulbs burning through the night. Miss Wine moved quickly along the dusty Land Rover ruts toward them, swinging her walking stick lightly in front of her like a blind man, while the lantern highlighted the dark outlines of the tamarind trees and the sandy drip castles of the termite hills, almost as tall as she was. The only sound was the monotonous drone of locusts. Miles to the east, bush fires burning on the table-flat savanna that ran to the Camaroon highlands cast an eerie glow.

In the obstetric ward, a low, squat mud-and-cement building in the Lassa hospital compound, a pregnant village woman was writhing in final labor pains, her body glistening with sweat. Beside her bed, speaking softly in tribal dialect, was the Nigerian night nurse waiting for Laura Wine to arrive.

The baby was born safely shortly after dawn, and Miss Wine made her way back to her house to get some rest. In one of the other three houses of the Lassa mission compound, Esther Hamer began preparing Sunday dinner with her own grown-and-canned vegetables, fresh yams, and some goat meat bought at the local market. Flies had clung to the meat like clumps of raisins, and it would have to be thoroughly cooked. Since 1952, when she had arrived fresh from the Western Reserve School of Nursing, Mrs. Hamer had learned how to handle the small wood-burning stove with great expertise.

She had come to Lassa with her husband, John, the only

doctor at the mission station. Each had had youthful dreams of becoming a medical missionary in Africa. They had known each other slightly at Manchester College in Indiana but never dated until they met again at Western Reserve, where John took his medical degree. When they arrived in Nigeria, carrying forty-four pounds of luggage apiece, they were too excited to be apprehensive, too dedicated to let the remoteness and loneliness of the western Sudan bother them.

The Sudan, that mysterious and ill-defined slice of Africa that runs from west to east across the wide belt of the continent below the Sahara, has always had a magnetic appeal for everyone: from commercial barons to explorers, missionaries, and slave traders. Lassa, a lonely herdsmen's village of thatched-roof mud huts with some 1,000 inhabitants, is typical of the remote towns of the northern Nigerian Sudan. Lying in the Yedseram river plain, at the base of the serrated and ominous ranges of the highlands that divide Nigeria from the Cameroons, Lassa is practically inaccessible for half the year when the rains come and the tire ruts turn to a hopeless pudding of mud. But it was here that the Church of the Brethren Mission stubbornly built its hospital in the 1920s to serve the Hausa, Fulani, Margi, Higi, and other tribesmen whom the mission passionately felt needed both conversion and medical care.

It was January now, and in place of the mud was dust—bitter, red, and everywhere. With it in the dry season came waves of cerebrospinal meningitis, striking the northern plateau savannas with a vicious impact, riding on the clouds of dust that rise with despairing persistence. At times, there would be up to 500 cases in the Lassa area alone.

Offsetting some of the discomfort of the dust was the harmattan, the dry, ghostly wind that sweeps down from the Sahara, bringing a gray canopy of talcum-fine desert smog that seems as thick as cement. But it is cooling, bringing some relief from temperatures that occasionally soar to over 120°. It is also somber and mystical. Pushing through the leaden cover of the harmattan, the sun—if it can be seen at all—looks like an Alka

Seltzer tablet floating in the froth of a vanilla milkshake. As the Hausas say: "It often happens that when the harmattan blows, madness seizes people."

With Sunday dinner under control, Esther Hamer joined her husband for the church services in the village and was surprised to discover that Laura Wine was not there. Even when she made her frequent deliveries in the obstetric ward in the middle of the night, Miss Wine was always at the service, struggling to sing her favorite hymns in Hausa or Margi, though she never could master either tribal tongue.

After church, the Hamers were relieved to see Miss Wine walking toward their house across the compound, exactly on schedule for her usual Sunday meal with them. While Laura Wine was independent, she was no recluse. She had never married, but some felt that she was married to her work, putting in so much voluntary overtime that her associates begged her to rest. Her work at Lassa was also the fulfillment of a dream— one that she had expressed years before while training in public health at the Universities of Chicago, Minnesota, and Northwestern. A history of tuberculosis had prevented her from practicing in Africa, however, and she had to content herself with heading the medical nursing program for the Oak Park school system near Chicago.

In addition, she had worked and taught at Bethany Hospital in Chicago's black ghetto. She was devoted to her work, and spunky. Once she beat off a mugger in the Chicago streets and went on to work unruffled. At the age of sixty-five she convinced the Church of the Brethren Board of Missions that her medical history was not a handicap and that she was just the right age to begin a career in Africa. She went over as an unpaid volunteer. Money was of little interest to her. In years past, she frequently was called up by the Internal Revenue Service because she habitually gave more than 30 percent of her modest income to charity—a fact that skeptical tax officials found hard to believe.

As Laura Wine crossed the compound, one thing was obvous to Esther Hamer: Miss Wine was not herself. She walked stiffly, not as erect as usual. When she greeted the Hamers' two preteenage daughters, home on vacation from missionary boarding school, she lacked her usual sparkle and smile.

Halfway through dinner, word came that a Margi tribeswoman had just delivered a baby alongside the dusty ruts that led to Lassa. As head of the obstetric section, Laura Wine rose from the table to go to the waiting Land Rover, but the pain in her back dropped her down into the chair again. Esther Hamer insisted on taking the assignment herself and urged Miss Wine to let the Land Rover drop her at her house.

Laura Wine accepted without protest—another most uncharacteristic thing for her. She got out of the Land Rover with difficulty, moved slowly into her house, pushed aside the cumbersome mosquito netting, and dropped on to the bed fully clothed. Neither she nor anyone else knew at the time that her malaise and backache would set into motion one of the most frightening episodes of modern medical history. It would reach from Africa to the United States in a series of unpredictable incidents that was to bring into action many of the leading medical scientists of the world.

By Sunday evening Laura Wine felt somewhat better. She showed up at the Lassa hospital in uniform, although Esther Hamer protested that she should rest. Nearly everyone, including Miss Wine, attributed her setback to a touch of arthritis, plus exhaustion from the long early-morning hours at the obstetric ward. She went about her chores with much of her usual vigor, mixing the powdered milk for orphan babies, bathing them, feeding them, changing their diapers. The hospital was busy, with the dry season and the harmattan at hand. The sixty-two-bed station was bulging with nearly one hundred patients—some of them sleeping on the floor. In the African tradition, the hospital served no food. The compound sparkled with the fires of the Hausa, Fulani, or Margi families—whether Muslim, Christian, or pagan—cooking food for their sick and bringing it carefully, tenderly into the wards.

Laura Wine left the hospital early that evening and walked back to her home. It was a tidy and comfortable house, brick-faced over hardened mud walls. Like the three other missionary homes on the compound, it looked like a small house in a Chicago suburb in contrast to the round mud huts in the village, with their conical thatched roofs. Inside, it was sparsely furnished with somber mission furniture.

In addition to the Hamers, she had Elsie and Von Hall as neighbors, two veteran missionaries who turned their efforts to community development. Prenatal care was also a specialty for Elsie Hall. She could be seen almost every day on her motor scooter, moving out to the small villages even deeper into the bush than Lassa, to bring information and care to the tribal mothers. With her husband away for a series of community development meetings and her young children home from boarding school, Elsie Hall was too preoccupied with her work to notice any change in Laura Wine's activity. Nor was there enough change for anyone to be concerned about at that time.

Change is constant in this land of awesome beauty and loneliness. Emergencies often spring up and have to be handled with whatever ingenuity one can muster. "Persons serving with the World Ministries Commission," states the policy manual of the Church of the Brethren Board of Missions, "are inevitably liable to be involved in situations of risk. These hazards cannot be lightly evaded, and considerations of personal safety will not likely be the determining factor in making their decisions."

In the remote northeastern corner of Nigeria where Lassa sits, turmoil has died down considerably since the British—sometimes ruthlessly and sometimes benevolently—wiped out the Fulani slave raiders of the nineteenth century. Scars from these slave raids remain in the memories of the Higi tribesmen in the remote mountain villages of the Cameroon highlands. Many are still hostile, fearing to come down to the savanna and keeping poison darts or arrows in readiness. Only a few years ago, a British district officer wandered too far in the highlands and was found screaming and insane with wounds from poison darts. But this sort of incident is rare, a defensive reaction by tribesmen who make no distinction between the former British colonials and the Fulani slave raiders.

There were British colonial officials who claimed that all Africans were idiotic and worthless, just as there were Africans who claimed that all the British were ruthless and cruel. The truth lay somewhere in between. The early missionaries, blinded by their fanatical passion to convert, often were without regard for the customs and culture of a region rich in history. But the wise colonial official would go to them for the most authentic information on the tribal people, because they were involved in more than religion. Politics and social conditions were a part of their lives as well. Up to the 1960s, all but a fraction of the schools in Nigeria were operated by the missions with only token government support.

Paul Bohannan, in his book *Africa and Africans,* writes:

> Missionaries are very often blamed because they destroyed and misunderstood and so they did. But so did everybody else. And missionaries are the only people who *built* below an institutional level. In many cases, I do not myself like what they built. That is beside the point. They did build, and are still building. Many of them are in even closer touch with citizens of new nations than they were with the colonized people of the first part of the twentieth century.

There is little doubt that the early Protestant missionaries planned their strategy like military generals in a battle against both Muslims and Catholics. The competition was fierce, with the Muslims having an edge because their dogma required less cultural change than that of the Christians.

In the present day, in Lassa and elsewhere in Africa, the intelligent missionary is trying to work himself out of a job. Because of missionary training, Nigerians are moving into more responsible positions in the hospitals and dispensaries. Schools are being staffed by Nigerians and turned over to the government in increasing numbers. The missions have considerably matured, and so have the Africans.

Life at the Lassa mission in 1969 was almost placid, though strained and pinched by the brutalities of the civil war raging in southern Nigeria below the Benue River.* Supplies were skimpy in the stores at Jos, a two-day drive away over rough and punishing roads. Provisions had to be piled high in the Land Rover and had to last for many months.

But there were gardens; each of the missionaries had his own. Laura Wine worked hard in hers, in spite of the frequent appearance of spitting cobras. There were also lush fruits that grew with ease and abundance: oranges, tangerines, grapefruit, lemons, limes, guavas, mangoes. The meats at the local market were acceptable, in spite of the flies and the wartime scarcity: mutton, scrawny beef, goat, some pork. On rare occasions there was wild baboon meat, python, crocodile tail, even lizard. In the dry season came the burning of the bush. Village youngsters armed with clubs would move out to the deeper savanna, set fire to the tinder-dry grass, wait on the edges for the rats to rush out in panic, club them, and take them to their compounds and the cooking fires. Here the hair would be burned off, the carcass skinned, and either spitted or boiled or fried with okra in peanut oil. The meat would taste not unlike chicken, with a peculiar sweetness. Ninety percent of the pro-

---

* There was bloodshed and starvation on both sides, with the Ibos in their newly declared state of Biafra (there has been no nation by that name before or since; the name was borrowed from the Bight of Biafra) creating a massive publicity program through a Swiss public relations firm to try to convince the world that the suffering was exclusively theirs. The war had its roots in newly discovered offshore oil. The issue was whether one state could claim it in a military coup and leave the rest of Nigeria without its benefits. The result was a national tragedy for both the Nigerian government and the insurgents. Many new facts were just emerging when the author was in Nigeria.

tein diet of the tribesmen is reported to come from rats. The missionaries also eat it with no qualms whatever.

At mealtime at the mission houses there was always grace, short and simple: "Our kind Father in heaven, we give Thee thanks for this food, and pray that Thou will bless it for our use in Thy service. Amen."

With all its secular and medical problems, the mission always remained close to the cause that had brought its people into this strange country, so many thousands of miles away from their homeland.

On Monday at 6:30 A.M. Laura Wine joined the dozen or so nurses and attendants of the hospital staff for the regular morning service. It was held in the hospital storeroom, where rough wood benches lined the wall of the dark and musty room. The service began, as usual, with a scripture reading in Hausa by the soft and mellifluous voice of Ngamariju Mamza, who was not only the supervisor of the Nigerian nursing staff but also pastor of the Lardin Gabas Church in Lassa.

While she yearned for the service to be in English, Laura Wine could sense the devotion of the Nigerians as they prayed and sang hymns in their tribal tongue. Mamza, whose smile and ebony face were as infectious as his warm voice, prayed and read with a conviction that transcended the language barrier. Miss Wine often commented that she understood him as if he spoke in English. It was always a touching scene in the storeroom: the tiny congregation surrounded by cartons bearing the trademarks of various companies—Parke, Davis; Smith, Kline & French; Squibb; Lilly; and others—while the staff implored its Savior for guidance in the work to follow that day.

The service ended with a brief report—in English—about the activities of the night. There were births, deaths, and sudden crises to consider as the conditions of the patients were reviewed.

Immediately afterward, Laura Wine went to the mission

shortwave radio in the hospital office, where she took her turn monitoring and reporting the news and information bulletins from the ten different mission stations of the Church of the Brethren scattered throughout the bush in northeast Nigeria. The self-built Heathkit radio served as a lifeline for the lonely mission outposts—the only link with the outside world in Lassa for six months of the year. Each morning the radio routine began with a Bible reading from the main mission base in Garkida. Then, after a series of general bulletins, each station would come on in round-robin fashion for its own communications. Though reception was scratchy, the communication was adequate.

Laura Wine handled the radio well, but her voice was noticeably weaker on this Monday morning as she enunciated the usual "Brethren Lassa, calling Brethren Jos. Over to Jos," followed by a wide variety of special messages. She completed the routine with some effort, then joined Esther Hamer in the drug supply room to fill prescriptions for the various wards. It wasn't long, however, before Miss Wine mentioned that she thought she had a sore throat, and Esther Hamer insisted that her husband should check it out.

Dr. John Hamer, like his wife Esther, was quiet, modest, almost diffident. He had had his own problems with schistosomiasis, the snail fever that lurks in practically every sluggish river or pond in Africa. For the tribesman, the disease is endemic and constant. For the missionary, it is acute, painful, and sometimes fatal. The victim can get the disease simply by putting a hand or foot in the water. Cercariae, an early development stage of the liver flukes, hosted by fresh-water snails, seep through the pores of sound and healthy skin and make their way to the liver. With an antibiotic named stibophen it is now possible to keep the disease under control. John Hamer, pale but youthful-looking with well-chiseled features, took the disease in his stride, as he and his wife did with all the hardships and inconveniences of their long tour at Lassa. The same was true of the other missionaries at the station: they accepted the stress as a matter of course, the most acute being the necessity of sending even first-grade children off to the missionary boarding school at Jos, 400 miles away. When the Lassa mission station was founded in the 1920s, an incredulous British officer asked the first Church of the Brethren missionaries: "Why on earth have you chosen this place?" The reply was: "Because there are people here."

There were people there, and they were being well served by the hard-pressed staff, which habitually ignored its own illnesses, often to the extent of considerable physical damage. Laura Wine disliked above all to inconvenience anyone else, and it was only the insistence of the Hamers that persuaded her to submit to a medical examination.

But there was very little for Dr. Hamer to note. Her throat looked normal. There was no lymphadenopathy or edema, no gray or white membrane discernible in the throat. Her temperature was normal. Her complaint, however, was a little strange. The soreness was above and behind the soft palate, an atypical symptom. Dr. Hamer told her to rest and take a simple course of aspirin. She protested vigorously, saying she had some patients to prepare for discharge and wanted to come back after breakfast. Reluctantly the doctor agreed, making her promise to go home and rest immediately afterward.

Laura Wine walked home for breakfast, then back to the hospital again to take care of her patients. But she did keep her promise to rest. A brief visit that noon revealed nothing new to John Hamer, but he put her back in bed on the strength of the persistent soreness in her throat.

Diagnosis in the tropics is difficult at best. There are many strange conditions that require elaborate tests and sophisticated laboratories—which are simply not available. There is also a spectrum of diseases that doctors in the temperate zones don't often have to contend with. In the western Sudan there is always the threat of malaria. If a missionary fails to take his quota of chloroquine or Aralen in any single week, there is no question that he will come down with malaria. Even those who are conscientious in taking their preventive pills can be stricken with it, though usually in a milder form. By going to bed and increasing the dosage of the antimalarial drug, a patient can reduce the attack to the proportions of a light case of flu. The common practice of the tropical doctor is to give any noncrisis condition forty-eight hours or so to let the symptoms either develop more fully or disappear.

On Monday evening Esther Hamer brought some light food over for Miss Wine, and John Hamer again examined her. He reacted sharply to a new condition that had emerged: there were several blisters on the front portion of the neck. But the chances of anything illuminating coming from the symptom were dispelled when Miss Wine said she had burned herself with a hot water bottle earlier in the day in an attempt to alleviate the pain in her throat.

At 6:15 Tuesday morning Dr. Hamer again stopped by. Miss Wine seemed considerably worse. She told the doctor that she could hardly swallow, that the pain was still deep behind the soft palate. He looked at her throat. For the first time something specific was appearing. Far in the back of her throat was a group of yellowish ulcers with halos around them. At first Dr. Hamer thought they might be simply cankersores, more technically known as stomati. But they were markedly different from any he had seen. There were also some on the inside of each cheek, on the posterior buccal mucosa. She seemed more nervous than usual, and her temperature had now climbed to just over 100°.

John Hamer lost no time in prescribing procaine penicillin, which was available in the hospital's supply room. Almost automatically when a patient develops a fever in Lassa, he is put on the antimalarial choloroquine phosphate. This was so done.

There was still no reason for alarm. Hamer had seen a considerable number of strep throats in the area, and even though Miss Wine's throat lesions were a bit unusual, he was confident that she would respond to the penicillin. If the condition persisted, he could also prescribe streptomycin, which teamed up very well with penicillin in such cases. Aside from her uncharacteristic nervousness, Miss Wine did not seem in too much discomfort and certainly showed no signs of being critically ill.

Meanwhile, life went on as usual in the village and in the hospital. John and Esther Hamer took over the chores of the obstetric ward, along with their other duties. In additon to the cases of cerebrospinal meningitis, which came with the advent of the dry season, there were snakebites (mostly viper or spitting cobra, and mostly critical), pneumonia (on the increase because of the dust), wounds from occasional fights, and hernias (a constant complaint among those who lifted heavy loads). For some reason, the Fulani tribesmen had an inordinate tendency toward hydroceles, necessitating the amputation of swollen testicles, which sometimes hung down to the knees and weighed up to sixty pounds.

At least John Hamer could be thankful that there was no massive wave of yellow fever, which had raised such havoc on occasion in the past. Nor was there any new evidence of the unidentified "African fever," which had mystified tropical doctors from the time the white man first came to Africa. The little hospital at Lassa was not equipped for such emergencies.

It did, however, have a comfortable supply of pharmaceuticals, shipped in during the dry season before the rains cut off the village from the rest of the world. There were antimalarials, both in capsules and in intravenous form for those who were seized with vomiting and could not hold the oral dosage down. There was stibophen for the schistosomiasis so widespread in the area, and the usual group of broad-spectrum antibiotics and other common drugs, including tranquilizers. The perishables—kept in a small kerosene refrigerator—were dominated by both specific and general antivenom for snakebites. A rough-hewn operating room was equipped for major surgery, but the ubiquitous and ineradicable bats shook down dust and dirt from the eaves and made sterile conditions difficult. Twice a year a young tribesman would go up to the attic and club 300 or 400 bats to death. In spite of the conditions, many lifesaving operations were performed there.

Along with the crowded medical schedule, there was evangelical and service work. In the latter, the missionaries worked ecumenically with Muslims, pagans, and Christians to dig cement wells, to teach practical skills, and to improve farming, housing, and sanitary conditions.

The Church of the Brethren, born out of German Baptists and active in America since colonial times, supports its own missionaries from its headquarters in Elgin, Illinois. Other missions prominent in the region are the Sudan Interior Mission, a highly active group of varied Protestant denominations (including British and Canadian churches) that emphasizes fundamental adherence to the tenets of the Bible; the Sudan United Mission, another interdenominational group with heavy Danish, British, American, and Swiss participation; and various Catholic missions.

For an outsider, it is hard to define the collective personality of the African missionaries. There is little doubt that they are a breed unto themselves. They are often somber, and yet a constant sense of humor leaks through at unexpected times. They are often obsessional and proselytizing, yet they show remarkable restraint in not forcing their views openly on the unsuspecting visitor. They can be dull and boring and suffused with an overbearing plainness, yet many are erudite and sophisticated. Physically there is a predominent paleness and wanness of complexion, an undefinable pallor that may result from subclinical tropical disease or from what could be a masochistic compulsion to overwork. They are selfless to a degree that is hard to conceive—yet the self-denial is there and it is genuine.

The cliché "missionary zeal" is a reality to them. Almost without exception, they feel they have been individually called upon to serve their particular theologic God. They believe what they preach, and they believe it literally. Their inner faith may sometimes seem manic and overly euphoric, but its sincerity cannot be doubted. The extent of their works is reflected in the impressive hospitals, schools, dispensaries, and churches they have carved out of the deep bush.

There is a guarded edginess among the different missions, in spite of the very real attempts at ecumenical cooperation. One mission, for example, will grudgingly suggest that another mission refuses to give penicillin unless the patient sings a hymn first. Newer missionaries will tend to grumble against the uncompromising fundamentalism of the older ones, and will down a scotch or two with no qualms whatever. The Protestant groups will assume a tacit respect for the territorial imperative of a rival group, but the Catholics are said to move in wherever they please, and let the hymn books fall where they may. It is rumored that one Catholic priest said to a Protestant missionary: "We let you fellows go in and take the rough edges off. Then we go in and make them Christians."

The medical missionary, invariably with superb technical and scientific training, seems to live on two planes. Dr. John Hamer could slip effortlessly from a discussion of erythroblastosis or hemolytic anemia to his favorite Bible verses. When he examined Laura Wine on Wednesday, January 22, he was determined to try to get at the root of her illness, because there was no improvement and yet nothing specific to go on beyond the strange lesions in her throat. They were still there, with their bright yellow centers and brilliant erythematous halos. He took a blood smear and urine and stool specimens and went back to the hospital to check them.

Lassa was hardly equipped for exacting blood counts, and Dr. Hamer was forced to do it himself. He regretted that he was out of practice but went about it as best he could. If the leukocyte—or white blood cell—count were high, it would be evidence of a bacterial infection. Instead the count was on the low side, indicating a condition known as leukopenia. This was not of much help in diagnosis. It occurs in many diseases: typhoid, measles, influenza, dengue fever, many of the anemias,

and malaria. Alcohol or morphine could also bring it about, to
say nothing of lead, mercury, or arsenic poisoning. Some plate-
lets were seen in the blood—those tiny fragments from large
cells in the bone marrow that play a key role in blood coagulation. Their presence could indicate a blood dyscrasia—any one
of a number of pathologic blood disorders.

The urine test was likewise inconclusive. It was dark, but
there was no albumin present, which would have been a sign of
kidney problems, Bright's disease, or bladder infection. The
urine output, though, was a little disturbing. It was very low
and would have to be watched. It could be the result of the dry
season, and Dr. Hamer urged Laura Wine to take as many
fluids as she could.

She was helped in this by frequent visits from Elsie Hall
and Esther Hamer, who brought fruit drinks, Jello, and ice
cream, quietly urging her to drink and even spoonfeeding her.

By Wednesday evening Dr. Hamer found her temperature
had nudged up to over 101°, although her blood pressure and
pulse remained normal. But he was surprised to see a small
hemorrhagic mark on her left arm, just above the elbow. This
was something new, but he could find no explanation for it.

On Thursday the oozing ulcers in the throat had faded
somewhat, but there was swelling in the neck. Her temperature
had dropped slightly, but she was drowsy and extremely lethargic.

John Hamer admitted he was stumped. Nothing seemed to
add up to a clear clinical picture. There was no evidence of
meningitis, because swollen as it was the neck was not stiff. No
known tropical disease quite seemed to fit.

On Friday morning he got up before dawn and pored
through a back file of medical journals in the little hospital office. As the sun came up over the Cameroon mountain ranges,
he began to think more and more about the possibility of an
unusually stubborn virus. Laura Wine was not responding to
penicillin or streptomycin, another sign that a virus rather
than bacteria might be at work. And the leukocyte count re-

mained down, indicating that no army of white cells was assembling in the blood to fight bacteria. If immature white cells were present, this would indicate the body was working overtime in defense, equivalent to a nation losing a war and sending out fifteen- and sixteen-year-olds to replace its decimated regulars.

Dr. Hamer rose from his medical journals at 6:15 A.M. and walked to Miss Wine's house. He was surprised to find that she was a little brighter, and her temperature was at least not any higher. Encouraged, he went about his rounds at the hospital, checking and visiting over one hundred patients in the crowded wards. He finished before noon and came back again to her bedside.

But the mercurial progress of the disease had shifted again. She was sleepy and her speech was extremely difficult to understand. There seemed to be acute renal failure—a kidney shutdown. Her urine output had dwindled almost to zero. Her face would alternately flush and turn pale. She could barely swallow. Her mouth was dry and caked, looking like that of a patient who had been on broad-spectrum antibiotics for a month.

Again a new symptom appeared: a patch of discolored skin on her thigh, with minute, veinlike hemorrhages beneath the surface, called a macular and petechial rash.

Convinced of the gravity of the situation, Dr. Hamer decided he would have to move Miss Wine to the Sudan Interior Mission hospital at Jos as fast as possible. There was a larger, better-equipped laboratory there, with trained technicians. Further, there were more nurses for round-the-clock care, which was now obviously needed.

The shortwave radio round robin was not available until 5 P.M. Friday, and Dr. Hamer waited impatiently. Because of the civil war in Nigeria, both radio communications and air flights were under severe government restrictions. Civilian craft were permitted to make only the most urgent emergency flights, and those at specified times and to specified airstrips. The nearest airstrip was at Mubi, some fifty miles away. There was a question of whether it was even operating. Two of the large missionary groups, the Sudan Interior Mission and the Sudan United Mission, had their own airplanes, both based in Jos. The Church of the Brethren Mission, with administrative posts in Jos and the more remote village of Garkida, had no planes or pilots but could lease emergency flights from one of the other two missions if a plane were available. Strangely enough, it was often more economical to fly to the crude airstrips near the lonely missionary stations than to drive there in a Land Rover. Some posts had an airline distance of 200 miles and an overland route of six or seven times that. Cost figures showed that a Piper Comanche could be operated at 13 cents a mile, which was fully competitive with a Land Rover or car.

Dr. Hamer went to the five-kilowatt Lister diesel generator promptly at five and turned it on. It was of World War II surplus vintage, but it was serviceable and could usually be relied on.

The reception on the Heathkit was not good that evening. He repeated over and over again: "Brethren Lassa calling Brethren Jos . . . Brethren Lassa calling Brethren Jos. Come in, please. Come in . . ." Finally, a weak voice from the Church of the Brethren office in Jos came over the 400-mile distance, but it was barely discernible. Hamer repeated his message five or six times in the hope that it would be understood: Could Brethren Jos contact either the Sudan Interior Mission or the Sudan United Mission for a plane for the next morning, along with a stretcher and a nurse? The readback was unintelligible, and he wondered whether his message got through at all.

It was frustrating and distressing, especially when he found Laura Wine's condition getting rapidly worse. Her lips and mouth were cracked and dry, and her dehydration was critical. With a wheelchair and the help of his wife and Elsie Hall, he pushed her to the hospital compound, the chair sticking and bumping in the dusty ruts. In a small room behind the hospital office, they prepared a bed that could be raised and lowered and propped her up at an angle known as Fowler's position. An intravenous stand and bottle were wheeled in, and a solution of saline-free commercial dextrose was introduced into her veins. Dr. Hamer and two of the staff took turns on two- to three-hour shifts around the clock during the night.

There was no question in his mind now that this would be a close race with death, even if his message about the plane did get through. Laura Wine was in a situation of acute renal failure—etiology, or source, unknown—and her kidneys might shut down altogether. In addition, the cumulative evidence pointed toward a serious, even deadly virus infection. But, what kind? Where did it come from? And what could be done to combat it?

Resting in the hospital office, Dr. Hamer prayed that a confirmation of the plane would come over the radio in the morning, and that Laura Wine would be able to survive until they could get more extensive diagnostic and medical care at the larger hospital.

Chapter Two

Before the age of the jet, which can whisk thousands of people across the oceans in less time than it takes a traveler to sense the slightest discomfort from a deadly tropical fever, research on tropical diseases progressed at a steady, if erratic, pace. Major conquests had been made, of course, against viruses and bacteria. Over one hundred laboratory scientists and technicians had in fact died in the line of duty from the early days of virus research alone.

But the jet age brought with it sudden and dramatic problems of a new character. There was a concern among the medical profession about a whole new spectrum of diseases just emerging on the scene, many of which had been simmering for decades, undiagnosed, some of them viciously lethal, some entirely unknown and baffling.

Nearly five years before Laura Wine took to her net-covered bed in Nigeria, Dr. John Frame of the Division of Tropical Medicine at Columbia University had been giving considerable thought to this new set of conditions. He was concerned about how little the medical world actually knew about the strange fevers that could now be transported to the United States and elsewhere in a matter of hours.

Frame, a lean, graying, distinguished-looking man who

wears a vest with his conservatively cut suits, was particularly puzzled about a number of cases he had examined among the children of missionaries when they returned to the states after a tour of duty in West Africa. In several instances the children had been stricken with an unknown virus, had come down with a high fever, and had gone into severe convulsions, resulting in permanent brain damage. He was also mystified by constant reports of unidentified fevers, many of which had been fatal, among his adult missionary patients.

In seventeen years of practice with returning missionaries, Frame had become suspicious of clinical diagnoses of malaria, typhus, and typhoid fever in many of the medical histories.

One day in 1965, soon after his appointment at Columbia, Frame talked this over with Dr. Harold Brown, the head of his department. Brown promptly suggested he talk further with Roger Williams, a Columbia entomologist who had helped to set up a new virus laboratory at Nigeria's University of Ibadan. Williams in turn recommended that Frame get in touch with Dr. Wilbur Downs, head of the Yale Arbovirus Research Unit in New Haven.

Arboviruses are simply viruses that are transmitted by insects—arthropods. The name "arthroviruses" was considered too clumsy, and the shortened form came into scientific use.

Wil Downs, as he is called, has an impressive list of credentials, from his medical degrees from Cornell and Johns Hopkins through his international work with Yale, the Rockefeller Foundation, and the National Academy of Sciences Environmental Studies Board. Bronzed from his field studies and frequent fishing trips, he wears a clipped mustache and tweed jackets with ease and comfort. His colleagues call him one of the world's great naturalists, entomologists, pathologists, and ornithologists—an ungrudging portrait that reflects the proportions of a Renaissance man. But more important to his colleagues are his kindness and good humor, both of which are essential in establishing morale in a laboratory where death can spring at any moment from a broken test tube or a careless scalpel. Downs and his staff at Yale had been thinking along lines similar to those of John Frame at Columbia. Yellow fever and malaria were endemic in large sections of Africa and South America but would often lie dormant and undiagnosed until a major outbreak occurred and ravaged a wide geographic area. There were provocative and unanswered questions about these fevers, and about many newly emerging viruses that were commanding serious attention.

Frame's ideas appealed to the researchers at Yale, and an agreement was made for Frame to send along blood serum specimens from returning missionaries who had reported unusual fevers in their past. Yale would analyze and catalog them, and build up a data bank that might reveal fresh information on both known and unknown viruses. It was a fairly simple program and, at the time, not of any startling interest. By 1966 Frame had managed to gather some twenty-eight blood specimens from his missionaries. Finding this pace a little slow, he increased his harvesting of missionary blood, taking specimens from every missionary returning from Africa, whether he had a history of a tropical fever or not.

A few interesting facts began to emerge, but they were not earthshaking. Of sixty-one missionary patients who reported histories of fever, nearly half revealed antibodies to known arboviruses, indicating that at some time in the past they had been stricken with insect-carried viruses of greater or lesser strength.

By the summer of 1968 Frame had decided to step up his program again. He asked Dr. Jeanette Troup, who was going back to the Sudan Interior Mission hospital on the Jos plateau in Nigeria, to draw blood from unusual fever patients there every week for an entire month. She left for Africa with the promise to send the samples along as soon as they became available, and Yale agreed to process them promptly.

The interest in the unknown areas of virology at Yale and Columbia was matched by that of the Center for Disease Control

(CDC) of the U.S. Public Health Service in Atlanta, Georgia. For some time Dr. David Sencer, director of the center, had been growing progressively alarmed about the newly emerging diseases in both man and animal, many of which were ill-defined and some of which were ominous in their implications.

Among the known diseases, he noted an increase in malaria cases, which had jumped since 1966 to more than 4,000 per year, much of it traceable to returning Vietnam servicemen. And with Wil Downs at Yale he shared a growing concern about the arbovirus diseases such as Eastern, Western, and St. Louis encephalitis, which had long been rampant in the United States. But two emerging viruses, California encephalitis and Venezuelan equine encephalitis, were of particular interest because of the potential public health hazard.

California encephalitis was scattered lightly throughout the States, drawing most attention in the Midwest, where it struck the central nervous system most dramatically in victims under fifteen years of age. Carried by *Aedes* mosquitoes, which feed on wild rodents that host the virus, the disease had been around since the 1940s. But in the 1960s its impact and medical importance surged with the growing recognition by doctors of its dangers.

Venezuelan equine encephalitis had been around for several decades too. But giant new outbreaks between 1962 and 1970 in South America and Mexico brought the violent and explosive disease to U.S. borders, where its pattern of progression threatened the entire South from Florida to Texas. Again the death rates have been highest among children, who show a more severe involvement of the central nervous system than adults.

Most critical in the eyes of both Yale and the CDC in Atlanta was a newly recognized complex of severe hemorrhagic diseases caused by LCM viruses. The initials come from the medical term "lymphocytic choriomeningitis." The new viruses were emerging into such prominence that a whole new classification was proposed: arenaviruses. What distinguished the new group from arboviruses was that they were borne by rodents, not insects. Ultrasliced, these viruses reveal under the electron microscope fine, sandlike granules in their makeup.

Argentinean hemorrhagic fever was among the first of the arenavirus group to receive attention from the virologists. It was not even recognized until 1955, and details of its background are still clouded. The fever is caused by an agent known as the Junin virus.

Yellow fever, with a fatality rate of between 5 and 10 percent, is a dread disease of great concern. But the Junin virus of Argentine hermorrhagic fever, rising from the cornfields near Buenos Aires, buffeted workers with a mortality rate of 20 percent, double that of yellow fever. The virus, excreted in the urine of wild, chronically infected rodents, would mix with the dust, creating a fine, lethal aerosol to be inhaled by the harvesters as they worked.

An even higher death rate prevailed in 1963, when Bolivian hemorrhagic fever came into prominence. Infected wild rats spread their urine into the dust around the village of San Joaquin, Bolivia, bearing a virus similar to the Junin, called Machupo. Ironically, the wave of rats that swamped the village resulted from the decimation of the cat population of the town. It is believed that a vigorous DDT campaign to rid the area of insects caused severe neurological disorders among the cats. As they died, the rats moved in. More recently another village was stricken, and the threat of the virus moving northward in the jet age remains serious.

One of the most dramatic new viruses came to light for the first time in 1967. It sprang without warning from the tissues of African green monkeys and turned out to be strikingly different from any other virus particle known to man. Alarmingly, it broke out not in Africa but in the town of Marburg, Germany—thousands of miles away from Uganda, the home of the monkeys. Primary victims of the disease suffered from an incredible death rate of nearly 30 percent. Seven of twenty-five laboratory research workers were felled. Beyond that, six secondary cases resulted from the accidental slip of a hypodermic needle used on the sick victims, or from contact with their tissues or blood.

The monkeys had been imported to Germany and Yugoslavia for biomedical research and vaccine production. Their kidneys provide cell lines that can be maintained in cultures for critical medical studies throughout the world. The United States alone requires some 12,000 African green monkeys a year to keep up with research demands.

The disease—now called Marburg disease in dubious honor of the town where it broke out—strikes its victims with a vengeance after incubating only four to seven days. First come high fever, headache, vomiting, diarrhea, and conjunctivitis. These are quickly followed by the blooming of skin eruptions, bleeding from the nose and intestines, and the ravaging of the liver, kidneys, and lymphoid tissues.

In some cases the Marburg virus lies dormant. One patient passed it along to his wife nearly ninety days after the onset of the disease. As distressing as this was, it at least suggested to pathologists that this might well be the way in which the virus is spread among monkeys in nature. But the green monkeys themselves remain aloof to the agony they transport to man. They show no symptoms at all. The disease has baffled and mystified all the epidemiologists who have tackled it, and the potential of disastrous focal outbreaks remains.

"There is definitely a danger of importing an increasing amount of disease," Dr. David Sencer told a reporter. "It's a symptom of the fact that the world is growing smaller."

Dr. Wilbur Downs of Yale shares this sentiment and goes a step further. "The Marburg virus could just as easily have gone to Chicago as to Germany," he says. "In these times, the unpredictability of viruses creates a situation which is as delicate as a hand grenade with the pin pulled. The only answer is constant vigilance."

The literature of the Center for Disease Control points out

that every day thousands of American citizens and foreign visitors enter this country. "About one in five," says a recent bulletin, "comes from a country where smallpox, cholera, plague, or yellow fever still exists. An international traveler incubating a disease could circle the globe and touch down in many areas and expose many people before developing recognizable symptoms."

In light of the bizarre incidents that were intensifying in the remote mission station of Lassa, Nigeria, in mid-January 1969, it would prove to be a particularly ominous warning.

All night long, as 300 cc of dextrose dripped into her veins, Laura Wine's condition remained steady, but she was desperately weak. The Hamers and the two staff members were red-eyed and exhausted from a night of fitful sleep and watching.

Quietly, John Hamer closed the door to the little room off the hospital office and went to the radio. He did not want Laura Wine to overhear his plans, because she had protested through the last few days that she did not want to leave Lassa, no matter what the circumstances. Her fear of being a burden was almost obsessional, despite her sickness.

Elsie Hall joined Dr. Hamer at the radio desk. Again, the contact was miserable. But scattered words came through, fragmentary sentences. The messages of the previous evening had definitely been garbled. There was a flight of the Sudan United Mission, the Christian Reformed Church operation, but it was scheduled to go to Biu, more than 150 miles from Lassa. To meet the plane would require a brutal drive over devastatingly rough roads. It was difficult enough to conceive that Laura Wine could survive the fifty miles to the Mubi airstrip. The day was already scorching, and the temperature was almost certain to rise to 115° in the shade in spite of the harmattan cover. Even with the intravenous injection, Miss Wine's dehydration was more marked than ever.

John Hamer, in the stifling hospital office, was sweating as he tried to explain the situation over the radio again. Enough information came through from Jos to indicate that the Sudan United Mission plane had been planning to bring a missionary dentist to Biu, but that it would shift plans and drop him at Mubi instead. It would arrive at 10 A.M., if the harmattan cover didn't block visibility. Even major airports in Nigeria are shut down for days when the harmattan closes in. Pilots are often unable to see their own wing tips as they fly through it. None of the small airstrips such as Mubi has a control tower or radio beacon. Instruments are practically useless.

At last the flight was confirmed. Not a moment too soon, because the radio signal broke into hopeless hash immediately afterward—before Dr. Hamer was able to request additional oxygen bottles and a stretcher. This was serious. Laura Wine was already showing signs of cerebral anoxia, where not enough oxygen reaches the brain. The amount of oxygen on hand in the single bottle at Lassa was pitifully small.

The mission's Land Rover was already gassed up and waiting outside in the hospital compound when John Hamer and Elsie Hall went to prepare Miss Wine for the trip. She was sleeping when they entered the room; her face and neck were swollen and her lips more cracked and dry than ever. Dr. Hamer woke her gently, and she opened her eyes. She was coherent enough and recognized both of them, putting her hand out and holding Elsie Hall's arm. She had great difficulty in speaking, tried to protest when they told her of the trip, but dropped back in exhaustion after a few words. She showed strong signs of dyspnea—extreme difficulty in breathing.

Gently, but with considerable effort, they slid her off the bed and into the wheelchair. Then, as they rolled her through the radio room toward the front door, she convulsed. Her skin suddenly began turning blue, a condition called cyanosis. There was not enough oxygen getting to the blood. Within seconds Dr. Hamer brought the oxygen mask to her face, and almost as quickly she recovered.

The back section of the waiting Land Rover was cleared, and a mattress was placed on the floor. The vehicle did not make the best of ambulances. Esther Hamer, who would join her husband on the trip, came running up just as they were ready to put Miss Wine into the Rover. She had been making arrangements with Elsie Hall to take care of their young daughters, age eight and ten, who were old enough to realize the seriousness of the crisis and the trip and young enough to be extremely apprehensive. She had tried, not quite successfully, to comfort them in a hurried good-by. Plans for getting them back to the missionary boarding school in Jos, where classes were to resume the next day, would simply have to wait.

Transferring Miss Wine from the wheelchair to the back of the Land Rover was awkward and difficult. As she was lifted from the chair, she went into convulsions again. Once more, Dr. Hamer clapped the oxygen mask over her nose and mouth, rapidly using up more of the precious supply. There were signs now of the beginning of cardiac failure, as well as kidney shutdown.

By 9:30 A.M. the jury-rig ambulance was ready. John Hamer jumped into the driver's seat; Esther squeezed into the back and gently supported Miss Wine in a half-reclining position. The temperature in Lassa was well over 100° now, but the windows of the Rover would have to be closed most of the time because of the acrid, stinging dust that coated everything with a thick, gray-red layer.

It is fourteen miles over incredibly rough dirt ruts to Michika, the first town on the gravel road that runs south to Mubi. There are two wide rivers to ford. Even in the dry season, the water can come up over the axles.

Sometimes, in unexpected places, a vehicle can sink in a river-bottom hole; water floods the engine and stalls it out. John Hamer drove as fast as he dared, trying to dodge the deep ruts and enormous potholes in the sandy tracks that led toward Michika. On each side the dry brown grass towered over them. At any speed, it was impossible to keep the Land Rover from pitching and yawing over the rough surface. In moments the interior was caked with dust. In the back, Esther Hamer and her patient tossed back and forth with the violent lurching.

Then, to Esther Hamer's horror, Laura Wine began convulsing again. She tried to hold the oxygen bottle and the mask to Miss Wine's face, but there was no way to support herself and the mask kept slipping off, spilling out the precious oxygen. She piled blankets against the metal sides in a feeble attempt to stop the punishment of the unpredictable slamming and jostling.

At best, it is an hour-and-a-half drive from Lassa to Mubi. John Hamer knew it was senseless to try to reduce that time, especially under the conditions in the back of the vehicle.

At the first river he cautiously shifted the car into four-wheel drive and crawled toward the edge of the water. Then, as he drove with infinite caution, the wheels churned through the water, leaving a wake as the Rover sank into the river mud up to the axles, rolling at times like a boat. The flat hood momentarily dipped down toward the water, as if to submerge, then leveled off. All four tires spun in place for a moment, then jerked forward. Near the far shore, the Rover began its climb out of the mud and onto the dusty stretch ahead.

By the time he had splashed across the second river, Hamer felt a sense of immeasurable relief. In back, Miss Wine had recovered from her third set of convulsions.

The crude ambulance emerged from the ruts and the tall savanna grass. Ahead was Michika, a welcome sight. From there the gravel road, euphemistically labeled Route 4, would have its share of ruts and potholes, but the speed could be increased up to forty or fifty miles an hour in stretches. Huts lined the route, tucked into individual compounds by walls of herringbone woven straw matting or rough mud brick. Barebreasted women could be seen pounding millet or carrying calabashes piled high with fruits or firewood on their heads. Hamer turned to the right, south toward Mubi and pushed the Land Rover into higher speed.

Within moments he was flagged down by the Nigerian national military police, edgy, alert, and trigger-happy in the war-time atmosphere. They were carrying Sten machine guns and didn't look at all hospitable.

It was a routine check. In addition to the military hazards, there were smugglers from the Cameroons on the other side of the mountains, constantly infiltrating into Nigeria. Practically every vehicle on Route 4 was stopped at one place or another. When the police learned about the missionary plane flight to the Mubi airstrip, they were surprised. Did the Hamers know that the strip was piled high with large oil drums, chunks of metal, and other junk to prevent any enemy planes from landing there?

John Hamer did not know. He could only push ahead at the fastest possible speed, because Laura Wine was going into another convulsion.

Ray Browneye, the missionary pilot for the Sudan United Mission, was blond, rugged, and athletic, an inveterate hunter who had once been gored by a wild buffalo. He was pleased to note that the harmattan was thin that morning. He went through his preflight checklist in his blue-and-white single-engine Piper Comanche, registered as 5N-ADT. Then he notified the tower at Jos that he was ready for takeoff.

As a tin-mining center of some 100,000 people, Jos had the rare privilege of both tower and radio control at its airport in the middle of the Jos plateau. Like all the missionary pilots in the area, from both the Sudan United and the Sudan Interior missions, Ray Browneye would check his rudder, elevators, magneto, and other preflight details, run up the engine to the specified RPMs, ease the throttle back, and bow his head in a brief vocal prayer. To the uninitiated passenger in the cockpit, this procedure would be noted with mixed emotions. Was the prayer intended to serve as a substitute for adequate maintenance or lack of navigational and pilot skill? The answer, fortunately, was no. Neither mission had had a fatality or injury since the air services began in 1948.

There had been some close calls, of course. On one occasion, a valve went through a piston of a Sudan Interior Mission plane forty miles from the nearest airstrip. The plane shook violently but limped in for a safe landing. Often, a pilot would have to buzz a strip to scatter cattle on the runway.

Strange things sometimes happened in the flights over the untamed territory of the Nigerian savanna and rain forest. One missionary pilot had the unsavory job of picking up the corpse of a man who had been accidentally electrocuted near Maidugari, in the northeast. He had strapped the body to a stretcher designed for air rescue work. The stretcher had been cut out of plywood in an elongated pentagon shape to fit into the cockpit. The pilot reached altitude, leveled off, and thought he heard a voice coming in over the radio. This was surprising because he was sure the radio was turned off. He checked, and it was. Then the voice came a second time. His hand traveled down to the mouth of the corpse, which was open. The change in air pressure at the higher altitude had caused air to be expelled from the dead man's lungs and out through the vocal chords.

Later, at the Jos airport, he learned that a fellow pilot had run into a similar situation, with a corpse that was only partially strapped down at the waist. When the plane had reached altitude, the change in the pressure contracted the muscles of the corpse, and it sat straight up in the cockpit.

The Sudan missionary pilots face stiff requirements to qualify for the job, yet their pay is the same as that of a neophyte missionary. They must have a commercial pilot rating and must be checked out for instrument flight as well as multi-engine craft. They must be able to double as aviation mechanics, and have at least one full year of religious training in an accredited Bible school. They must convince the missions of their dedication to the Christian faith. They clock an average of seventy to eighty hours a month, flying in all kinds of weather over the most rugged terrain imaginable. An engine failure over the rain forests of southern Nigeria is tantamount to death. Even if he crash-landed safely, few pilots could survive swamps, insects, and snakes underneath the jungle canopy. But Sudan Interior Mission planes have flown over 70,000 hours with no engine failure, all with self-overhauled engines. As one nonmissionary pilot wryly observed: "Maybe there's something to that prayer of theirs."

Pilot Ray Browneye rolled down the hilly Jos runway on schedule, with his missionary dentist as passenger. He was not sure what to expect at Mubi, because the radio messages had been so garbled. He knew that someone was desperately ill and needed transport, and that was about it. He leveled off over the jagged mountains of the Jos plateau and headed almost due east toward Mubi, about two hours away. Because of the lack of radio beacons and directional signals, he would have to rely considerably on his road map, which was none too dependable. Rivers and mountains also made commendable landmarks—if you could find them in the harmattan. Even when the harmattan was light, it was treacherous. The Hausas call it the Wind of the White Horseman.

Fortunately, the military police at Mubi had received word by missionary radio that the rescue plane was on its way to the bush strip. Troops were rolling away the heavy barrels and carting off the metal junk from the strip in a race with time. Not long after the last of the hazards had been cleared, Browneye's Comanche was making its descent toward the grass runway.

On the road to Mubi, John Hamer was pushing the Land Rover hard toward the airport. Muslims in their white robes, Higi tribesmen with their spears, Fulani herdsmen with their straw helmets and herds crowded the road at times, creating exasperating obstacles. Donkeys with their back feet tied together to prevent them from running far astray, pigs, goats, sheep, lambs, chickens frequently strayed out into the road without warning, causing Hamer to veer suddenly and to jolt the passengers in the rear. Overloaded trucks, jammed with goods and people, tilting precariously to one side, rolled by, spraying up clouds of dust and often propelling stones against the windshield. Hamer used a familiar Nigerian trick to save the windshield from being pulverized from the flying stones: he placed the back of his hand against the inside of the windshield whenever a truck went by and pressed hard. With this counteracting pressure, the stones would bounce off and leave chip marks. Without the pressure, the windshield could explode in a thousand pieces.

Laura Wine was still convulsing at intervals, and the oxygen bottle was nearing the end of its supply. Esther Hamer prayed.

The Land Rover pulled into the Mubi airstrip at about eleven. Browneye's Comanche was on the ground, and the strip had been cleared of its obstacles. Hamer was immeasurably relieved.

His first concern was about a new oxygen supply, but the message had never gotten through, and there was none. Nor, of course, was there a stretcher. He pulled the Land Rover as close as possible to the plane and was distressed to note it was a three-seater—for four people. Ray Browneye reassured him about the extra weight, and the Hamers squeezed into the single seat in the rear of the cockpit, helping from inside the plane as Laura Wine was lifted in beside the pilot.

Her blood pressure had dropped to 60 to 80 systolic, and her pulse was irregular at about 80 beats a minute—signs of cardiac failure. The seat was reclined as much as possible, leaving very little room in the back of the plane for the Hamers. Esther Hamer kept her hand on Laura Wine's pulse constantly.

Getting into the pilot seat beside her, Ray Browneye noticed that she was conscious and that she seemed to be communicating with her eyes and facial expression but was unable to speak. He could see her lips move, but she was not making any sound. He remembers being very moved by what appeared to him to be peace in the face of desperation. He was convinced that she was trying to express gratitude for the help she was getting, rather than concern about her own condition.

He pushed the throttle forward, and the plane rumbled down the bumpy bush airstrip. It seemed to strain to get off the ground, yet it climbed steadily, banked over the village of Mubi, and headed back westward toward Jos.

Below, the savanna and mountains of the plateau stretched to the horizon, still with only a light harmattan overcast sweeping down from the Sahara to the north. The plane flew over thousands of years of turbulent history, the kingdoms of ancient Muslim emirs, pagan villages, jutting, hostile mountain ranges, and sweeping grasslands that seemed to go on to infinity. In the 1920s the first Church of the Brethren missionaries, their supplies transported by head carriers, had made their way across this country, fighting off malaria and yellow fever through lands branded as the White Man's Grave. Frequent white crosses along the roads of the plateau mark the graves of missionaries who had to be buried where they dropped.

The plane droned along over Garkida, over Biu and Bauchi, following the customary bush-pilot, seat-of-the-pants navigation, until Jos town loomed ahead high on the plateau. At least Laura Wine was not convulsing now. There was practically no oxygen left in the bottle, and little could be done in the crowded cockpit if she convulsed again.

Perched 4,000 feet above sea level, Jos town looks out on a magnificent view of the plateau that bears its name. To the east, the Shere Hills reach 6,000 feet, with dramatic escarpments and precipitous cliffs of awesome beauty. The climate is salubrious, so much so that Lord Frederick Lugard, the first British governor of Nigeria, had the fantasy of establishing a health and rest station there for Europeans. His dream was shattered when the same quota of tropical diseases was discovered in Jos as elsewhere in Africa. Later, when malaria and yellow fever came under reasonable control, the Hill Station Rest House was established, bringing with it pink gins, roast beef, and Yorkshire pudding and all the amenities of British colonial grace.

Jos town's rich tin ore, almost pure metal, was a lure for the British. Early in the 1900s the British West African Frontier Force moved in with Maxim machine guns, Guinness stout, and the famous British square. This military ploy, with British officers and native troops formed into a hollow square for maximum firepower, soon discouraged the mounted native warriors, and the Royal Niger Company took over. The British squeeze against Africans in any capacity but raw labor is still felt but fading rapidly in the new independence.

The Sudan Interior Mission had its own problems in this regard. Having established the Bingham Memorial Hospital in 1947 for white missionaries of varied faiths, it created the Evangel Hospital, also in Jos, in 1959 as a definite separatist facility. This bit of missionary chauvinism gradually eroded as African Christian leaders were admitted to Bingham, and the practice was soon to be changed forever. But as the plane bearing Laura Wine approached Jos town, a bed in the Bingham Hospital was being prepared for her.

The small staff of the Sudan Interior Mission hospitals consisted almost entirely of missionary women, including the only full-time doctor at the hospital at the time, Jeanette Troup. When the radio message from Lassa was received and verified on Saturday morning, the chief nurse, Lily Pinneo, went into action to prepare for the new patient's arrival. Penny, as she was called, was an energetic, vital, and motherly woman from a devout Presbyterian family in New Jersey. Her father had been a general practitioner; a brother was a missionary doctor in Alaska; a sister was a missionary teacher in India. Like so many of her colleagues, she would say: "The Lord wanted me to be a missionary in Africa." And she became one.

The information that nurse Pinneo and Dr. Troup had to go on in preparing for the arrival of Laura Wine was skimpy. Jeanette Troup, known as Dr. Jeanette, had taken her medical degree from Philadelphia's Hahnemann College of Medicine, of high repute in medical circles. She had moved through residencies in pathology and pediatrics. She was in her middle forties. Both she and Penny Pinneo were known for their warmth and personal interest in both Nigerian and expatriate patients; both shared an admiration from the staff that bordered on veneration.

In the compound of the Bingham Hospital, they prepared the mission's Opel Caravan with an air mattress and stretcher and an ample supply of oxygen. By the time the Comanche approached the Jos runway, they were waiting and ready to go into action.

The Hamers, stiff and tired from the flight and the punishment of the Land Rover, greeted Penny Pinneo and Dr. Jeanette as the Opel pulled up beside the plane. They rushed the fresh oxygen to the cockpit, where Laura Wine was showing more signs of cyanosis. She responded, but her pulse was not good.

All the way to the Bingham Hospital, Penny Pinneo and Dr. Jeanette administered oxygen. At the hospital they lost no time in starting the patient on intravenous fluids, and together with the Hamers they assessed the situation in detail.

The signs of cardiac failure were now obvious, and the possibility of a strange viral complication was a strong part of the consensus. Since Laura Wine appeared to be fading rapidly and could be near death, radical therapy was indicated.

Lab tests were immediately ordered. Every possible treatment was utilized: digoxin, hydrocortisone by injection, nasal oxygen, and phenylephrine. Tourniquets were rotated on her extremities, to sacrifice blood from the limbs in favor of getting more blood to the brain and vital organs. Her leukocyte count had soared from below the normal count of around 6,000 to a massive 21,900. This was strange and confusing if a virus instead of a bacterial disease were involved, but it could be the result of excessive dehydration. A critical effect was shown by the bleeding time. Normally, it takes one to four minutes for a small skin puncture to stop bleeding. The tests on Laura Wine showed a rate of over twice that. Her blood coagulation time was also ominous. The tests showed that the process took nearly an hour—up to twelve times the normal rate. All this suggested the possibility of massive internal hemorrhaging. And all the signs indicated that she had gone into shock during the flight from Mubi.

Nurses were ordered around the clock. Mrs. Hamer volunteered for two shifts. Dr. Jeanette, recalling the request of Dr. John Frame at Columbia, drew a specimen of blood and put it in the freezer. Later, this was to have major significance. At the time, it was routine.

Charlotte Shaw arrived for night duty as usual. Fair, slightly built, quite plain-looking, with blond hair and blue eyes, she was in her forties, like so many of her colleagues. She had not slept well after her previous night's work and had gotten up much earlier than she had wanted to. She had recently returned to her nursing job in Jos from a furlough in the States and was troubled by vague, floating anxieties that she couldn't define and didn't quite know how to handle. A close friend had died not long before, and that, coupled with her anxieties, had brought her to a crisis as to whether she would return from her furlough or not. She was never a strong person but was known to be a loving and conscientious nurse who put the needs of others ahead of herself.

She had sought advice, trying to work herself out of her *angst* and trying to make the critical decision of whether to come back to Jos. Her physician recommended that she not return and tried to convince her that her many years of service in Africa had more than fulfilled her obligations. But her affection for her colleagues was overwhelming, and against the advice of many she returned. No one would have faulted her if she had not.

On the morning of Laura Wine's arrival Charlotte had been in her flower garden, a great source of comfort, which she cared for in the brief hours when she was free from her work at the hospital. She had heard about Laura Wine's emergency flight, and knowing that she would be on duty that night, Charlotte felt she could better prepare herself by working off her tensions in the garden during the morning and catching up on her sleep in the afternoon.

She was cutting a bouquet of roses to take to the hospital with her that evening when, reaching high for a particularly striking blossom, she punctured her finger with a thorn. It sank in deep, and the wound bled considerably, which of course was desirable. She went back into the house, washed it off and dabbed it with some Merthiolate. It soon clotted, and she promptly forgot about it.

Now, rested from an afternoon nap and ready to take up her night duties, she familiarized herself with the case at hand. It was obvious that Miss Wine needed special attention, and Charlotte was prepared to give it to her. The night was soft and, as usual on the Jos plateau, refreshing in contrast to the steaming heat of the rain forest or the burning dryness of the lower savanna. Outside the low-slung, bungalow-type hospital, the night lights revealed very dimly a pleasant gravel court-yard, framed with flame trees, palm trees, acacia, and bougain-villaea so rich and purple it could hurt the eyes in daylight. Along the gravel walk were poinsettia and flowering hibiscus.

Inside the hospital wing it was deathly quiet, except for Miss Wine's labored breathing. Charlotte Shaw watched and waited. Though hardly able to speak, Laura Wine complained of her throat, and the nurse went to a nearby cabinet for a gauze swab.

She wrapped it around her finger and softly, gently swabbed the ulcerated throat. As the fluid soaked through the gauze, she became aware of a slight stinging sensation in her forefinger and suddenly realized she had forgotten about the rose prick in her finger. She disposed of the gauze, flooded her finger with water and green soap, dabbed it with more antiseptic, and put a Bandaid on it. Then she went back to her duties, checking the IV, or intravenous, fluid and the nasal oxygen apparatus. With Miss Wine resting fairly well, the night passed without further incident.

Esther Hamer was on duty the next morning when Laura Wine stirred restively in her bed. Across the hospital compound the Sunday morning services had begun. The mission colony, suffused with enthusiasm for old-time religion and bursting with ecclesiastical energy, respected neither the slothful nor the ailing when it came to hymns. The staff sang lustily and with herculean vigor. The first hymn of the morning was "A Mighty Fortress Is Our God," and it bounded and resonated across the courtyard.

The hymn had its impact. A wan smile appeared on Laura Wine's swollen face, and she rolled her head lightly on the pillow. Without opening her eyes, she said to Esther Hamer: "Oh, I'm so glad the hymns are in English today!" Then, realizing that in distant Lassa the services were always in Hausa or Margi, she said: "But where am I?"

They were just about the last words she uttered. She convulsed again on Sunday afternoon. There was no more urine output. She went into shock. Two ministers arrived in midafternoon for an anointing service, laying on the hands in prayer and rubbing olive oil lightly on the forearms.

Shortly after nine that evening, she took a turn for the worse and went into convulsions again. By 9:30 P.M. she was dead.

As saddening as Laura Wine's death was, she had lived a full life and had died in the fulfillment of a lifelong dream. Now those she left behind were faced with urgent, pressing decisions, because all the medical personnel involved agreed that an autopsy should be performed in light of the elusiveness of the strange disease that had killed her.

Dr. Hamer, checking on the alternatives, decided that the best plan was to fly the body back to the Church of the Brethren's main medical mission station in Garkida. There an autopsy could be performed, and Miss Wine could be given a burial near the region where she had worked and the people whom she had loved. The body could not be embalmed before the autopsy, and it would begin to swell within twenty-four hours.

Hamer obtained a certificate of death from the city of Jos, and a Sudan Interior Mission plane was chartered to fly to Biu, the nearest bush strip to Garkida. The Hamers felt numb, but the strain and the crisis were over, and there was much accumulated work to be done back at Lassa.

On Monday morning the plane climbed again to altitude, and the trip to Biu was made in silence. There was no longer the terror of the sudden convulsions; only the quietness of death.

As the plane left Jos town back on the horizon, Dr. Hamer turned over and over in his mind the strange convolutions of the sickness that had killed Laura Wine. He still believed his diagnoses several days before were at least partially correct. There must have been a viral throat infection, and it must have been powerful. Dr. Jeanette agreed. Known tropical diseases such as malaria and yellow fever could be definitely ruled out. Whatever it was, it had killed within six days—or perhaps a few more if Laura Wine had hidden some of her early symptoms, as she would have been likely to do.

There was definitely renal failure. There was also cardiac failure, with some possible cerebral edema. But she had no history of cardiac disease.

The most powerful agent for all this was likely to be a virus, but certainly a virus neither he nor Dr. Jeanette had dealt with before. Then there were the peculiar rashes under the skin, indicating hemorrhaging just below the surface.

The high leukocyte count, emerging suddenly at the terminal stage from an early low count, was also puzzling. Normally, this didn't happen with a killer virus. Was this an exception?

The unpleasant but vitally necessary job of the autopsy fell on the shoulders of Dr. Beryl McCann, head of the Church of the Brethren's large leprosarium in Garkida. The heart muscle appeared to be firm, but there was a slight thickening of the mitral valve, which regulates the blood flow. There was evidence of gross internal hemorrhaging and kidney damage. This was reminiscent of the hemorrhagic fever viruses from South America. But other signs varied considerably. The death-dealing agent was as much of a mystery after the gross autopsy as it was before. Microscopic examination would have to wait until tissue specimens could be sent back to the United States and a more sophisticated laboratory.

There was great sadness in Garkida and Lassa. News had come over the mission radio Monday morning, and those who could made their way from the remote mission stations to Garkida for the services on Monday afternoon. The church was packed with both Nigerians and missionaries. Laura Wine was buried on a hillside in the Garkida mission compound, near the graves of several other missionaries and children who had died so many miles away from their homeland.

A few days later, when the Hamers had settled back into their strenuous routine at Lassa, Esther Hamer wrote to Laura Wine's sister:

> We did not know Laura until she came to Nigeria, but we do know from what she had told us that she was supremely happy in doing this work out here. This was evident from her smiles and the radiant face which she had every day as she went about her work. She was *really* needed here at the time she was here and she did *much* for the hospital and the community. She was a real friend; she was as a mother to us, and a grandmother to our children. Her life was beautiful and useful to the end.

After a memorial service at Lassa, Esther Hamer and Elsie Hall sorted and straightened out the little house where Laura Wine had lived, removing the elaborate mosquito netting and still pondering the strangeness of the disease. No one knew whether it was infectious or not. No one knew where it came from. No one knew how to deal with it if it came back.

The house cleaned, Esther Hamer and Elsie Hall shut the door and left. There were still the bats in the attic, but they could not cope with them. They made a note that the next time the bats were cleared from the operating room, Miss Wine's house should also be cleared.

The harmattan continued to blow. The drums in the village echoed back to the mission in the evening. The bush fires blazed at night in the distance. The hospital continued to house the sick, the lonely, the dying, and the promise brought by a new birth.

Life returned to normal too at the Sudan Interior Mission hospitals in Jos. With Dr. Jeanette and Penny Pinneo as the anchormen, the staff was pressed under a load of some 8,000 patients a month, the outpatients alone numbering almost 300 a day.

Another doctor would be coming soon to help take some of the pressure off the all-woman staff. Meanwhile, Dr. Hal White, a gentle but determined man in his middle thirties, took time off from his teaching to help when needed. He was head of the medical school affiliated with the hospital. The consolidation of the Bingham Hospital with Evangel would help too, both in making the work more efficient and in breaking down the color barrier that had been so long raised in the outworn tradition of the past.

In spite of the rigors of the overloaded schedule, there was time for relaxation, though trade talk often intruded on the simple teas and coffee breaks the staff would hold. Dr. Jeanette liked to give what she called pie socials, baking over a half a dozen different types of pies for her colleagues. She also liked to sing her favorite hymns, accompanying herself on an autoharp. Her voice was almost professional. Her rather severe, disciplined features contrasted with the warmth and gentleness her friends noted.

Charlotte Shaw, subject to inordinate feelings of guilt, was reassured by her fellow nurses when she expressed concern that she might not have done enough to save Laura Wine in her illness. Dolores Rohe, who was one of Charlotte's closest friends, reprimanded her gently for feeling this way. Wasn't all this in God's hands? Didn't they all believe in the absolute veracity of the Bible? Is there not victory in sadness and death?

The hospital routine automatically did its part in tempering Charlotte Shaw's unwarranted feelings of guilt. There were charts to check, medications to prepare, lab tests to follow, patients to prepare for surgery, temperatures to take, supplies to order. These and other details of the crowded mission hospital kept Charlotte Shaw too busy to dwell on morbid thoughts for long.

Just eight days after Laura Wine died in her bed at the Bingham Hospital, however, Charlotte began to notice severe back and leg pains. She also had a slight headache, but she had frequent migraines and was used to that.

When she began to feel chills, she was convinced that she was coming down with malaria, common on the Jos plateau as well as in the savanna and rain forest. She was reluctant to bother anyone about her problems and almost automatically went to the hospital pharmacy and took three tablets of amodiaquine, .2 base each, one of the many antimalarials on hand, all of which were basically the same. She was certain that by the next morning she would shake the mild attack and get back to her usual routine with little or no loss of time.

But in the morning there was no improvement at all. In fact, her temperature had shot up to 102°, and she realized that she was in no condition to go to work. Dolores Rohe, stopping by to join Charlotte on the way to the hospital, knew something was wrong the moment she looked at her. She could not put her finger on it, but she instinctively knew this was not malaria. She was further disturbed when Char, as she was often called, who had been with her for many years at the mission, said something that suggested she didn't feel they had too much time left to spend together.

Dolores Rohe took immediate action in persuading Char to

enter the hospital as a patient. She was reluctant but she finally agreed, especially since she felt nauseated on top of the chills and fever.

Penny Pinneo, hearing that Char was sick, went immediately to her bedside at the hospital. She assisted Dr. Jeanette in giving the patient a thorough examination and took the necessary specimens for the laboratory tests. The fever had now risen to 103°, and a stiff course of the antimalarial hydroxychloroquine was prescribed, the usual precaution. There was no discussion whatever about a thought that was on everybody's mind: Was there any relation between Charlotte Shaw's condition and the tragic course that Laura Wine's disease had taken?

Dr. Jeanette and the nurses were further disturbed when Char told them about the small wound on her finger and the stinging sensation she had felt when the fluid had soaked through the gauze while she was swabbing the patient's throat. They reassured her that there was nothing to worry about, especially since she had washed the cut and put antiseptic on it.

When they left Char so she could get some sleep, Dolores Rohe was still almost certain that it was not malaria but found herself desperately hoping it was.

As head nurse, Penny Pinneo was most concerned when any of her staff became ill. She was known as counselor and friend to all of them, and she tended to wear herself out trying to help them over any difficulties they encountered, either in or outside their work. "She's a *lovely* person," one of her staff commented. "And the most even-tempered person you could ever find. Do you know, I've never seen Penny angry?"

Whether the loneliness of an African mission post engenders an extra dimension of uncritical homage or not, this feeling continually dominated the ambience of the Sudan Interior Mission, especially as far as Penny Pinneo and Dr. Jeanette were concerned. Commenting on the extreme closeness of the nursing staff, one member said: "Maybe plasma is thicker than water. We're always fighting death and disease all the time, we're all united in a strange land and in what we feel is one Lord. I think it brings us together in a bond that you're not likely to find anywhere else. It's very special, and it's very hard to describe."

Penny Pinneo followed the lab tests on Charlotte Shaw with intense personal interest. Her training at the Johns Hopkins School of Nursing and the University of Pennsylvania equipped her aptly with many facets of nursing in addition to anesthesia, which was her specialty. She buttressed this with continued study. Before she and Dr. Jeanette reviewed the first of Charlotte Shaw's lab tests, they went over those of Laura Wine. There were certain similarities, but this could be a coincidence. It was always easy to jump to conclusions in diagnoses, especially when gun-shy from a particularly dramatic and mysterious case. The total leukocyte count was markedly down for Charlotte Shaw—one of the puzzling factors in Laura Wine's condition early in the progress of the disease.

The various forms of the white cells—neutrophils, lymphocytes, monocytes, and all the rest—were, as usual, broken down in what is called the differential count. They showed striking similarities to those of Miss Wine. But there were no signs of ulcers in the throat or the buccal membranes inside the mouth, no indication of a macular rash, no swelling of the face and neck, no dyspnea or difficulty in breathing, no cyanosis, and no drop in blood pressure or a weak pulse. Nor was there any sign of the subsurface bleeding of a petechial rash. Beyond that, Charlotte Shaw was considerably younger than Laura Wine and could be expected to withstand more rigors in the course of whatever disease it was. There was comfort in that.

Without being unduly alarmed, Penny Pinneo concentrated on giving Charlotte the best possible attention and as usual left the rest to her Lord. But the patient did not improve; nor did she measurably worsen over the next several days. Her temperature remained several degrees above normal. Her friends on the staff and the patients prayed.

Seven days after she became ill, on February 10, 1969, a macular rash discoloring the skin appeared on Charlotte Shaw's face, neck, and arms. It spread to her trunk and thighs that evening and was followed by the appearance of a petechial rash.

Her temperature moved up to 104.8°.

The strange ulcers appeared in her throat and buccal membranes.

The leukocyte count inexplicably rose.

By the evening of February 12 her face and neck were swollen, and she experienced severe dyspnea. By midnight the blue discoloration of the skin set in and she became cyanotic. There was a marked drop in blood pressure.

At 3:45 A.M. on February 13, the eleventh day of her illness, Charlotte Shaw died.

Chapter Three

News of the tragedy spilled across the plateau and savanna with incredible speed. Dr. Jeanette announced it over the Sudan Interior Mission radio in flat, measured tones. By breakfast time nearly every mission post was aware of it. Prayers were said. The missions at Jos were stunned. On everybody's mind, whether medical personnel or layman, was the same question: Was there a direct link with Laura Wine's death? What kind of disease was it that killed in a matter of days, defied diagnosis, and had no respect whatever for nearly every therapy that modern medicine could offer?

But there was still no absolute certainty that the two cases were related. It would take a laboratory more sophisticated than that at Jos to shed light on the riddle. A gross autopsy would reveal little aside from how death came about. It would not pinpoint the cause.

The autopsy had to be done, and done fast. One hope for enlightenment came from getting the tissue specimens and blood samples of the victims back to Dr. John Frame at Columbia University for analysis.

Over the years Penny Pinneo had proved herself to have courage and stamina. But she also had feelings. She was shocked at the death. Her Lord was very real to her, and she drew on this resource to keep her stability as she went through her regular eight-hour shift at the hospital that day, preparing herself for assisting at the autopsy. It could not be done until late that night. The uncertain thought of a positive link between the cases of the two nurses was painful and frustrating.

Just before Charlotte Shaw's condition had become critical, Penny Pinneo and Dr. Jeanette had tabulated the symptoms, since their suspicions were growing. When the hemorrhagic petechial rash, the ulcers in the throat and mouth, the swelling of the neck, the cyanosis all appeared, the evidence became overwhelming that the two cases were the same—that both nurses had died of some strange, elusive virus. *But evidence is not proof.* The thick membrane in Laura Wine's throat suggested another possibility: diphtheria. Remote as the chance might be, this had to be weighed and considered, along with the possibilities of infectious mononucleosis, dengue fever (prevalent in Africa), and typhoid. None of these could at the moment be ruled out from either case.

Penny Pinneo was exhausted when the time for the autopsy arrived. It was after midnight, and all except the operating room was quiet. She and Dr. Jeanette put on their gowns and gloves and prepared for the unwelcome job. They did not need gauze masks, they felt, because, unlike an operation, an autopsy presented no danger of infecting the patient.

The major incision was made by Dr. Jeanette, as Penny Pinneo assisted. One by one, the organs of the chest and abdominal cavity were removed and biopsies were taken. *Dear God,* Penny remembered thinking, *what a shocking experience to look inside your good friend and co-worker. What a horrible shock!*

She steeled herself, helped by Dr. Jeanette's outward professional calm. The body cavity was abnormally filled with amber serum fluid, literally cupfuls. She sponged this out, squeezing it into a bowl, trying to maintain her own professional posture. Little was said between them.

There had obviously been massive internal hemorrhaging.

There was lung, liver, and kidney damage. There was no specific clue to the killer. Just what kind of contamination the organs contained was shrouded in mystery.

The specimens and blood were carefully saved and put in the freezer. They would be sent to John Frame in New York, with the fervent hope that some light would be forthcoming. They took off their robes and gloves in silence, and scrubbed. Dr. Jeanette went to her office to prepare a cable for John Frame, to be sent in the morning.

When he had started his modest research program some time before, to screen the blood samples of deceased missionaries, no one, including Dr. Frame, had had any thought that a crisis situation such as this would come up. Some strange serendipity seemed to be at work. It was almost as though the Frame-Yale program had set a trap for a wildcat and was about to catch a tiger.

The services for Charlotte Shaw were held in the nearby village of Miango, where she was buried. Beside the red clay houses and the thatched roofs of the pagan-Christian Nigerian village, the Sudan Interior Mission had constructed an impressive school, a modest holiday rest station for missionaries, and a church. It was a strange juxtaposition, with the church facing the steep cliff of the sacred rock of the animist worshippers, where a leopard was rumored to live and where the benevolent ju-ju man and the malevolent do-do man practiced their witchcraft.

The Christian service was muted. Charlotte Shaw was laid to rest in the small, flowered graveyard beside the church. There would be no headstone, as was the custom with the other missionaries buried there; simply a slab and a modest bronze plaque to mark the passing of a fellow nurse who was loved and mourned.

But beyond the mourning, intense as it was, was a feeling of apprehension that was only partially mollified by the unquestioned faith in religion. Something was happening that was strange and unfathomable. The question, mainly unspoken was: Where would it strike next? Or would it strike again? And if it did, what was it? No one knew the answer.

While the atmosphere at Jos remained subdued, morale was lifted somewhat with the arrival of Dr. David Christensen, the new staff doctor awaited so long. Tall, slim, and aggressive in contrast to the quiet calm of Dr. Hal White, he was to fall in love with a nurse from a nearby mission and marry her within a short time. Together with Dr. Jeanette and Hal White, he re-studied the tragedy, but the usual blind alley was reached in the absence of microscopic studies, which would be a long time in coming. All three doctors agreed that they were facing an im-ponderable unknown.

About a week after Charlotte Shaw's death, Penny Pinneo, on the eve of her fifty-second birthday, lay in her bungalow at the Sudan Interior Mission in Jos trying unsuccessfully to sleep. She was feeling vaguely uncomfortable and didn't know quite why. She was still awake at three in the morning, when Dr. Jeanette rapped on her door to ask her assistance at the ob-stetric ward.

They had been summoned by Dorothy Davis, a soft-spoken veteran nurse from Merchantville, New Jersey, who was on night duty when one of the Nigerian nurses on staff went into a particularly difficult labor. It soon became apparent that a Caesarean section would have to be performed, and Dorothy had sent an associate for Dr. Jeanette and Penny Pinneo.

Now the two colleagues made their way across the com-pound to the obstetric section. Although she felt weak and slightly dizzy, Penny Pinneo administered the anesthesia while Dr. Jeanette operated. The Caesarean was a success, and nurse Pinneo went immediately home and back to bed. Checking her temperature, she noted that it was a little over 100°, and this had apparently been responsible for her earlier discomfort.

She stayed in bed the next morning, with a feeling of mal-aise, slight headache, and some nausea. Her temperature re-mained slightly elevated. In spite of her moderate fever, she put her portable typewriter on her lap in bed and tried to catch up on some letters. She had some difficulty in typing, and when she reached the sentence "I'm not feeling very well today . . . ," she put the typewriter aside and tried to get some rest.

Later, she was barely able to finish the letter. It was to her sister Rose, the only sibling who was not in the mission service. Like Penny, Rose Pinneo had studied at Johns Hopkins and the University of Pennsylvania. She was now an associate professor of nursing at the University of Rochester, a specialist in cardiovascular nursing. Penny Pinneo wrote:

> We've had difficult times here. On February 13th, our dear Char Shaw, one of our nurses, went Home to Glory. She had been sick for two weeks with shooting fevers, bad throat and mouth, aching, not responding to antibiotics—a viral infection. A week before she got sick a missionary was brought here who died 24 hours later, with the same terminal symptoms that Char developed. At the time of this missionary's death, Char felt that she had gotten contaminated when caring for her.
>
> Yesterday and today I haven't been feeling well, with a low-grade fever, and so I am off duty. Trust this is short-lived. There is no time to be sick. Do pray with us for permanent health.

By Sunday, February 23, three days after she had helped with the Caesarean operation, the thought entered Penny Pinneo's mind that she might have the same illness that had stricken Laura Wine and Charlotte Shaw. If this were so, she was thinking, she would have just about ten days longer to live.

Her next thought was that if the disease were diphtheria, there was no antitoxin available. Whether it was diphtheria or not, if her case were the same as the others, she fully realized that there was probably no treatment, no therapy that would be of any help. In spite of this, she had a feeling of perfect peace. When she found that she was so weak she couldn't lift a glass of water, she admitted herself to the hospital.

When the news trickled out to Jos town that a third nurse was laid low with strange and unidentifiable symptoms, concern grew to major proportions. Whatever feelings of apprehension there were at the hospital, however, were shielded and repressed. Among staff members, there was a transference to the God in which they believed so devoutly. In her journal Dolores Rohe wrote:

> As another day's work begins, I am aware that just anything can happen! It may be a day in which everything runs like clockwork, or it may be a day packed with emergencies, admittances, crying babies, questions, countless visitors, constant interruptions, and never-ending work. But I know, Lord, that whatever the situation I am to represent You: the apostle Paul calls me Your ambassador. Be with me in a special way today, that I may not fail You!

Like Dolores Rohe, the others on the staff had no reticence or embarrassment in expressing similar feelings. This personal theology was perhaps the key that distinguished the missionaries' subculture, that enabled them to function in the face of extreme crisis without stumbling under the gargantuan responsibilities they so willingly assumed. It was always difficult for an outsider to realize this was not a display of superficial emotion; it was etched in their lives.

Nurse Dorothy Davis, praying for courage and sustenance in the face of the new crisis, found herself propelled by some urge to clean out her house. And, although it was not scheduled until April, over a month away, she began preparing to pack for her furlough. It kept her busy in her off hours and diverted her mind from the tragic series of events that was unfolding at the hospital.

There, all three doctors were studying Penny Pinneo's condition with grave concern. A small ulceration was now clearly observable inside the cheek, on the right buccal mucosa. The tonsillar pillars were turning slightly red. The leukocyte count had dropped, and leukopenia was evident. Almost in despair, the usual antimalarial hydroxychloroquine was given. Then crystalline and procaine penicillin, 1.2 million units, was administered twice daily.

Dorothy Davis remembers seeing the trio of doctors in the corridor. They looked tired and distressed. Usually cheery and cordial, they went down the hall with their eyes diverted, somber and silent. Their first conference had lasted for over an hour.

In her hospital bed, weak but rational and conscious, Penny Pinneo kept thinking: *If only we had diphtheria antitoxin in Nigeria.* She had seen how the new disease—and again no one was sure this was the same disease—had mocked the usual effectiveness of both "miracle" drugs and the antimalarials, and anything else that had been tried. Maybe, just maybe, the diphtheria antitoxin would work, if only because it was something that had never been tried.

On February 14 Penny Pinneo received gamma globulin, along with the rest of the staff, as a prophylactic measure. But the antibodies in gamma globulin are general, not specific. A new, strange virus would easily skate around the improperly armed defensive forces, punch into the healthy cells of the patient, and begin its ruthless hijacking of the RNA (ribonucleic acid) and DNA (deoxyribonucleic acid), the life forces of the cell, converting them to the virus' own use: specifically, to make more viruses. The new viruses, geometrically increased in number, would repeat the same process, fanning out with incredible speed and aggression.

Dr. Jeanette, whose professionalism could not fully block her intense emotional concern for Penny Pinneo, held constant conferences with the other doctors, Hal White and Dave Christensen. The result was always the same: a dead end. At the same time, they were doing everything within their power and resources. Finally, the three doctors agreed on one thing: they would set a deadline of Wednesday, February 26. If the fever did not drop by that day, they would make immediate plans to ship their patient to New York, where more elaborate facilities were available.

Meanwhile, Penny Pinneo found strength and sustenance in Psalm 23, which she said to herself repeatedly. Later, she was to write: "Then peace came and I thought I would just enjoy the Lord, even if my days might be few. 'Though I walk through the valley of the shadow of death, I will fear no evil, because Thou art with me.' His presence was real from then on, and there was no more fear."

Then, on the day of the deadline, February 26, after another meeting with Dave Christensen and Hal White, Dr. Jeanette sat down at her typewriter to report on the patient's condition and the consensus of the meeting. She wrote, in part:

Significant in her [Penny Pinneo's] history is the fact that she helped to care for Miss Laura Wine, who expired on the 26th of January 1969, and Miss Charlotte Shaw, who expired on the 13th of February 1969. The diagnosis on both these cases was somewhat obscure, but it was felt that both died of viremia [disease caused by virus] . . .

Treatment has been symptomatic, related primarily to the headache and muscular pain for which she was given paracetamol. Prior to admission she took a course of Plaquenil in spite of no malarial parasites being seen in her blood smear, but these appeared to make no improvement in her clinical picture. On the 24th of February, she was started on Vitamin C, 200 mgm q.i.d., Vitamin B-1, 60 mgm t.i.d., Vitamin K, 20 mgm I.M. daily, Vitamin B-12, 1,000 mcg I.M. daily, and Vitamin B-complex 1 cc daily . . .

The impression is that her illness is due to viral infection, and it would seem as if her illness is following the same pattern as that of the last patient whom she cared for, also a nurse from this hospital, especially in regard to the pattern of fever and blood picture. Also significant is the prolonged coagulation time in this case and the two previous cases [a frequent sign of hemorrhagic fever].

Blood was taken for viral studies on the 24th of February, and will be sent along with her to Dr. John Frame in New York, for processing.

It is felt because of the inability to make a specific diagnosis and therefore inability to give specific treatment, also because there does not seem to be improvement, that it is wise she be sent to New York for diagnosis and treatment.

Dr. Jeanette wrote one other report that day, a summary of Charlotte Shaw's case to be sent to New York.

"This staff nurse," she wrote, "was admitted on the 4th of February after having been working night duty for three weeks . . . After admission she had spiking fevers to 102° or 103° with associated chills . . ."

Then, after considerable medical detail, the report continued:

> The impression was that this patient died of viremia, mode of death being possible cardiac failure. It is significant to note that her illness began one week after the death of a patient whom she cared for in the hospital, Miss Laura Wine. This patient was also thought to have died as a result of viremia and terminal cardiac failure. Miss Shaw had cared for her one night, and stated thereafter that she had used a gauze on her finger to clear secretions out of the patient's mouth. Miss Shaw had a small cut on her finger, and later washed well and applied antiseptic to this wound.
>
> Treatment in the hospital included aspirin, IV fluids, 10 cc gamma globulin intramuscularly on two occasions; hydrocortisone and Vitamin K and penicillin in massive doses during the last eight hours of life . . .
>
> No obvious cause of death was found at post-mortem examination.

The reports were signed "J. M. Troup, M.D." Along with the accumulated specimens of tissues and blood samples from all three victims of the unfathomed disease, the reports were put aside to send with Penny Pinneo on her long, painful journey back to the United States.

The logistics for the trip were imposing. There would have to be a Sudan Interior Mission plane flight from the Jos plateau to Lagos, nearly 700 miles away. The plywood stretcher would have to be fitted into the plane in place of the front seat. Clearances would have to be made in Lagos for customs and immigration. Permission would have to be obtained from Pan Am in New York for transporting a stretcher case, necessitating the purchase and removal of four first-class seats and the installation of special curtains to screen off the patient. The tissue and blood specimens would have to be iced and put in containers so that whatever virus might be lurking in them would withstand both the trans-Nigeria and transoceanic flight. And someone would have to accompany Penny Pinneo, give her close care and attention in her precarious condition.

The natural choice was Dorothy Davis. Since her furlough to the States was due to come up within a month, it would be a reasonably simple matter to shift the date with minimum disruption. Dr. Jeanette, having made the decision to send Penny back, called Dorothy Davis to her office and explained the situation. She accepted the assignment immediately.

It was strange, Dorothy was thinking, that she had already begun packing. But there were many details remaining. In addition to packing and cleaning her own house, she had to do the same for Penny Pinneo. She went to Penny's house with divided feelings about leaving. If there were to be more tragedies brewing, she felt she should be on hand to help. But Penny, whom she deeply loved, needed the best possible support in her ordeal. The problem was not too difficult to resolve when she weighed the circumstances. Penny's survival was on the line; the rest was speculative.

She entered Penny's modest but cheerful living room. The house seemed bleak and vacant without her. She had spent many pleasant times there with Penny and others.

Not knowing quite what to do first, she decided to feed and water Penny's two canaries, since she had assumed that responsibility from the time Penny had entered the hospital. She went to the cage and looked in. Although they had been alive, bright and lyrical the night before, they were now dead, lying on their sides at the bottom of the cage.

She carefully buried the two birds in the garden and resolved not to let Penny know about it under any circumstances. It was strange, though, that they had died so suddenly. They had been given food and water regularly. She made a point of reporting this to Dr. Jeanette. They added it to the list of imponderables that was already growing long but not providing any real clues.

She packed the most essential of Penny's belongings and hurriedly tried to get her own house in order for the four-month furlough in the States. The details seemed endless, almost overwhelming. Penny Pinneo, barely holding her own in the hospital, was too weak to make any judgment about what was best to do and willingly left all the decisions in the hands of Dr. Jeanette.

They put Penny on a stretcher on Thursday, February 27, loaded her into the Opel Caravan—the same one that she had ridden in when she met and took care of Laura Wine—and drove her to the airport. With them was a large, iced thermos jug containing the tissues of the first victims and tubes full of blood samples for study. There was a large group from the Sudan Interior Mission at the airport, and a tacit undercurrent of feeling: Would this be the last time they would ever see Penny?

Paul Rogalsky, a Russian-born naturalized American with a shock of gray hair and rough-chiseled features, was the Sudan Interior Mission pilot selected for the long flight to Lagos, over the thick rain forest to the jammed and crowded city on the Atlantic coast of Africa. He had checked out the twin-engine Aztec plane and was satisfied that it was ready for the trip.

It was larger than the Comanche, and the plywood stretcher slid easily in next to the pilot's seat. Penny Pinneo was strapped down on it, terribly pale and weak. Some of the group who watched her thought that she managed a forlorn smile. They gathered around the plane, and an administrative officer of the mission said a brief prayer. "We know that God can heal and help the doctors find a solution," he was saying, "but His will is what counts, no matter what." Pilot Rogalsky said his own prayer, then waited for clearance.

Because it was wartime, all planes from the Sudan Interior Mission hangar were required to taxi to the passenger airport, nearly half a mile away, for inspection by the Nigerian troops. Out of deference to the desperately sick patient, however, the soldiers obligingly came to the hangar in a jeep and cleared the plane for takeoff. Pilot Rogalsky gunned the two motors and taxied out to the runway.

It was only after the plane was airborne that Dorothy Davis realized she had mislaid her yellow health certificate booklet, so important in clearing the ubiquitous health authorities at every intercontinental airport. She was distressed but realized there was nothing she could do about it at least until she got to Lagos, where she would hope for the best. Meanwhile, she turned her full attention to Penny.

The harmattan was again forgiving, being light and only slightly muddying the sky. The plane skirted the war zone to the southeast, riding over the reaching fingers of the plateau mountains, over the dry savanna, then over the tangled green rain forests.

The decision to send Penny Pinneo to New York had not been made lightly. By letter, Dr. Jeanette had advised the public health authorities in Lagos that it was possible, but not established, that the patient could be suffering from a communicable disease, and that all precautions should be taken. She *could* certify that Penny was not suffering from any known quarantinable disease, but she again warned that proper precautions should be taken in isolating behind curtains the portion of the plane that was to carry the patient.

Alerted to this, the Nigerian health authorities met the mission plane at Lagos as it taxied in from the runway.

Penny stayed on her stretcher in the Aztec mission plane, which was already beginning to bake in the tropical sun. Dr. Stanley Foster, a U.S. Public Health Service official in Lagos, had heard about the impending arrival and was on hand to consult with Nigerian authorities when the plane arrived. The consultation was long and involved. Clearance from the Pan Am New York office had not come through, and there wasn't another flight to the States for four more days. The patient would have to be given a complete examination at the Lagos University Hospital and kept in isolation until she could be loaded on the next plane—if she were permitted to be put aboard. Even if the clearance came through, there was a question of whether the flight was entirely booked. It might be impossible to obtain the four first-class seats necessary for the stretcher room. Further, there was the question of the essential yellow health book of Dorothy Davis.

The conference lasted for an hour. Inside the plane, now oven-hot, Penny Pinneo prayed through her aching mouth and cracked lips.

If Nigeria was known as the White Man's Grave, Lagos could be called the White Man's Coffin. The heat is often unbearable. In contrast to the Jos plateau, where the highlands temper the broiling sun, Lagos sprawls broodingly on a swampy lagoon surrounded by mangroves just off the Bight of Benin in the Atlantic. The port of Lagos steams in its heat, as mounds of groundnuts, tin ore, cotton, and tank after tank of palm oil are loaded on an endless parade of freighters in its harbor. Once a notorious slave market, Lagos is now suffering the growing pains of the new Nigeria, desperately trying to erase its former image and miraculously beginning to do so.

The road from the airport to Lagos, an hour away, is sheer hell. It is jammed with diesel trucks and buses packed like pickle barrels, spouting clouds of noxious black fumes as the traffic moves bumper to bumper, sheathed in an envelope of gray smog and dust. Along the sides of the roads countless cyclists and pedestrians often move more swiftly than the traffic, sometimes darting in front of it with total disregard of limb. Accidents are legion. Mufflers are unfashionable; the noise is deafening. Horns are pushed as much as accelerators; motors are revved incessantly. Crumbling, dirty-yellow houses from the days of British colonialism line the road, shutters wide open, people staring out hypnotically at the incredible jam.

It was along this road that Penny Pinneo was driven in the Lagos University Hospital ambulance, lying on her stretcher, looking to her Lord. The ambulance was nauseatingly hot. She was sweating, losing body fluids vital to her in her state of dehydration. A verse from II Corinthians went through her head constantly: *Blessed be the God of all comfort who comforteth us in all our tribulations that we may be able to comfort them which are in any trouble, by the comfort wherewith we ourselves are comforted of God.* She later felt it had given her strength to endure the trip from the airport.

Dorothy Davis rode with Penny in the back of the ambulance van, watching her pulse and vital signs, trying to comfort her. After what seemed like an endless hour, the van pulled into the outpatient ramp of the Lagos University Hospital.

Penny was wheeled into the stifling emergency room, which was jammed with outpatients, from babies to grandparents. Children were crying constantly, whether from pain or impatience. She lay there over an hour before she was examined by the Nigerian doctors, and then there was a parade of them. They could find nothing specific about her condition and went into consultation.

Finally, two agonizing hours after she had arrived at the hospital emergency room, the decision was made. She could not stay at the hospital but would have to be put in isolation. She would be driven to what was called the Pest House outside the city, back toward the airport and another hour away. She would be under the supervision of Stanley Foster, the American public health doctor, and the Nigerian nurses at the Pest House. Efforts were to be continued to follow up on the Pan Am arrangements for the Boeing 707 flight, four days away. Dorothy Davis would have to find some doctor qualified to certify that Penny had had typhus, yellow fever, smallpox, and cholera shots. All through the endless palaver, Penny Pinneo lay stoically on her stretcher, her dehydration increasing, her sheets wet with sweat, her throat and lips parched, in spite of the small sips of water she was able to hold down at ten-minute intervals.

It was dark now, but the heat does not lift when night comes to Lagos. It even gives the illusion of intensifying, as if the city were wrapped in a heating pad whose controls had gone wild. The trip back along the airport road was painfully slow. The van jerked, stopped, jerked, and stopped in monotonous sequence. The sides of the road were filled with market stalls lit by a glittering carpet of candles and Tilly lamps. Purveyors of fruits and kolanuts moved alongside the crowded road, trays on their heads and tiny kerosene lanterns on the trays. Vendors hawked Vicks cough drops on cardboard displays.

The Pest House was a crumbling building set aside for contagious diseases, with rough plaster walls and the inevitable corrugated tin roof. The principal occupants were children and babies with measles and chicken pox, the former being a serious threat to the lives of younger Nigerian children.

As crude as the Pest House was, it was an improvement over the arrangements made in former days when tribesmen in the bush villages came down with contagious diseases. A tribesman who was found to have smallpox was taken to the deep bush miles from the village, given a certain amount of food and water, and left to die. The practice was not as cruel as it sounded: there was no other defense against the disease. Half the village might die otherwise. Lepers were accorded the same treatment. Plague or cholera victims often were taken up to the top of a sheer cliff and simply pushed off by their fellow tribesmen. In spite of the efforts of the Nigerian government to stop these practices, there are reports that they still occur on rare occasions in remote areas.

There were no fans or screens in the Pest House. The windows looked out on the naked night sky. Word had been sent ahead to the Nigerian nursing staff that the two American nurses would be arriving. Penny Pinneo was carried in on her stretcher to a little room that usually held six beds. Three beds had been cleared away to accommodate the new isolation patient and her mission nurse. A Nigerian woman with a very sick child lay mutely in the only other bed. The room was dimly lit and suffocatingly hot.

Penny was eased into her bed, and Dorothy Davis checked her over carefully, professionally. She was weak and lethargic.

The rigors of the trip and the long hours in the van and hospital had taken their toll. Her fever was up, her neck swollen, her throat ulcerated. Her respiration was labored; she had much difficulty in breathing. *There is nothing I can do except pray and make her comfortable,* Dorothy Davis was saying to herself. Dr. Foster would be returning in the morning: there was some comfort in that. But could Penny live through this night?

She prepared for bed slowly, keeping an eye on Penny as she did so. For some reason, she never once worried about herself and the close contact she had with her patient, who might or might not have the same disease that had killed two of her colleagues. Her main thought was: *Get Penny home before she dies. Give her strength to survive in the face of these tribulations. The trip is a gamble that must be taken. The others have not survived.*

Within minutes she became aware of the mosquitoes: hoards of them coming in through the open windows. The small sink in the little room off theirs was black with them, and with flies. There were no nets on the beds. How could she keep them away from Penny, too weak to brush them away herself? Penny needed intravenous fluid for the dehydration. Something must be done in the morning, she knew. Tonight she would have to concentrate on survival.

As she got into the bed beside Penny's, she saw the bedbugs, wingless blood-sucking insects with a faint acrid odor. But she was exhausted. Everything would have to wait until morning. There was a single, bare light bulb hanging down in the center of the room. She didn't dare turn it off, in case of an emergency. She propped herself up in the half-century-old bed, trying to stay half awake, half asleep to get the rest she knew she would need. She stretched her arm over to the side of Penny's bed, so that all that would be needed was a light touch for her to wake. A rat scurried across the floor, darted erratically back and forth, then disappeared. It would return again and again throughout the night. *Strange,* Dorothy thought, *Penny never had any fear of rats or mice.* She would have to be the same.

An enormous loneliness came over Dorothy. She and Penny were distant from their homes in both Africa and America. The sights and sounds and smells were strange. She prayed.

Then she became aware of the sounds of the crying children down the hall. Their loneliness and pain touched her, as the sobbing rose and fell on the other side of their doorway. The baby and mother in the next bed grew restless. The child began crying, then suddenly convulsed. Before anyone could do anything to help, the baby was dead. The mother broke into uncontrollable wails, shrieking in supplication. It was impossible to comfort her as she held the dead child to her, alternately moaning and wailing. They were eventually taken away, but the cries of the other children continued through the night.

The mosquitoes were relentless. Dorothy tried to keep them away from Penny, but it was hopeless. Her fever was slowly rising. The dehydration, without intravenous fluid, was increasing. When Penny would summon the strength to question Dorothy about her condition, she would answer evasively. It was not good; she was slowly failing. But it was still surprising that she had not gone into a more precipitous decline. *I feel so helpless,* Dorothy Davis was thinking. *There is nothing I can do to really help. But there is always God.*

Dr. Stanley Foster arrived in the morning. Just his presence strengthened the morale of the two mission nurses. But more than that, he brought over half a dozen bottles of intravenous fluid, with all the equipment to administer it. It was rushed in to use, but the fever continued to climb, slowly and relentlessly. There was deep concern. Antibiotics were continued in order to prevent complications, but if the real villain were the unknown virus, it would remain untouched by the most potent antibiotic conceivable. Unfortunately, what works against bacteria will not work against a virus.

A further boost to the morale came later that day with the

arrival of Dr. and Mrs. Herman Gray of the Christian Reformed Church. They were stationed in Lagos. Appalled at the thought of Dorothy Davis serving what amounted to twenty-four-hour duty, Mrs. Gray volunteered to relieve her on regular shifts. The relief would be of immeasurable help. Dorothy had had practically no sleep the previous night and was almost ready to fall in her tracks. Mrs. Gray would return in the evening. Meanwhile, Dorothy prepared to make the best of the conditions they would be facing for at least three days. She gave Penny a sponge bath, then did the same for herself at the small sink in the little room next to theirs.

The Nigerian nurses, shy at first at having unexpected foreign visitors, tried to do everything possible to help. It was the first time in their memories that the Pest House had served anyone other than a Nigerian. A strong Nigerian trait is warmth and hospitality—a devout dedication to making strangers feel welcome. This trait came to the surface immediately, as the nurses did their best to try to cook European food, restraining themselves from lavishing the dishes with tongue-scorching peppers and spices and sending out for whatever scraps of European food they could locate. They closed off the room to other new patients to give the mission nurses privacy. Before evening came, two smiling Nigerian nurses appeared in the doorway with brand-new mosquito nets for each bed, some insecticide, and an ancient electric floor fan.

But still the heat hung in the room, and by nightfall there was the same loneliness and despair. Again Penny's temperature edged up, and again Dorothy read and prayed with her. When Mrs. Gray arrived, Dorothy dropped on the bed in exhaustion and tried to sleep. She did so only fitfully. The cries of the children seemed more agonizing than ever and tore at her heart, which, despite all her professional experience, never failed to respond emotionally to a child in pain.

On the next morning, Sunday, March 2, she despaired when she noticed Penny's temperature up again, and she came to the sudden realization that it was now the tenth day since the beginning of Penny's illness. Neither Charlotte Shaw nor Laura Wine had lived much beyond that. She was aware that Penny knew this too, and there was an unspoken tension hanging over them as the day went by.

But there were some notes of cheer. The plane reservations had been cleared and confirmed. By some miracle, Dorothy found her health certificate jammed into a corner of her suitcase. Penny was still conscious and her mind was clear, in spite of great pain and discomfort. *Lord, give her strength and healing if it be Thy will,* Dorothy prayed that night. *Bless and protect the people back at Jos.*

In her pain, Penny's mind scanned her past kaleidoscopically: begging her missionary mother at the age of nine to teach her the East Indian dialect she had used in her mission, thinking that if she learned this she would be able to be a missionary anywhere in the world . . . remembering the inscription inside her mother's wedding ring: "God be merciful unto us and bless us and cause His face to shine upon us" . . . recalling her days at Johns Hopkins and the University of Pennsylvania, where she polished her technical skills to match her passion for service. *I do not want to die,* she kept thinking. *There is too much work to be done in this service.*

In New York City, Dr. John Frame had been unaware of the growing terror in the Sudan, although he had continued his routine studies of missionary blood samples from several parts of West Africa in collaboration with Wil Downs and Jordi Casals at Yale. There were still not enough data assembled to shed any significant new light on tropical febrile sicknesses.

These mysterious fevers continued to be as elusive and unyielding as ever. A plaque on the wall of the lobby of the U.S. State Department in Washington honors the memory of American ambassadors who died in the line of overseas duty. Name after name appears with the notation: "Died of African fever." A distressingly vague term, a symbol of the frustration the medical researchers have been facing. A commemorative plaque for missionaries could easily read the same way, only with a much longer list. Frequently, medical reports from the tropics will use the term "fulminating febrile sickness"—a fever that literally explodes with sudden violence. This especially characterized the hemorrhagic fevers.

Of the first three men who went to Nigeria in 1893 to found the Sudan Interior Mission, two died of fevers within a few months. The third nearly died of malaria but was able to return home.

It wasn't that they were not warned. Before they set out for the interior, the head of the Methodist mission told them when they arrived in Lagos: "Young men, you will never see the Sudan; your children will never see the Sudan; your grandchildren may." Expeditions of Europeans and Americans were constantly being walloped by "African fever" at that time. Six missionaries, landing in Lagos that same year of 1893, headed for their target on the lower Niger River. Four were dead before the expedition arrived; one was stricken with a fulminating fever but was lucky enough to get back to America; and the sixth died within a year.

British officers of the West African Frontier Force who would arrive in Lagos and head for the Sudan met a similar fate. In one unit, 87 percent were either dead or sent home within a year after their arrival. They were felled not by bullets, but by fever. This pattern was consistent. The White Man's Grave designation was more than badinage.

When John Frame finally got news of the events in Jos, it arrived in a confused and inverted way. Mail and cables from Nigeria were often unreliable. In his private office in Manhattan's East Sixties, he received a cable from the Sudan Interior Mission in Jos stating laconically that a second nurse had just died. He was puzzled. He knew nothing about any first nurse who had died. Very quickly after that another cable arrived, stating that Penny Pinneo was on her way to New York in very serious condition.

The information was disjointed. He could draw no real

conclusions from it. But on Saturday morning, March 1, a mission executive called from the main office in New Jersey to say he had received a very disturbing communication from Jos. It was only a brief paragraph, part of a general letter, which simply stated that a mysterious series of lethal illnesses had struck the Sudan Interior Mission at Jos with a vengeance. There were few details.

Mulling it over, John Frame came to the conclusion that either the Jos mission hospital was dealing with an unfortunate series of coincidences or, just possibly, a hitherto unknown hemorrhagic fever from Africa had sprung up, apparently highly virulent and quite contagious.

With Penny Pinneo already being prepared in Lagos for her transatlantic flight, he got on the phone to Dr. John Baldwin, one of his colleagues at Columbia Presbyterian Hospital, to arrange for her immediate admission. Even with the sketchy information they had, it would be better not to take chances. The strictest possible isolation measures should be arranged, coincidence or not.

It all seemed too unlikely, too fortuitous that something like this should develop in the light of his recent research efforts in conjunction with Yale. Such things just didn't happen in the routine of medical research.

At home in Forest Hills, Long Island, that Saturday evening at dinner, he told his wife Veronica that he had a hunch this might be something important. A striking, affable woman of Hungarian birth, Veronica's first thought was, quite understandably: *My goodness, John, do you have to get involved in this?* She often felt this way in connection with his work; she consistently made it a point never to express her feelings. She bit her tongue this time too, keeping the thought to herself and hoping for the best.

After dinner, John Frame went over his notes and records and medical journals. His extensive knowledge of tropical diseases enabled him to eliminate quickly a wide spectrum of possibilities and to narrow down the field. Aside from a fulminating form of malaria, always a likelihood, the only possibility he could come up with was the Marburg virus, which had recently stricken laboratory workers in Germany with a vengeance.

But he still had such meager information on the Jos and Lassa patients that it was useless to speculate. He could only gather what relevant material there was to prepare himself for Penny Pinneo's arrival. He would then pass along what he could to the front-line doctors at Columbia Presbyterian Hospital, who would be carrying the bedside burden of the case in the isolation ward.

He noted the essentials about the symptoms and mode of contagion of the Marburg disease: contact with tissues or blood of the monkeys or patients; accidental pricking of a finger with hypodermic needles infected by the patients; fever, nausea, headache; damage to the human liver and kidneys in the fatal cases; and hemorrhaging that included the gastrointestinal tract. He would keep an eye out for these clues when Penny Pinneo arrived, although he was still not sure when it would be. Whatever the time of arrival, there would be a medical crisis on hand.

It took some time for the letter Penny Pinneo had written from her sick bed in Jos to reach her sister Rose in Rochester, New York. Returning to her home from her busy day's work at the University of Rochester nursing school, Rose Pinneo was elated to get the letter. She had not had any news for some time.

She opened the letter and read it. Her elation faded. It was not like Penny to be sick, and if she were sick in bed, it would have to be something of major proportions.

She was disturbed at the news that two nurses had died, and that one of them had felt she might have been contaminated in taking care of the first. She knew that Penny would be in the thick of things and would certainly have taken a commanding role in caring for both the sick nurses. As a highly skilled and trained nurse herself, she was also perturbed about the news that the symptoms had not responded to antibiotics. She knew of Dr. Jeanette's skill as a physician, and of Penny's capacity for giving the patient the best possible medical care.

Just two days after the letter arrived, on Monday, March 3, she received a call from the Sudan Interior Mission office in New Jersey. The news was not good. Penny would be arriving at Kennedy International Airport around midnight via Pan Am Airways—*as a stretcher case.* The gravity of the situation was immediately evident.

Rose Pinneo was not in the mission service. Her work at the hospital was secular, involved with the intricacies of cardiovascular disease. But she was deeply religious in her personal life. Prayer was her immediate thought and only help in this situation. After she prayed, she picked up the phone and made a plane reservation for New York City for the following day.

John Frame got a similar phone message in his New York office and quickly called Dr. Baldwin at Columbia Presbyterian to confirm the arrival of the patient late Monday night. He was assured that a private room in the isolation ward would be made ready for immediate admittance.

In calling the Yale arbovirus lab, Frame found that Wil Downs was away until Thursday on a field trip, but he got hold of Jordi Casals. Frame was aware of the dangers of undue alarm and presented the problem in low key: Miss Pinneo was arriving from Nigeria as a stretcher case and was obviously quite ill from an unidentified fever. There had been two similar cases, both fatal, but no concrete evidence had been found that the same disease was involved or that the cases were related. There were a considerable number of ifs that would have to be clarified when more data came in. In the meantime, it might be worthwhile for Yale to give special attention to the blood specimens that were being shipped with the patient.

The isolation of a virus is a long, ponderous, and highly

complex problem. It involves tedious, drawn-out manpower hours, hundreds of specially bred laboratory mice and other animals, an exasperating length of time for signs of disease to incubate, careful preparation of monolayer cell lines and tissue cultures, painstaking statistical correlation of data, electron microscope observation after complex preparation of the cell materials to be observed, ultracentrifuges, and infinite patience. It is a process that cannot be hurried, for it must wait for the virus to reveal itself and its insidious destructive power over extended periods of time and over repeated verification experiments.

Both Frame and Casals realized the Yale lab could do nothing that would be of immediate help to Penny Pinneo if she were facing a life-or-death crisis when she arrived. Whatever could be done in this regard would have to be taken care of by the doctors at Columbia Presbyterian. Unless the conventional laboratory tests done quickly at Columbia showed something beyond what had been noted in the Jos hospital, the only hope would be the most meticulous symptomatic and supportive treatment. This is simply a semitechnical way of saying: keep the patient comfortable, the fever down, and the pain reduced.

What Yale could do, however, was to begin the cumbersome machinery of the search so that the enemy could be identified and an attempt made to counteract it by the slow development of possible vaccine or plasma containing antibodies. But this could take months or years, if it could be developed at all. However, if some kind of outbreak were occurring and spreading, at least the medical world would know what it could or could not do to prevent and forestall the disease. Further, if the source of the virus could be identified, at least prophylactic measures could be taken to retard its spread. This was critical.

But all this speculation was of little use until more information came in. Frame and Casals agreed that as far as they knew at the moment they might be conjuring up dragons that didn't exist. The two deaths and the serious illness of the mission nurse, tragic as they were, might have absolutely no connection with one another.

Rescheduling of work in the thirty-five-man laboratory for a crash program was another problem. With more than thirty meticulous, ongoing projects a year, from the testing of Near Eastern bird serum to studies on the "antigenic and biologic classification of dengue viruses," a halt in the Yale assembly line could throw everything seriously out of whack. The number and variety of viruses under study at any one time was staggering.

An alphabetic grouping in the list under "C" alone exemplified the wide spectrum of remote viruses being researched at the Yale lab:

> Cali 874
> California
> Candiru
> Capim
> Chaco
> Chagres
> Chandipura
> Changuinola
> Chenuda
> CoAr 3627
> Cocal
> Congo
> Corriparta
> Colorado tick fever
> Cotia

It is doubtful that more than a handful of doctors in the country were familiar with most of these—and the other 350 viruses under study at the arbovirus laboratory.

To cope with these problems, director Wil Downs had assembled a group of researchers considered to be at the top of their professions. There was Spanish-born Dr. Jordi Casals, a Rockefeller Foundation pathologist and microbiologist of great stature. There was Dr. Sonja Buckley, originally from Zurich,

Switzerland, whose research in tissue cultures had made her internationally famous. There was Dr. Robert Shope, who had come up from his work on viruses for the Rockefeller Foundation in Brazil to do outstanding research in virus epidemiology at Yale.

The Yale lab, built with the help of an outright grant of $2 million from the Rockefeller Foundation, had major assignments for special studies from the World Health Organization, the U.S. Public Health Service, the Department of Health, Education, and Welfare, the National Institutes of Health, and the U.S. Army. It could not exactly drop everything and pick up something new that quickly. The previous studies with Frame's materials had been done on an open-time, nonpriority basis.

Jordi Casals agreed that the new apparent crisis would more than warrant a priority commitment, but he could not make that decision himself. He would immediately try to get in touch with Wil Downs, however, and arrange to set up a crash schedule if he agreed, which he was sure Downs would do.

Frame said he would collect the serum and tissues from Penny Pinneo's plane the minute it arrived and take a new blood specimen from her before she was hospitalized. He would sort and prepare the material for analysis not only by Yale but by the New York City Bureau of Laboratories and the Columbia Presbyterian labs as well.

With this division of the load, not only would there be an independent check but the hospital would have something to go on directly without having to wait for the lengthier and more sophisticated tests at Yale.

The only thing to do at the moment was wait.

In Nigeria, the Pan Am Boeing 707 was already at the open ramp at the Lagos airport when the ambulance van bearing Penny Pinneo and Dorothy Davis pulled up. The entire first-class section was emptied of other passengers. Curtains were put up on poles to surround the area where a canvas stretcher bed had been installed in place of the seats. The stewardesses were helpful and efficient. By pure coincidence, Dr. Lyle Conrad of the Center for Disease Control in Atlanta, Georgia, was returning from Lagos to New York on the same flight. He volunteered to help take care of the patient on the thirteen-hour flight, which included stops at Accra, Monrovia, and Dakar.

Close to exhaustion, her uniform disheveled, nurse Davis was buoyed by Dr. Conrad's moral and professional support. Although Penny had survived longer than the other two nurses, she was acutely ill and gravely dehydrated; she could hold down only a few sips of water at widely spaced intervals. With persistent fever, continual sponging is necessary. Dorothy worried, since this was impossible to do. She also worried because it was the twelfth day of clinical sickness. If death was to come, it would probably come soon.

To get the plywood stretcher into the plane, the Nigerian bearers had to hold it high above their heads and maneuver it through the bulkhead door. A considerable wind had sprung up, making the operation difficult. Penny was convinced she was going to fall off, but by now she had become mentally confused. The ordeal of the unbearable heat of the Pest House, the vacillating but steadily climbing fever, the inability to swallow combined to make her disoriented and utterly exhausted.

In the plane the canvas stretcher bed made a sunken pocket under her weight, so that it was difficult to change position. Dr. Conrad and Dorothy Davis propped pillows underneath the canvas to raise it. A night table was improvised, and medicines and injectables were laid out on it, along with a glass of water and a straw for whatever fluids Penny would be able to swallow and hold down.

All that could be done had been done. Dorothy took a seat across from Penny and collapsed in it with total exhaustion. Dr. Conrad sat nearby and urged her to go to sleep. She closed her eyes and moved her hand across the aisle to the stretcher, just as she had done during the long days in the Pest House.

As the jetliner roared down the Nigerian runway for takeoff, she prayed that Penny would live through the flight.

Chapter Four

In midevening on Monday, March 3, 1969, John Frame prepared to leave his house in Forest Hills to go to Kennedy International Airport. His youngest daughter was home from school for a visit. It had been a pleasant family reunion. Veronica Frame finally broke her self-imposed code and said: "John, are you sure you have to become involved in this? Isn't it dangerous?"

Frame was in the process of packing a Becton-Diston Vacutainer, a tube and needle for drawing blood specimens. It was obvious why his wife asked the question: he would be drawing 10 cc of blood from Penny Pinneo even before she left the airplane. Columbia Presbyterian would be too busy getting its own specimens to divert the most up-to-date samples for either Yale or the New York City public health laboratory.

His daughter was apprehensive too. He reassured them that he would be extremely careful, and that they were not to worry. He had given a great deal of thought to the problem of contagion involved in these three strange cases. As a specialist in exotic tropical diseases, he was constantly taking certain calculated risks. These were occupational hazards, and he had to face them. The delicate balance lay at the point where he might shift that risk from himself to his family. This was a common hazard among doctors, virologists, and bacteriologists. The most important element in avoiding it was caution, which he was always at great pains to take. The other element was pure, subjective judgment. There was no pat slide-rule formula to follow. At a certain point the benefit-risk ratio had to be considered and acted on.

Going through his mind in this crisis was the courage shown by those who had been facing the terror from its beginning in Africa. Although his information was at the moment sketchy, it was easy to extrapolate and imagine the conditions there. Medical and nursing care was an intimate thing. There was constant, direct contact with those parts of a patient that were most likely to contain the infectious agent, whether it was bacteria or virus.

Dr. Jeanette Troup, in treating the three patients, would have been continually assaulted by the possibility of exposure to the micro-insults of the unknown agent, whether in taking a blood sample or in examining a throat. If she had done an autopsy—and this he did not know yet—she would have been especially vulnerable to lingering bacterial or viral agents.

For the nurses involved, there would have been similar risks: the handling of bedpans, the turning and helping of patients to move in bed, the collection of throat swabs and throat washings for analysis, the taking of temperatures, the changing of sheets, the taking of a pulse, even the raising of dust or the handling of dishes. Though these routines were not commonly hazardous, they could be in the case of an extremely virulent disease.

Frame admired the quiet courage of those who had exposed themselves to such danger. Under the circumstances, he could not blench in the face of his own task. He had to confess, though, as he drove toward Kennedy, that he had some trepidation.

At the airport, already waiting, were Rose Pinneo and Trevor Ardill, who headed the Sudan Interior Mission program from the main U.S. office—at that time in New York. Professional as she was, Rose Pinneo was upset about her sister. Many questions had gone through her mind since she had received word of Penny's illness. How would immigration authorities take to the situation? Would they even let her sister enter the country? Could Penny survive the incredibly rough trip from Jos to Lagos, and from Lagos to New York? Would there be any slip-ups in the arrangements for giving her the best possible treatment? Her survival depended now on expert and immediate hospital care.

Rose Pinneo found that she had no need to worry about the latter. The Scully-Walton ambulance was waiting at the airport before she and Trevor Ardill got there. The plane arrived ahead of schedule. After the regular passengers had disembarked, John Frame, Trevor Ardill, Rose Pinneo, and an officer from the U.S. Public Health Service boarded the 707 quickly. Penny recognized her sister even through her mental confusion and said: "I never thought I'd see you again."

Penny was obviously a very sick person. Her dehydration was marked, and she had extreme difficulty in breathing—the same dyspnea that had struck the other two patients in Jos. Much of Rose Pinneo's fear was allayed when the public health officer immediately and sympathetically gave permission for her sister to be taken to the waiting ambulance. Before Penny was put into a wheelchair to be carried off the plane, John Frame prepared to take the blood specimen. He simply said: "Good to see you back safe." She replied: "I can hardly swallow," and held her arm out for the blood to be drawn.

With the trepidation that he freely admitted, Frame drew the 10 cc of blood into the Vacutainer. In a brief conference with Lyle Conrad, he reviewed the latest information and got from him the large thermos jug full of the once-iced tissue and blood specimens from all three victims. Wet ice was far from an ideal mode of shipping. But dry ice or liquid nitrogen had, of course, been unavailable.

Assured that there was nothing more he could do, with the ambulance waiting and plenty of hands on deck, Frame left the

plane formulating plans of how he would coordinate the research work with Yale, the New York laboratory, and Columbia. He suddenly found himself heading toward the washroom
in the terminal, went directly to it, and scrubbed hard. On
viewing Penny Pinneo's condition, even briefly, he was convinced
that something serious was going on, and he wouldn't be worth
much if he didn't take whatever precautions were necessary to
follow this enigma through to the end.

It was bitter cold that March midnight. Rose Pinneo carefully wrapped her sister in a winter coat and tucked a blanket
around her as the ambulance attendants lifted her into the
wheelchair.

Dorothy Davis engineered the luggage and equipment at
the customs post, dreading the potential delay in getting Penny
to the hospital. Her fears were groundless. The customs officer
simply said: "I understand. Please go right through." She saw
her family waving to her on the balcony and bit her lip. The
reunion would have to wait until she got Penny safely to the
hospital.

She rode with Penny and Rose Pinneo in the ambulance to
Columbia Presbyterian. It was one more frenetic addenda to an
almost endless series of awkward, agonizing shifts, transfers,
probing examinations, red tape, and rudely shocking journeys
that had begun on the remote Jos plateau in Nigeria so many
days ago. *How much*, she wondered, *can a person stand, in this
condition—or in any condition?*

At Columbia Presbyterian's isolation ward the staff of residents, nurses, and doctors was prepared for the midnight arrival. John Baldwin and David Gocke, both colleagues of John
Frame and extremely able physicians, lost no time in getting
Penny Pinneo into her room and ready for the complex routine
of diagnosis. If the hunches about the three mission cases were
correct, the disease was a killer that gave little time for lei-
surely analysis or comfortable, conventional therapy. Tests
would have to begin right away, late as the hour was.

As a precaution, every staff member in the isolation ward

was gowned and masked—hardly a cheerful-looking welcoming committee for Penny and her sister.

Rose Pinneo was immediately aware of her peculiar position: she was a highly trained, highly qualified nurse who was also a member of the family and an outsider to the hospital. She wanted desperately to take care of her sister, but as a professional she knew that outside interference—even by an expert—could pose problems in hospital routine. She was admitted, however, given a mask and gown, and permitted to stay with her sister as a relative rather than a nurse. Faced with the reverse situation in her own hospital, she would probably have done the same thing. Dorothy Davis, having seen Penny safely to the hospital, finally went to rejoin her family.

The inevitable medical history would have to be taken anew for the Columbia doctors, regardless of the lateness of the hour. Lying on the bed with her neck and face swollen, and unable to swallow, Penny tried her best to answer the young resident. Rose Pinneo ached with every painful response and wondered if the resident had any idea how sick and exhausted his new patient was. Again, she felt the conflict between nurse and relative. A delay in taking the history might mean a delay in the commencement of therapy. The crisis came when Penny, breaking down for the first time since the long ordeal had started, began sobbing. "Please, please," she said, "Let me alone. I need sleep." The history taking came to an end, and Rose Pinneo sat by her sister through the night, wondering if she would live through it.

The following morning, on his way to his office at the Columbia School of Public Health, where he taught tropical medicine, John Frame stopped off at the isolation ward. He was impressed by the way the nurses and residents were handling the situation but was startled to find that they were not wearing rubber surgical gloves along with the masks and gowns. Checking Penny's chart, he found that she was neither worse nor better than the night before, which could perhaps be taken as a hopeful sign—or perhaps not. Rose Pinneo had gone to her hotel to rest; she would be returning later.

Since the patient was resting as comfortably as she could under the circumstances, Frame took the opportunity to hold an informal, on-the-job seminar in tropical diseases for the nurses, interns, and residents. In the conference room of the isolation ward, away from Penny's hearing, he used a word he seldom uttered. "Look here," he told the group, "this is a *frightening* disease, if our hunches are correct. I see that none of you are wearing rubber gloves. This is most essential and must be added to the mask-and-gown precaution."

In the best Socratic tradition, he asked the young staff: "All right—how would you handle this if it were the plague?" In a light vein, but with an edge of seriousness, the staff members agreed: We'd collapse. Then Frame continued: "All right—if this were a strep throat, what would you do? You'd have to have confidence that your procedures were working, and that you were following your procedures. That's why I emphasized the need for rubber gloves."

The nurses and doctors were edgy and a little unhinged, but they went about their work. Procedures were tightened, and the use of masks, gowns, and gloves became a ritual. They were put on any time Penny Pinneo's room was entered. (The term "ward" was a misnomer; it was a series of isolated rooms.) They were removed immediately on leaving. The masks and gloves were thrown in a special disposal unit to be incinerated. The gowns were put in a special hamper to be sterilized before being laundered. Risks were to be reduced to a minimum.

Back in his office at Columbia's School of Public Health, John Frame got a call from a jittery intern. "Can you give me any more information about this disease?" he asked. Frame told him all he could, which was not a great deal. He did know that two nurses who had cared for the first case had come down with it—always keeping in mind the possibility of coincidence —and that was why he had been so firm in his lecture at the isolation ward earlier in the morning.

There was a pause on the other end of the phone, and then the intern said: "Can you tell me this? Does *anyone* ever recover from the disease?"

There was no answer whatever that John Frame could give. Or anyone else, for that matter.

The lab tests at Columbia were drifting in with small chips of information, none of them very revealing. The leukocyte count had jumped dramatically to twice the normal—from a low count of 4,500 to 12,000. This was disturbing, since it was typical of the cases of both Laura Wine and Charlotte Shaw, and atypical of a conventional virus infection. Urinalysis: 1 plus, against 0 for normal, indicating slight difficulty with kidney function but not critical. Charlotte Shaw had shown 4 plus, the highest rating; Laura Wine, 3 plus. The hematocrit, which indicates the percentage of solid material in the blood, was well within normal range at 40. Blood urea nitrogen (BUN) was markedly high at 44, against a normal of 10 to 22, suggesting that the kidneys were not getting rid of their waste products. Overall, there was still nothing to grab hold of.

Rose Pinneo, who felt that she should remain discreetly away as much as possible, kept in touch by phone. As a family member, she was given evasive answers. Used to complete access to clinical information in her work, she found this rankling.

Reviewing his notes with Roger Williams, the entomologist in his department at Columbia's School of Public Health, John Frame was groping for other theories. Both agreed that Penny Pinneo's condition must represent some kind of hemorrhagic fever, although neither of them knew of any like it in West Africa. Yellow fever—perhaps? The chances were it would be ruled out. Dengue fever, commonplace in Africa, was unlikely. It certainly had not shown itself to be as deadly as this one. The symptoms didn't seem to match up closely enough with the terrifying Marburg green monkey disease. Yet if the three cases were not a coincidence, the new unknown agent could prove itself even more dangerous.

Williams then recalled that Jordi Casals at Yale had recently linked a virus affliction called Congo fever with a Crimean-type hemorrhagic fever discovered by the Russians in 1930. Both diseases apparently resulted from the same virus and differed only in geographic location.

Frame got on the phone with Casals at New Haven, and Casals confirmed this fact. Congo fever had been found in East Africa in 1968. It was related to the Crimea fever, and it was dangerous: mortality rate, 25 percent. Again, the facts about the three mission nurses didn't quite add up to the Congo fever hypothesis. But it could not be ruled out.

Another very real consideration, however, was a plague, never satisfactorily identified, that had sprung up in Upper Volta, the landlocked African country northwest of Nigeria with the same savanna-like topography. There had been a remote paper written on it in the *Bulletin de la Societé de Pathologie Exotique* back in 1946. The article had been lost in medical archives until a doctor from Africa, James Gear, dropped by Yale one day and told Wil Downs about it. Downs had been intrigued because research on the disease had never been followed up, and a big question mark remained.

Frame tracked down the twenty-year-old article and gave it a careful reading. The disease had been studied by French doctors as far back as 1944 and was dubbed Red Congolese fever, although it was not related to the newly discovered Congo fever. It seemed to create symptoms similar to epidemic typhus.

The French had done some other studies on "tropical typhus" (a most inexact and unscientific diagnosis) in the nearby Ivory Coast in the early 1940s. Two white priests from the Mission du Reo were seized with this devastating form of tropical typhus after accompanying some of their African parishioners on the traditional rat hunts so common in all parts of the western Sudan, including Lassa and the Jos plateau. The French colonists in Upper Volta called it *la chasse aux rongeurs*. The rats, crazed by the bush fires (*feux de brousse*) roaring above their holes, would stumble grotesquely out into the open, where they would be clubbed to death for the evening's dinner. After one such hunt, when some scorched rats sought refuge in their bungalow, an American missionary and his family living near a burned-out section of the savanna were seized with the same type of fever that had striken the two priests.

Shortly after that, a new French battalion arrived in the area and cleared the bush around its billets by burning the savanna grass. Within fifteen days several officers and subofficers came down with the ill-defined fever.

The medical article was not clear as to how many deaths were involved. But it pointed out the strangeness of this particular form of typhus and its relation to the bush rats, which made up such a generous portion of the tribesmen's diet and which also created such a hovering menace in the houses where they scurried for shelter after the fires.

The sicknesses were so commonplace during the peak of the dry season and the burning of the bush that the months of January and February were dubbed the Months of the Doctors by the local villagers. Among the many varied rats of the bush, the mahogany rat (*Mus ruffinus*) was recognized by nearby Ivory Coasters as the heavy villain. As a result, the eating of this particular strain was formally prohibited by tribal fiat. So the intuitive instinct of the tribesmen made the connection between the fire, the rat hunt, and the epidemic, whatever it was. The article also noted that during the rainy season no European contracted the disease, only farmers who encountered the red rats in the course of their work in the fields.

But the article had been written in wartime. There had been neither time nor manpower nor funds for research to follow up. Aside from that, the report carried no hard information, no clinical tests, no extensive laboratory follow-up. Its value to John Frame and Roger Williams and the rest at Yale was that there was a possibility of a source for a hemorrhagic

rodent-borne fever that could relate to the deadly South American viruses that carried the Argentinean and Bolivian fevers.
The virus from Lassa, if it existed, could conceivably be of the
same genre—but again, they were back in the area of wild
speculation.

At Columbia Presbyterian the tests continued, but they seemed
to be getting nowhere. Rose Pinneo dropped by on that first
day for a brief visit and noted that her sister's condition was
neither improved nor dramatically worse. She later wrote in
the *American Journal of Nursing:*

> During the severe illness, every system of her body was af-
> fected by the virus, and she was subjected to many diagnostic
> tests—spinal tap, thoracentesis, electroencephalogram, and
> electrocardiogram—to isolate the organism or determine its
> effect on the body organs. It was difficult for me to see her
> undergo these, especially the thoracentesis, for she could not
> sit upright without becoming light-headed, or the spinal tap,
> which required lying quietly in a difficult position.
> One of the persistent complications of great concern to
> me was lack of a swallowing reflex and an enlarged neck,
> perhaps from damage to the nerves supplying these areas.
> Would these be permanent? How can a person survive for
> very long with these complications? As she attempted to swal-
> low a few cc's of fluid with oral medications, her jaw muscles
> went into spasm from this small expenditure of energy.

Rose Pinneo tried hard to keep out of the way of the line
nurses, but could not resist falling into some of the hospital
routine. She volunteered to do some chores, and the other
nurses did not seem to object, especially since she offered to do
some of the most burdensome, which she was glad to assume.
Tension was mounting as the first day's tests trickled in, and
she went about preparing to empty the bedpan as a check on
the urinary output.

She was stunned when she looked down at it. A small, live
creature was floating on the surface of the fluid. Trying to
calm her already taut nerves, she took the animal immediately

to the charge nurse. In all Rose Pinneo's experience, she had never encountered anything like this. It was immediately sent out for laboratory analysis, but in only a few moments the results came in: it was a common, garden-variety slug that had dropped off the flowers in the room and into the bedpan.

The incident served a good purpose: it eased the tension among the nurses and for Rose Pinneo. Humor was scarce at these moments; it was needed badly.

Wil Downs of Yale, his affability muted by the serious condition of Penny Pinneo and its possible implications, had returned from his field trip, checked in at the Rockefeller Foundation offices at Columbus Circle, and grabbed a taxi uptown to John Frame's office at Columbia. The blood specimens of the three mission victims were waiting for him there, under refrigeration. No one knew what their condition would be after the harsh trip and delay in Africa during the stopover.

Downs was intrigued by the speculation Frame and Williams had indulged in. He had followed up to some extent on the Upper Volta fever outbreaks. Victims had shown an awesome fatality rate of 60 percent. If the current crisis turned out to be more than just a coincidence among three mission nurses, and if the sample was adequate—which of course it wasn't—the new African fever was already showing an unbelievable mortality rate of 66 percent.

The fact was that no one really knew anything. It appeared that the only real hope of elucidation would have to come from the sophisticated facilities of the Yale arbovirus laboratory, with a solid assist from CDC researchers in Atlanta, after they received some samples to work with.

At the doorway of John Frame's office, Wil Downs, holding the neatly boxed thermos jug of blood and tissue specimens, stopped for a moment and said: "You know something very interesting, John? The whole staff at Yale is in the middle of reading *The Andromeda Strain*. Does that kind of make you stop and think?"

Frame smiled and nodded, and Wil Downs left the office.

He taxied to the 125th Street station and caught the next train for New Haven. On the train, Downs struck on another horrifying thought: there must have been up to a hundred passengers on the jet flight from Lagos to New York. At this very moment, they were most likely fanning out to their homes in widely separated sections of the country.

The work at Yale was obviously cut out for him. He had better move fast.

The medical report, a joint effort of all the Columbia doctors involved in Penny Pinneo's case, revealed the frustration they faced in the jungle of medical alternatives:

> The clinical records suggested that the three illnesses were related, but they might have been merely coincidental. These cases suggested typhus, some form of typhoid fever, leptospirosis, ornithosis, fulminating African trypanosomiasis, amebic liver abscess, or chloroquine-resistant malaria; or more commonplace diseases such as Hodgkin's lymphoma, mycoplasma infection, or trichinosis. However, if all three cases are accepted as exemplifying the same disease process, we know of no African disease that fits the epidemiologic pattern. The high death rate, though not the clinical courses, suggests the Marburg virus disease. To our knowledge, this has not been reported in Africa [it had only broken out in Germany], but neither had any other identifiable syndromes that fit the features that have been noted in the patients.

The report continued: "The various alternative diagnoses were eliminated one by one. Bacteriologic and fungal cultures of blood, stool, urine, the nasopharynx, fluid taken by the thoracentesis, and spinal fluid were all negative. Serologic tests for salmonella, typhus, mycoplasma, and malaria were all unrevealing . . ."

There was one chink in the armor plate, however. A hospital parasitologist placed a blood smear from Penny Pinneo under his microscope and found what seemed to be a ring form of the parasite *Plasmodium faciparum,* a definite clinical indication of malaria.

This was a serious and not too common form of malaria. In

commenting on its prevalency, the CDC noted in one annual report: "There were only 3 malaria deaths . . . and all were due to *Plasmodium falciparum.* All occurred in persons who had *recently returned from Africa:* two foreign seamen and an American tourist [italics added]."

One of the seamen who died came down with headache, fever, chills, dizziness, and dyspnea. His fever shot up to 103°, then dropped to normal. But before the evening was over, he was dead. The other seaman experienced similar symptoms, and the same virulent malarial parasite was found in his blood smear. He went through a sudden jump in temperature to a searing 105°, and was dead in less than four days.

The American tourist was a seventy-two-year-old woman from Dallas, Texas, who came home after a camera safari in South and East Africa. She came down with malaise and nausea, followed by fever and progressive weakness. The similiarity of her case to those of the mission nurses was marked. Antibiotics were useless. Initial diagnosis was fever of undetermined origin. Her temperature suddenly spiked to a vicious 105°. She became cyanotic and was dead within ten days.

It was similarities of this sort, with one tropical disease easily masquerading as another, that made the job of the Columbia doctors so difficult.

It became all the more so when Penny Pinneo's temperature suddenly and dramatically soared to an incredible 107° within twenty-four hours after she had arrived at the hospital.

Back in Lassa, Dr. John Hamer was still puzzled and shocked by the death of Laura Wine. Cut off from the world by both geography and unreliable radio reception, he knew little about what was happening in the wake of her death. At the time Penny Pinneo was being wheeled into the Columbia Presbyterian Hospital, he had completed a summary of Laura Wine's case to forward to Dr. Joseph Schecter, the medical consultant for the Church of the Brethren Mission back in California. Dr. Hammer wrote:

I am enclosing a copy of the clinical record and illness of Miss Laura M. Wine, who lived here in Lassa and died in Jos on Sunday night, January 26, 1969. I believe you have already received a copy of her gross autopsy report.

We are suspicious that she may have been sicker than she let on during the weekend of January 17, 18, and 19.

In reviewing the situation at this point, of course there are some things that I would do differently, but that of course comes from hindsight instead of foresight.

Recently, in a letter from Jos I heard unofficially that one of the nurses who helped some with Laura during her illness also came down with a disease that did not respond to antibiotics. I've not heard anything official. Maybe you have heard about this. I believe the young lady may have died . . .

Of course, this thought reopened another enigma. John Hamer and his wife had been just about as close to Laura Wine in her illness as anyone could get: at her home, in the Lassa and Jos hospitals, in the Land Rover, in the tiny Comanche aircraft. Why had they been exempt? Why had Dr. Jeanette Troup and several other nurses remained unscathed? Or Dorothy Davis? Or Dr. Lyle Conrad? Would they *remain* exempt?

Hopes for further illumination from the detailed laboratory findings on Laura Wine dwindled after Dr. Schecter reviewed both the gross and histologic autopsy reports on March 5, the day that Penny Pinneo's fever shot up so rapidly.

Making his own report to the Church of the Brethren Mission, Dr. Schecter wrote:

I have just now received the autopsy report on Laura Wine. It is not at all helpful. According to the diagnosis, she died of kidney failure presumably due to a hemorrhage somewhere in her system that could not be detected from the autopsy. There was some hemorrhagic gastritis, that is, bleeding points in the stomach, though whether she was bleeding from this would have to come from the doctor who made the autopsy.

So all in all, I don't think the autopsy findings would

give any insight into the nurse passing away who was taking care of Laura . . .

Another blind alley. Hope continued to rest on what the Yale arbovirus laboratory might be able to come up with, which put Wil Downs, Jordi Casals, Sonja Buckley, and their colleagues in an uncomfortable position. All new serum, tissues, and fluid taken at Columbia were being forwarded to them.

Being neither supermen nor clairvoyants, they would have to work long and patiently, without even the assurance they would get anywhere in cracking the mystery. And they were well aware that nothing their slow-moving machinery could do would be of any help to Penny Pinneo's explosive crisis, much as they would like it to.

Wil Downs' train got into New Haven late in the afternoon. Within minutes he was on the sixth floor of the new high-rise building of Yale's Department of Public Health and Epidemiology, which houses the Arbovirus Research Unit. Most of the staff were waiting for him with considerable interest. He placed the package holding the thermos jug on the table, and the informal meeting began.

Inside the jug were the serum, pleural fluid, and urine specimens that had traveled from Africa. The Yale researchers would have to handle them carefully to stretch them over the long series of tests that would need to be done. The excitement about the job was tempered by the fact that the lab technicians had gone through many series of false alarms, and they were aware that this could be another one.

Wil Downs wasn't taking any chances. He prefaced his remarks at the meeting by laying down strict rules. First, everyone who handled the virus in any form was to wear mask, gown, and gloves, just as researchers were doing at Columbia Presbyterian. Second, Bob Shope—who was later to become director of the laboratory when Wil Downs retired—was not to become involved in the research under any circumstances. This was regrettable, because Shope was a crack virologist, with invaluable field experience. But he had four young children. Downs likewise issued an edict that no one in the organization who had small children would be permitted to work on the research. He said it very simply: "You guys will not touch the stuff!"

The only ones permitted to handle the specimens would be Sonja Buckley, Jordi Casals, and himself. Downs and Casals would begin work right away on their carefully bred mouse colony, while Sonja Buckley prepared her cell lines in bottles and test tubes. The latter would take several days to prepare.

A frontal attack on a virus is a complex process. No one, even the experts, knows exactly how to define a virus. It is a molecule that skates halfway between a living thing and a chemically inert thing, like sugar or table salt. It is made up of a protein or fatty-protein overcoat wrapped around a sliver of RNA (ribonucleic acid) or DNA (deoxyribonucleic acid), depending on what type of virus it is. Its form can range from a spherical glob to a particle shaped like an Apollo mooncraft, including a handy, four-pronged landing gear. Several viruses are beautifully geometric in shape, made up of numerous triangular faces. It would take a billion times a billion polio viruses to fill up a small salt shaker.

They are infectious. There's hardly a living tissue anywhere that is not a host to one or another virus. The only way they can reproduce themselves is to puncture a cell wall and inject their RNA or DNA inside the cell. The protein overcoat stays outside, its job over.

Once inside the cell, the virus begins its hijacking. Rudely, it makes the cell do the work. It even tricks the cell into thinking it's enjoying the job. There's no resistance once the spiral coil of DNA (or RNA—the effect is the same) gets inside. The cell begins giving the virus anything it wants. The entire machinery of the healthy cell is put at the disposal of the virus' nucleic acid. The cell hijacker may even decide to take it easy for a long time, curl up and rest. Then all of a sudden it may wake up and become a killer. Once the lethal DNA of the virus is inside the cell, no medicine, vaccine, or antibodies can help.

The DNA of a healthy cell is a blueprint, a diestamp, and a microcomputer that commands what the cell is to do and be and orders it when to divide. The DNA of the virus takes over these functions without ceremony. It orders the cell *not* to divide but to change over the assembly line and make more viruses.

It takes only a little more than five minutes for the healthy cell to turn out an ample supply of virus DNA. After a corresponding supply of virus protein is obligingly produced, the rest is easy. The two elements combine, and in less than fifteen minutes baby viruses are swarming all through the cell's fluid and cytoplasm—up to several hundred in a single cell.

Then a final-destruct signal is given, and the skin of the cell is exploded—lyzed, it is called—leaving the cell nothing more than an empty bag. Some viruses are content to puncture a little hatch in the cell wall and spill out like a crowd emerging from a subway. But they don't even have the initiative to propel themselves. They let the body fluids do it, and get a free ride. Whatever way they come out, the new herd swarms over other healthy cells, and the whole process begins again. A single virus can create an army of 10,000 new recruits in a matter of a few hours, and the forces swell geometrically as the invasion continues. In another few hours there could be 100 million viruses ready to search and destroy.

Except for the use of an electron microscope, all virus detective work is done by indirect methods. The tests at Yale would fall on the shoulders of Sonja Buckley and Jordi Casals, although Wil Downs would be taking an active part himself. Bob Speir, a Canadian out of Princeton, Columbia, and Sloan-Kettering, would be heading the electron microscope program —but he faced an immediate obstacle. The complex instrument able to magnify a particle more than 100,000 times was broken at the moment. Repairs were being rushed.

The infectious material brought to New Haven by Wil

Downs was for the most part blood serum and pleural fluid from the chest cavity. The test tubes had been carefully marked, according to which victim they were drawn from: L. W.; C. S.; or L. P. They had been repacked on wet ice at Columbia to preserve the virus, if any, because a virus has to be extremely tough to survive such a long trip. There was some doubt whether the virus had survived, even if it had existed in the specimens in the first place.

There wasn't much that Sonja Buckley could do with the specimens at the moment because she had to prepare her cell lines—tissue cultures—in a series of Roux and French Square bottles, test tubes, and plaque bottles. She went down the hall to her laboratory, which was spotlessly clean, brightly illuminated, and windowless. Eleanor Gilson, a limber, cheerful lab technician in her forties, was already waiting for her. They carefully put the serum and urine specimens in the freezers, unopened.

Then they drew out the large Roux bottles, shaped almost like quart hip flasks. Inside the bottles were carpets of living cells that they would later try to kill in various controlled ways with the infected blood serum and urine specimens from Africa.

There were two kinds of living cells, both bathed in a soft nutrient fluid that looked like Lavoris. The carpets of cells floated in a thin gray layer on top of the red fluid, barely visible but clearly discernible. The nutrient fluid bath that kept them alive (almost with a suggestion of immortality, because as they grew and divided some of the cells were drawn off to start another bottle) was a balanced salt solution, containing vitamins, some amino acids, and a bovine fetal broth.

The two types of cells were drawn from baby hamsters and from the kidneys of African green monkeys.

Since arboviruses grow abundantly in the kidney cells of African green monkeys, Sonja Buckley favored these cells, known as Vero cells. With the exactitude of a stingy bartender, she began pouring off the cells into scores of two-ounce flint plaque bottles, which were actually old-fashioned prescription bottles. When additional scores of test tubes and French Square bottles were filled with the cells in agar, a nutrient jelly, she closed down the work for the day to let the cell carpets set in their new environment over the weekend. Nearly 200 cell cultures sat in rows of tubes and bottles, like a regiment of soldiers. Her share of the infected specimens was safely packed in the freezer, and there was nothing more she and her assistant could do for the time.

For Wil Downs and Jordi Casals, the picture was different. The blood and urine specimens—which might or might not be lethal—would have to be injected immediately and directly into the brains of the purebred Charles River mice colony of the arbovirus laboratory. No race horses had been bred with any more care. The mice had to be identical, or the tests made on them would be varying and useless. They had to be free of other disease, or it would be impossible to tell whether they were being killed by the suspected virus or by some other agent. Only two years before, an epidemic of a mouse disease called ectromelia had swept through the mouse colony and paralyzed operations in the lab. A clean colony had had to be reestablished. Great precautions were taken to protect the mice, even though, ironically, they were being farmed and bred in order to die in the interests of science.

They were housed luxuriously in metal boxes called Horsfall isolators, which resembled row on row of large breadboxes. Each box had its own ventilating system, creating a negative pressure and reducing the danger of a mouse kicking and scratching up urine and feces dust. The foul air from the isolator would be drawn out and incinerated. The virus epidemic in the Argentine cornfield, when the farm workers had been felled by the deadly dust aerosol generated by the rats, dramatized the importance of that precaution. Without the Horsfall isolators, lab workers could be continually assaulted by similar aerosols, from mice injected with some of the deadliest viruses known.

After a conference, Downs, with his bronzed face covered by a surgical mask, and Casals, with his thick shock of gray hair covered by a laboratory cap, made a decision. They would select suckling mice for their first batch of inoculations, because there would more likely be a quicker response from mice at such a tender age. They were looking for some kind of immediate playback on the questions they faced: Was there a live virus lurking in the fluids they were unpacking from the ice? If so, how many mice would it kill? Or would it kill any?

The concept behind the experiments in the virus laboratory is simple; its rendition is infinitely complex. The experiments of Sonja Buckley with the tissue cultures and those of Downs and Casals with the live animals were basically designed for the same purpose.

First, you took either a carpet of healthy living cells in a bottle or a healthy live laboratory animal. Then you injected or inoculated them with a fluid or tissue juice suspected of harboring a virus.

Then you watched and waited.

You looked for damage to appear, either to the cells or to the animal. And you tried to find out what concentration of the suspected fluid or tissue it took to kill the cells or the animal.

You also took an equal number of other cells or animals and injected or inoculated them with the simple nutrient broth the cells were grown in or with a healthy serum. You did this to make sure there wasn't some kind of laboratory accident or atmosphere that might be doing the killing, rather than the suspected agent. This was known as a control group.

You later matched up the results of the cell-line experiments and the animal experiments. Then you repeated all the experiments over and over again, to assess the statistics. You never took anything for granted, and you always allowed for variables. It was precise, slow, painstaking work.

The animal inoculations were tougher and more dangerous than the cell-line or tissue-culture procedures. Cells don't move; mice wriggle unpredictably. Downs and Casals were not going to take any chances with this new and uncertain situation. They put the Charles River suckling mice under deep ether anesthesia.

Downs took a syringe with .02 milliliters of the suspected, straw-colored serum from Laura Wine, picked up a baby mouse in his hands, and plunged the needle into the cranium. Casals did the same. They continued until after midnight.

Casals, who usually commuted back to New York every evening, decided to stay the night with Wil Downs in nearby Branford, Connecticut. They were both exhausted. After they had finished, Downs said: "It might be a good idea, Jordi, not to tell your wife about this project."

Jordi Casals nodded.

Under conditions of crisis and pressure, even the best of scientists can make mistakes. As they drove along the Connecticut Thruway late that night, neither Wil Downs nor Jordi Casals knew it at the time but they had already made their first mistake—a mistake that would cost them time, the one element they could least afford to lose.

Chapter Five

With her fellow passengers of the jet flight from Lagos to New York now resettled across the country in their homes, Penny Pinneo lay in her bed in the isolation ward scorched by her incredibly high fever.

A fever of 107° in an adult is more often than not the threshold of death. Few can survive such an inner furnace. The nurses and doctors at Columbia Presbyterian had gone into immediate action. It was a question of treating the fever, not the disease, which continued to resist everything. Penny Pinneo was packed in ice. Intravenous fluids were continued. An oxygen tent was put around her. Aspirin was administered. There was not much else that could be done.

Rose Pinneo, on her way to the hospital, heard the news of the crisis from a friend at the main entrance. She rushed to the room and found her sister, limp and burning, in the cooled oxygen tent. She did the only thing she could do: pray and begin a vigil.

Slowly, the temperature began to fall. Even then, it seemed as if death would come at any moment. Penny's chest was filling with pleural fluid. She tried desperately to cough, but it was agony. Dyspnea became pronounced, as she gasped for breath. Her face and neck became more swollen from edema, the excessive accumulation of serous fluid in the tissues. There was nausea. Penny Pinneo remembered only one thought going through her mind that long night: *Lord, how can I take it? How can I bear it?*

Rose Pinneo, not even sure her sister could hear her, read from Psalm 103: "Bless the Lord, O my soul, and forget not His benefits; Who forgiveth all thine inequities; Who healeth all thy diseases; Who redeemeth thy life from destruction; Who crowneth thee with loving kindness and tender mercies."

Penny did take it, and did bear it through that long night. Her fever dropped to 102°. The question was: Would it hold —or soar up again?

The Columbia doctors removed 170 milliliters of clear fluid from her pleural cavity that day. There were signs of pneumonia gathering. With the erratic course the unknown disease was taking, no one could predict anything.

The detective story at Yale was beginning to unfold.

On Monday, Sonja Buckley went to her lab to begin the first assault on her healthy tissue cultures, which had obligingly prospered in their bottle garden over the weekend.

The concept behind the experiment was fairly simple. She would expose the cultures to the blood serum of one of the victims. If any virus were lurking in the serum, the damage to the healthy cells would begin to show up in a matter of days. If the serum from the victims was clean, the cells would remain a healthy carpet in each plaque bottle. Only if there were a virus agent in the serum would "moth holes" appear in the carpet, slowly at first, then multiplying until there was practically nothing left of the green monkey cells. The holes, or plaques, could be seen and counted through the flat side of the prescription bottle, each little white plaque ranging in size from a pinhead to the head of a small nail.

Granted special permission to assist in this precarious job was Clark Mullin, the sixty-five-year-old chief technician. Tall, slender, his face framed with white hair, he volunteered to take part of the burden off Sonja Buckley's shoulders. She could use all the help she could get, if only to relieve the tension of dealing with such a lethal virus.

No master chef works with greater artistry than a virologist. Their procedures read like a biologic cookbook. Sonja Buckley began by sucking out the old growth fluid from each bottle, using a glass pipette like a soda straw. Each pipette was plugged with cotton to prevent the fluid from coming up into her mouth, but at this point there was nothing to worry about because none of the bottles held serum that might contain any suspected viruses.

After the fluid was removed, the cell carpet, or tissue culture, lay neatly across the wide side of the bottle when it was laid flat. Then Sonja prepared a fresh nutrient fluid made with double-concentrated vitamins, fetal bovine serum, and some liquids known as Hanks' balanced salt solution and Eagle's basal medium, along with penicillin and streptomycin. The antibiotics were added to prevent any bacteria from getting into the bottles and confusing the picture. Viruses, of course, are untouched by miracle drugs. Any moth holes that showed up would definitely be from viruses, not bacteria.

The new solution would maintain the cell carpets in good health but would not cause them to grow; it was weaker than the broth Sonja had removed by pipette.

Now she added fresh agar to the broth. This would form a gel to fix or "paste" the carpet of cells in place to the flat side of the bottle.

At this point she prepared for the critical step: to inoculate the cells with the infected blood serum of those who had come down with the disease. She did this by pipette also, sucking the potentially deadly fluid up into the measured glass straw to the .1 milliliter mark. It takes some 30 milliliters to fill a one-ounce shot glass, so the amount for each bottle was small. She did not worry about being contaminated herself; the cotton plug was designed to protect her from contact with the serum fluid.

For the matching control group of bottles, she added only the nutrient broth without the diseased serum. Then she put all the bottles aside to incubate at about 70° Fahrenheit.

Later, there would be more complex and sophisticated tests: to determine the exact deadliness of whatever virus there was; to match it with known viruses; to find out if antibodies could be created to fight the disease; to determine the size; to catch it visually under the electron microscope. These would have to wait for the moment. The immediate question was: Would Sonja Buckley's healthy cell carpets be killed or mutilated by whatever was in that serum? The answer would not be forthcoming for several days.

In Jordi Casals' lab, surrounded by the rows of Horsfall isolator mouse cages, Downs and Casals were already looking for results. Their mice had been inoculated several days before, but nothing whatever was showing in open symptoms in the suckling mice; they looked normal and healthy.

If the situation stayed this way, it would be very doubtful that the blood serum samples contained a deadly virus. It was, of course, too early to draw any conclusions. Some laboratory mice could survive virus injections into the cranium for nine or ten days. The current colony had been so exposed only for four days.

And there was always the question of whether any virus in the blood serum of the mission nurses could have survived the long journey from Nigeria. Consequently, Casals and Downs were particulary interested in the blood specimens extracted from Penny Pinneo after she had entered Columbia Presbyterian. The primary concern was in determining the potency of the new virus, if it existed. Many other questions remained: How was it transmitted? Where was its main reservoir? Would it increase in potency? Of course, it could do just the opposite: mutate to become less virulent and relatively harmless. The need to know was there, overriding everything else.

On Tuesday morning, March 11, Jordi Casals came into Sonja Buckley's lab, somewhat disgruntled. Nothing was showing up among his mice, and he wanted to know how Sonja was doing with her tissue cultures.

"All my work is negative so far," he said. "How's yours doing?"

Sonja had nothing to report either. But she wasn't expecting anything to show up quite yet, and she said so.

Casals was pessimistic about the outlook, remembering many other false alarms that the Yale arbovirus laboratory had encountered. But there was plenty to do in getting ready for the more complicated tests, and they separately went about doing them.

That afternoon, as Sonja was working with her cultures in the stationary test tubes, Dr. Max Theiler, the Nobel laureate who had been given the award in 1951 for his work in developing the yellow fever vaccine, dropped by for one of his frequent informal visits. On these occasions a cup of coffee was a ritual, and Sonja prepared some for both of them. Theiler, who became affectionately known as "the father of the mouse" when his demonstration that mice could be given yellow fever led to the vaccine discovery, worked in close association with the Yale group in his semiretirement.

But Theiler liked lab animals better than tissue cultures. Sonja felt a slight strain in his presence, first because of his great stature in the field of virology and second because she felt a little defensive about working with cell tissue cultures. Before antibiotics, which kept the cells protected from bacterial invasions, tissue-culture techniques had been a stepchild of the researchers. Only recently had tissue cultures come into their own as a valuable virus research tool.

Theiler was interested, however. Over coffee he asked Sonja how the research was going. She had nothing to report but decided to take a look, just in case.

She took a wooden tray full of the plaque bottles out of the incubator and looked at them. She could hardly believe what

she saw. Every single carpet of cells was covered with plaques
—white spots or holes that made the carpet look as if it were
covered with chicken pox.

She felt a chill go through her. She took down a second
tray. Every bottle in it had come down with a rash of white
plaques. A virus was eating away with a vengeance.

With Theiler there in the lab with her, she tried to keep
calm. She went to the trays holding the matching control
bottles—those that simply had the noninfectious nutrient fluid
covering the cell layer. They were perfect, not a plaque to be
seen. Not a single hole in the carpet.

She went over to Theiler and said flatly: "I'm getting
scared. Every single tissue culture is down with a cytopathic effect." She was referring to the plaques. When they revealed the
damage done by a virus, they were known by that term—the
deadly effect of the infected serum on the cytoplasm of the cell.

"What I can't figure out," she added, "is why the mice
haven't shown up with anything."

Theiler put his coffee down and went over and looked at
the trays of bottles. There was no mistake about it.

It suddenly occurred to Sonja that somehow—although she
didn't know how it could have happened—the bottles might
have been contaminated with some other virus. It was strange
that her tissue cultures would come down so dramatically
ahead of the mice, which had been inoculated three days earlier. She was convinced she'd have to make a second try at the
whole process—a second passage, as the routine was called.

She begged Theiler not to say anything to Wil Downs. She
wanted to be sure before she reported her results to him. "I
don't dare open my mouth to him yet," she said. "I want to be
sure of my ground first."

Theiler smiled and promised. But within a few minutes
Wil Downs was upstairs in Sonja Buckley's lab. "Well, Sonja, I
hear you have something," he said.

She didn't like to admit it yet, but she showed him the
trays. There was no doubt that something radical was happening.

Downs was on the phone to John Frame in no time. "John," he said, "it looks as if Sonja's got something. It's hit every tissue culture in the first test. We don't know for sure why, and the infant mice haven't shown up with anything yet. So we're going to run the cell lines through another passage."

Frame was excited. For the first time in the long days of the attrition, there seemed to be something clear and definite in the wind.

At Columbia Presbyterian, Penny Pinneo's condition was still critical. A parade of intravenous bottles was rolled to her bed through the long days and nights. To maintain her electrolyte balance—the proper proportions of water and inorganic salts —the doctors fortified every other intravenous bottle with potassium. This caused the veins to go into spasm as soon as the needle went in, creating agonizing pain. There was constant nausea. The neck glands remained so swollen that Penny found it almost impossible to swallow. Even to take a capsule, she often needed a local anesthesia for her throat.

Then impending pneumonia developed, bringing with it a flooding of the lungs and a racking cough. This was followed by encephalitis—inflammation of the brain. It specifically attacked the eighth cranial nerve, which goes to the ear and critically affects both hearing and sense of balance.

An incessant ringing in the ears developed, along with deafness, dizziness, and light-headedness. Penny's eyes were inflamed and painful.

The virus also attacked the blood-clotting mechanism, causing internal bleeding of the tissues. The heart, kidneys, and other vital organs were affected.

But she had survived longer than either of her compatriots stricken with the new disease. The question was: Would she be able to withstand the new assaults in the wake of the fever crisis she had met and overcome?

Sonja Buckley, excited but slightly fearful of what now appeared to be a highly virulent virus, lost no time in preparing her material for a second passage. She used extreme care. If her first results were true, the African virus was not to be trifled with.

Over the years she had found herself becoming more and more cautious about the deadly microcargo she had dealt with almost since she had completed medical school at the University of Zurich back in 1944. A blonde, affable, blue-eyed woman brushing her fifties, who spoke with a slight accent, she was a favorite among her colleagues, and her exacting work was internationally known and respected.

She was proud of her research in tissue cultures, proud of her pseudo-immortal cell lines, which she and her assistant cultivated with meticulous care. She much preferred them to Jordi Casals' laboratory animals. They didn't make excretion, didn't spit, cough, kick, or bite. Therefore they were safer. She didn't envy Jordi and his work.

In her second passage, she harvested both the fluid and the cells from the bottles that were showing the cytopathic effects and pipetted both together into new cell carpets in fresh bottles. It was necessary to harvest both the nutrient fluid and the plaque-ridden cells, because the virus might be just in one or the other. Then she again put the new bottles away to incubate.

By the following Tuesday, March 18, she had her answer. Every single bottle again came down with the telltale moth holes. She knew now that she had a virus—or agent, as an unknown virus is called on discovery.

Wil Downs was elated and again called John Frame to pass the results along. "More news, John," he said. "Looks like the second batch has come down. But still no mice!" Frame joined in the elation—a very special kind of elation that occurs when a scientific mark is reached. It is not one that lacks respect for the gravity of the situation. It is more of a relief at the chipping away at a frustration.

Sonja Buckley could not help feeling that the virus in all its potency seemed to resemble an LCM-like virus, of the Machupo virus of the lethal Bolivian hemorrhagic fever. She knew enough not to jump at that conclusion. The big question still remained: Why weren't the mice showing anything? Verification would have to come from that quarter as a double-check on her tests, before any speculation could be made.

Sonja reviewed her results carefully, making meticulous notes. She wrote:

> Cytopathic changes in Vero cells were similar with all isolates. The following changes were noted: a) the presence of single necrotic [dead] cells throughout the monolayer, along with minute holes caused by the falling out of such cells; b) the occurrence of groups of ten to twenty rounded, granulated cells localized within focal areas, as well as large, empty spaces left by the detachment of such groups from the glass.

Downs and Casals had great respect for Sonja Buckley's precision and skill in conducting her tests. One of her tries might have been a fluke. A second fluke would be highly unlikely. Any virus agent that did so much damage to her cell carpets should by all rights do the same damage to the mice.

But continued checks showed the fragile suckling mice to be as healthy as ever, withstanding the direct infusion of the infected serum through the cranium and into their brains.

For the moment Downs and Casals were stumped for an answer. Then a rather obvious thought occurred to them: What if they tried the tougher, adult mice? There were strange variations in the nature of viruses, and this attempt might just work.

They put the baby mice aside and began work on the plump Charles River colony of adult mice, sucking out the infected African serum from their supply and into their needle syringes, anesthetizing the mice and jabbing their skulls, cataloging them, and putting them back in their cages. They did the same with a matching control group, using uninfected serum. Though they didn't realize it yet, they had just corrected their first mistake.

The following day Jordi Casals went to his cages, not really expecting anything in the light of his first tests. In a standard preliminary test, he picked up one mouse by the tail. He was startled to feel a very fine tremor coming up from the mouse and into his hand. It was a feeling he couldn't describe; he simply felt it and knew it.

The same thing had happened to him several years before. He had been working with rabies, with his characteristic lack of fear in the face of the ugly, unseen enemies in his specimens. He had picked up a mouse and felt the same vibration he was feeling this day. What had happened was that a tissue culture intentionally infected with rabies had become accidentally contaminated with an LCM virus of the kind that causes the dreaded Bolivian and Argentinean hemorrhagic fevers. When injected into the mouse, it created a syndrome that was later to be associated with LCM symptoms: the body of the mouse became rigid and stiffened like a board in convulsion; then it became loose again, producing the strange tremor.

Casals' surprise at finding an immediate response to the previous day's test was tempered by the thought that once again an LCM virus might have accidentally contaminated his specimens, overriding the effects of the new, unknown African fever. *Well, that's too bad,* he was thinking. *It throws the whole thing off.*

Where the LCM contamination would have come from he did not know. There was no work being done with it at the lab at that time. Sonja had also mentioned to him her hunch that the mayhem done to her specimens seemed to resemble her previous work with LCM viruses. Nothing quite added up. But one thing was certain: practically all his adult mice showed the unmistakable tremors and convulsions as he lifted them by the tail; his matching control group showed none.

Casals talked with Wil Downs, who agreed that the likelihood of accidental LCM contamination of the specimens was practically nil. More likely, the new African agent was similar to, maybe even more deadly than, the LCM virus and was perhaps carried by rodents that acted as a reservoir to keep the virus propagating in perpetuity. Whatever they were, the viruses must have been as tough as lead pellets to survive the trip from Africa.

Another interesting coincidence was that the Bolivian and Argentinean hemorrhagic fevers occurred in children in less virulent form than in adults. Could this be why the baby mice were resistent compared to the adult mice in the laboratory tests?

Only more refined and complicated tests and more field research would tell, and these would take considerable time and patience.

Meanwhile, the lethal potency of the new virus was revealed with shocking suddenness a few days later when practically all the adult mice inoculated with the infected serum were found dead in their cages.

John Frame's research project was turning into a blockbuster.

Jordi Casals, whose gentleness, warmth, and soft-spoken charm made him as popular as Sonja Buckley around the laboratory, began the extended tests right away. Convinced now by the joint impact of destruction on both the mice and the tissue cultures that it was a new virus of extreme deadliness, Casals got on the trail of several questions: Was the new virus an African duplicate of the South American LCM-related viruses? Was it closely related to them? Just how powerful was this agent? What was its size? Could it be seen and identified under the electron microscope?

The answer to these questions would involve many decisions with regard to the hazards in working with the infected material. From the clinical information recorded in the cases of the three mission nurses, the slightest slip could be disastrous. Experienced virologists have a tendency to slough off the dangers of their work. They sometimes get jaded and careless, though they rarely consciously take chances. Even when they use extreme caution, disasters can happen. Among the early

Rockefeller Foundation researchers on yellow fever in the era before the vaccine, 25 percent were killed as a result of their work in the laboratory.

Because of the dangers associated with this new African project, especially with laboratory animals, Wil Downs gently but firmly imposed a further restriction: once a specimen was determined to be virus-positive, no attempts to reisolate those specimens would be allowed. Downs was also having some problems with Bob Shope, who had been kept away from work on the special project because of his young children at home. Shope's frustrations were somewhat relieved when Downs promised him that he could do limited work on matching the new virus against a long battery of known viruses, including the LCM suspect.

The overwhelming power of the new African virus was obvious, and to find its exact strength Jordi Casals and Sonja Buckley independently went about a process called titering, which is designed, among other things, to see how weak a solution of the infected material it takes to kill 50 percent of the animals or destroy 50 percent of the tissues inoculated with it. Since it is impossible to count virus particles, even under an electron microscope (which reveals at best only a handful of dead ones), virologists must have some scale on which to judge their potency. The titering process provides a means to do this. Both Sonja Buckley and Jordi Casals used basically the same methods.

Casals used ten test tubes. He took a pipette, sucked up the infected serum, and dropped it full strength into the first test tube. In the second tube he dropped in the same serum diluted on a 10-to-1 basis. In the third test tube he dropped in serum diluted 100 times, and in the fourth tube he diluted the serum 1,000 times.

By the time he reached the sixth test tube on the rack, Casals was using a solution of one part serum to 10 million parts of watery solution. A solution as weak as this would have to include an extremely potent virus to kill an animal or infect a carpet of tissue-culture cells.

At the end of the procedure, Casals and Buckley would take their weakest solution—which might be as thinly diluted as one part infected serum to 100 million parts fluid. Then they would inoculate a group of ten mice or tissue cultures with it and see what happened.

If none of the mice died or none of the tissue cultures was destroyed, they would try the next weakest solution, and so on down the line until roughly 50 percent of the animals or tissue cultures were destroyed. The weaker the solution that killed 50 percent of the animals inoculated—which scientists call Lethal Dose 50—the stronger the virus.

One serum specimen taken from Penny Pinneo was found to riddle 50 percent of the tissue cultures with cytopathic damage at a dilution of 1 to 10 million. There was a terrifyingly lethal virus here, and all the precautions the laboratory was taking were more obviously needed than ever.

What's more, every specimen tested showed up virus-positive, whether it was from the serum of Penny Pinneo, Charlotte Shaw, or Laura Wine. There was no ambiguity whatever. Always, the specimens in the matching control bottles or test tubes remained healthy and normal.

On March 23 Wil Downs officially notified the Columbia Presbyterian doctors that all initial serum specimens had grown out cytopathogenic agents on tissue cultures that had been maintained for two passages, and that they had reacted in a complement-fixation system with serum drawn from Penny Pinneo on March 20. The complement-fixation system is a complicated series of tests to determine the titer of antibodies in a specimen. The Yale researchers would be working constantly with these tests as they began to refine further information about the new enemy.

While the virus hunters at the Yale laboratory were reaching into the unknown geography of their ominous and elusive agent, Dr. Donald Carey, a research professor and assistant director of the virus research laboratory of the University of Ibadan in Nigeria, was going about his own routine. Carey, whose handsome, youthful face belied his whimsical complaints about middle age, was an old hand at tracking down tropical viruses. After his studies at Princeton and his internship at Johns Hopkins, he had trailed epidemics around the world for more than a decade.

With his wife Barbara and his children, he lived a demanding life, filled with research administration and teaching, plus the general trivia of academia similar to any American university. There were extensive field trips to the bush and long hours in the virus laboratory working with exotic diseases. The research done by the lab fell under the wing of the Rockefeller Foundation, in conjunction with the University of Ibadan.

Ibadan, a large, sprawling city that sits on the edge of both the rain forest and the savanna, is 600 tortuous miles by road from Jos. During the crisis at the Sudan Interior Mission hospital, events moved so swiftly that there had been insurmountable difficulties in coordinating or exchanging information with the Ibadan staff. It is ironic that communication within Nigeria can be more difficult than communication overseas. At that time, it was often easier to reach London or Paris or New York by phone than to call from one town in Nigeria to another.

In fact, by late March, nearly a month after the Sudan Interior Mission crisis, Don Carey and his Rockefeller Foundation colleagues at Ibadan knew nothing whatever about the strange threat that had spawned in Jos. The awesome implications that were incubating there had revealed themselves slowly.

Oddly enough, the first word Carey received about the events at Jos was a cablegram from Wil Downs at Yale. It repeated the information that Downs had already sent to Frame and the other doctors at Columbia. A new virus agent had been isolated. It was dangerous. Two of the first three cases had died. Third near death. Etiology, or source, unknown. Rodent host suspected as a reservoir. Did not appear to be an insect-borne arbovirus. Mode of transmission: an aerosol of dust —in other words, airborne? Contact through perforation in

skin? If rodent or other animal, what animal? Or bird, perhaps?

First three cases: white, Caucasian. Any Nigerian nationals?
Original case from Lassa—the index case—now deceased. Any
clue as to where she got it? If so, what? Household environment? Hospital? Pets? Contact with any special type of patient?
Exposure to wild animals?

The number of alternatives to be explored was appalling.
The lab at Ibadan was understaffed and geared at the moment
for a long series of other virus studies: dengue fever, Congo
fever, a new disease called Kata virus related to rabies in goats,
another called Mokola virus, and especially yellow fever, a
major threat.

Scientists throughout the world constantly monitored this
mosquito-borne disease because it was so unpredictable. An epidemic may strike in Brazil or Africa, for instance, after years of
inaction. A jet landing in a tropical airport could pick up an
accidental cargo of mosquito vectors—hosts—and bring them
to New York, where only a handful of travelers among the population had been vaccinated against it.

The vaccine from Theiler's yellow fever strain 17-D was
amazingly effective, but to prevent massive outbreaks it had to
be administered universally. And great islands of the population of the developing countries and even developed countries
have not had the vaccine. It requires delicate preparation.
Fresh, fertile hen's eggs are incubated for over a week. If the
eggs show the development of a live embryo, they are inoculated with a fractional amount of the 17-D yellow fever virus
that has been put through up to 300 passages in tissue culture
to weaken the strain. At this stage the viruses are attenuated—
made so limp that they can't stand up without falling over and
therefore can't produce the disease in the body. What they do
is fool the body's lymph system into thinking it's being invaded
by the real thing.

Thus the lymph system gets to work and produces
antibodies—globs of protein molecules that have a special

shape for each kind of invader, or antigen, that dares to come into the bloodstream. A virus is simply one of many different kinds of antigens. Bacteria or foreign blood cells are other types of antigens.

It is thought that the human body has at least one antibody molecule that is shaped exactly right to clamp on to and neutralize any possible antigen invader. Almost miraculously, as soon as the body's immune system gets word that a yellow fever virus is in the bloodstream, it begins manufacturing specific yellow fever antibodies. They will rush out in a counterattack and literally lock into the crevices and notches on the surface of the virus, rendering it useless. The specific antibody can do this, because its shape is exactly like a negative cast of the virus it's designed to fight. It cannot help in the fight against other viruses of different three-dimensional shapes.

Theoretically, any virus disease can be fought to a standstill by the miraculous action of the antibodies—but only if enough of them are manufactured in time. Often a potent virus bursts so many cells that the defending antibodies can't recruit defenders quickly enough.

But once antibodies have been established and the patient survives, there are plenty of them ready and waiting if the same virus antigen is brash enough to attack again. This is what an effective vaccine does—stimulates the making of antibodies against a weakened and harmless form of a virus. If a real one should then come along, it's overwhelmed before it can begin its insidious work.

What applies to yellow fever also applies to many other forms of virus antigens. Some, however, like the antigens that cause hepatitis, are so elusive and unmanageable that scientists still can't crack the problem, even though they know the rules of the game that could theoretically immunize the body against the disease.

Don Carey's problem on receiving Wil Downs' wire at Ibadan was that a combination of scientific statistics and hunches indicated there already might be a yellow fever epidemic brewing on the Jos plateau, and he had to be ready for it. There had not been any since a murderous epidemic in 1953. In addition, Graham Kemp, his chief epidemiologist and virologist, was somewhere in the deep bush tracking and trapping African hedgehogs suspected of propagating Congo fever. It would be hard to redirect the resources of the lab quickly.

Kemp was a favorite of Carey's because he was not only an energetic and resourceful field worker but a meticulous laboratory technician. A congenial, rugged Candian in his forties, Kemp had taken his Master's degree in epidemiology at the University of California at Berkeley, after completing his requirements in veterinary medicine at the University of Toronto.

Kemp's job at the University of Ibadan was to investigate the occurrence and prevalence—and especially the role played by wildlife—of the West African virus diseases of men and animals. What viruses did they store in their physiological reservoirs? What insects acted as vectors of the virus diseases across the Sudan and elsewhere? What was new and undiscovered about them? In addition, Kemp was training Nigerians to gradually take over the direction of the lab after the Rockefeller Foundation men finished their development job.

Don Carey sensed the urgency in Wil Downs' cable. He realized that Kemp was the logical man to do some preliminary investigation of the Jos situation, but he hated to sidetrack Kemp's present assignment. Both the trapping of the suspected Congo virus animals and the monitoring of the possible new yellow fever outbreak in the north were important, although there still didn't seem to be any direct evidence of the latter.

Somewhat reluctantly, Carey drafted a telegram to Kemp, aware that the chances of him getting it were fairly skimpy. Kemp always moved with the speed of a gazelle in his wildlife scavenging. Carey decided to send the same wire to four places —Zaria, Kaduna, Kano, and Maiduguri—all of them strung along the possible route Kemp might be taking with his trapped animals on the way back to Ibadan. Kaduna, the nearest, was about 500 miles away; Maiduguri was about 1,000 miles away, in the extreme northeast corner of Nigeria, not too far from Lassa.

Graham Kemp had already trapped live samples of wild African hedgehogs and had them jammed into cages in the back of his dusty, battered Peugeot station wagon with over 60,000 miles on it. He would be bringing them back to the Ibadan lab, over 1,000 painful, hot miles away, to check their capacity for storing the Congo fever virus.

Kemp never seemed to worry about his constant contact with animals that might be carrying such a fearsome cluster of viruses. When he set out to get his animals, he got them. He extracted them from their traps and unceremoniously dumped them into cages in the back of the Peugeot. His tenacity was held in awe by his associates.

He had worked his way back from the swampy desolation of Lake Tchad, had passed through Maiduguri and Kano, and thought that he just might skip Zaria and make Kaduna by nightfall. The best accommodations were there, and he had been working in searing heat and dust that caked him like chocolate frosting from head to foot.

Reaching Kaduna, he drove directly to the Hamdahla Hotel, a remarkably civilized hostel that was a favorite of former British colonial officers. It had all the amenities of civilization, including scotch and soda and pink gins. After settling his animals down for the night in the back of his station wagon, he went to the desk to register and found one of Carey's repeat telegrams waiting for him.

His immediate thought was that there must be some new information on the yellow fever problem. Instead, he read the news of the crisis at Jos and the request for him to go there for further information and details about the cases from which Yale had isolated the unknown virus.

He wasn't at all enthusiastic about the idea. He had his live animals with him, and he didn't see how he could possibly detour to Jos—about 300 miles away over murderous roads—and keep the specimens alive. They represented a lot of sweat, time, and effort. They could be kept alive only underground, and they were the only known carriers of the Congo virus. Again, like most virologists, he was used to false alarms, which were more often than not the case. Then there were the constant military roadblocks, which would slow down the trip. His Peugeot carried a lot of funny-looking trapping and diagnostic equipment that consistently aroused suspicion on the part of the military.

He was tempted to wire Carey and say that he had better bring his animals back to Ibadan. But then he decided he might as well go to Jos, just in case it wasn't a false alarm. He got into a hot tub—his first bath in many days—dressed, downed a couple of double scotches, and went to bed early.

He was on the road to Jos early the next morning, passing village after village of conical thatched-roof huts surrounded by baked-mud walls, dodging the Fulani shepherds with their goats and sheep and cattle, veering into ditches to avoid the wild, appalling Nigerian truck drivers, who kept awake by smoking hashish and counted on the ju-ju man's symbols dangling from their rear-view mirrors to keep them out of accidents. Within minutes he was covered with red laterite dust and could feel it crunch in his teeth, even when he rolled the windows up and roasted in the heat.

As Kemp came up off the savanna and climbed toward the heights of the Jos plateau, the road became precipitous and twisting, rough enough to shake his teeth. But Graham Kemp was used to that, took it in his stride. Aside from his concern about his precious hedgehogs, it was part of his usual routine. Then the road straightened, and large, isolated sugar lumps of mountains loomed ahead. Breaking the monotony of the villages were the brilliant robes—in indigo, bright red, and yellow—of the Fulani horsemen, who rode in arrogant elegance. Occasionally, there would be a ju-ju man in his grotesque mask, a couple of stately barebreasted women, or a small boy urinating on the road and waving at the same time.

Up ahead, about halfway to Jos, he saw the military road-block. Even when he expected one, it was always a little nerve-wracking. He slowed down carefully, eased the Peugeot up to a squadron of helmeted soldiers, who stood with rifles cocked and ready.

His technique was simple, and he found it worked. As soon as the soldiers approached his car, generally in twos or threes, he would say: "Sannu-ka!" the usual hello in Hausa. Then he would point to himself and say: "Magani." This was the Hausa word for doctor.

The soldiers were still suspicious. What were the animals doing in the back of the wagon? What was all this equipment? Where was he going? Where had he come from?

Kemp explained as best he could, and then gradually turned the conversation around to benefit his own research. Speaking in Hausa, he said: "I'm here to study any diseases that are breaking out in this area. Have you noticed anything happening among the troops?"

Yes, the sergeant told him. There were many men in his battalion who were turning yellow. Kemp got down all the notes he could on this condition. It sounded more like infectious hepatitis than yellow fever, but he would try to correlate this information with anything else he could gather.

He pushed on, past several burning bush fires, some of which he could feel like furnaces from the road. Finally Jos town loomed ahead, perched on its plateau mountain, a lovely, breathtaking sight, as if some giant had taken toy boulders, thrown them in a mound of disarray, then taken toy houses and set them on the top. It was a shame that he had such nasty business in so lovely a setting.

He found Dr. Jeanette Troup at the Sudan Interior Mission's Bingham Hospital and lost no time filling himself in on the background of the strange series of cases that had passed through the hospital. He still suspected yellow fever, though he knew enough not to draw any conclusions on the basis of his meager knowledge of the situation. But after going over the records of the two deceased nurses, he became convinced that the villain was not yellow fever. There was no jaundice present. There was no *vomito negro,* the terrifying gushing of black vomit that characterizes yellow fever victims. There were no intractable hiccoughs that rack the patient; no delerious, maniacal seizures that cause panic during yellow fever epidemics among both the sick and the well.

Kemp also figured that whatever the virus was, it wasn't one of the insect-borne arboviruses. He felt the arboviruses could never have survived the alternate thawing and cooling and nonlaboratory conditions of the thermos jug on the trip from Jos to New York.

Now he was getting interested, even though he was forced to let his hedgehogs die. He put them on ice for further study. The most important task was to find the original source and mode of transmission of the new virus from Lassa. This wouldn't be easy, since there was no live primary, or index, case to work from, to trace with direct questioning.

Lassa was a punishing two-day drive from Jos, and since this was a preliminary investigation Kemp settled for the two-way Sudan Interior Mission radio to get through to John Hamer at Lassa. The reception was surprisingly good. He questioned Hamer on the routine Laura Wine had followed, what her living conditions were, the type of work she did, and how she did it.

There was not too much information. Laura Wine had no pets, which Kemp was particularly interested in. But his curiosity was aroused when Hamer mentioned the bats in her attic. This was one thing that would have to be followed up on, and he made a note to that effect. Bats had been found to be a reservoir of one virus in Trinidad some years before. They could not be excluded from study by any means.

The rest of the records and interviews at Jos were not very revealing. There had been no new cases, either fatal or convalescent, and the atmosphere was more relaxed.

Kemp looked up his friend George Stroh, who was stationed in Jos as part of the smallpox eradication program of the U.S. Public Health Service. Stroh was cooperating with the Nigerian government in trying to wipe out smallpox in Nigeria. They were miraculously succeeding, with the use of the high-speed jet gun for the vaccination program. This device, which literally fired serum into the arm, provided a fast and almost painless method of mass vaccination. Stroh wondered what the picture shaping up on the possible yellow fever outbreak was, but Kemp had no precise information to pass along to him, except the reports from the military, which had sounded like infectious hepatitis.

There wasn't much more that Kemp could do at the moment. It seemed obvious that the sicknesses of both Charlotte Shaw and Penny Pinneo were hospital-transmitted, through close contact with an initial case. This was important to note but was of little use in getting at the root of the problem: What animal was the virus hiding in, and how was it transmitted to a human to cause the disease?

Just before he left, he got news that both of Penny Pinneo's pet canaries had died shortly after she had gone to the hospital. This was extremely interesting, but frustrating. There were no specimens to check. Even if they were dug up from their graves, they would now be of no use in the laboratory.

Kemp got into his buffeted and pummeled station wagon and drove off with his dead African hedgehogs on the long road back to Ibadan.

What he didn't know was that he would be returning to Jos town much sooner than he thought.

Chapter Six

With the existence of the new virus now confirmed, Sonja Buckley went about her work on the research refinements. She knew what the virus could do, both from its ravages of the victims of the disease and from its devastating effect on mice and tissue cultures. But what about its size? Could it be seen under the electron microscope?

Sonja took up the job with her usual care and precision, scrupulously following the safety guidelines laid down by Wil Downs. Since a virus can't be measured directly, virologists must assess its size indirectly by forcing it through an instrument known as a millipore filter chamber. The chamber consists of porcelain filters with increasingly small pores, so that cells cannot pass through: only the tiny molecules of the size of various viruses.

A virus is so small that it can be measured only in millimicrons. A millimicron is hard to conceive. An ordinary micron is about one-millionth of a yard. The millimicron is 1,000 times shorter than that. The millipore filters Sonja Buckley was using varied from 450 to 100 millimicrons in diameter. By experience, she figured the vicious micromidget to fall somewhere within this range.

She took her ubiquitous pipette and sucked up a small diluted and measured portion of infected tissue-culture fluid, which had been harvested six days after she had inoculated it. Then she pipetted it into the casing that held the largest-sized millipore filter. She turned on nitrogen pressure and waited for the squeezed essence of the virus juice to work its way through the filter holes.

She repeated the process three times, with progressively smaller filters, and ended up with three finely strained juice samples. She was now ready to find which of the tiny filter pores had blocked most of the virus from passing through. To do this, she had to inoculate each of the juice specimens into her healthy tissue cultures again. Each specimen would be given its own array of plaque bottles. From observing how each of the three virus essences killed off the healthy cells in her tissue cultures, she would be able to determine which size filter made the lethal effect drop off.

In other words, she was after that 50 percent cell damage factor again. Whichever filter solution demonstrated a marked drop-off in killing power would give a good idea of the diameter of the virus.

The juice that filtered through the 450 millimicron filter showed that the cell destruction of 50 percent of the specimens required a dilution of about 1 to 1 million.

The juice that filtered through the 220 millimicron filter showed that a stronger concentration was needed to destroy: 1 to 100,000.

The juice that came through the small 100 millimicron filter showed a marked decrease in its power to destroy. It needed a concentration of almost 1 to 10 to destroy 50 percent of the cultures tested.

On the basis of the tiny size of the filter hole that reduced the potency of the virus, Sonja Buckley figured the diameter of the virus to be somewhere between 70 and 140 millimicrons— fairly big for a virus but about 9,000 times smaller than a small animal cell.

This estimate of the size of the agent would be helpful

when the electron microscope studies were made. She would be working with Bob Speir, the microbiologist who specialized in electron microscopy on this phase of the detective story. Speir knew his business well, knew what to look for, knew how to find it.

Sonja went about the complicated job of preparing some of Penny Pinneo's infected serum for observation under the giant electron microscope. She made sure first that her specimen was infective by again testing it in her cell layers. It was. She incubated the sample for five days then got ready to transfer it into a centrifuge.

As she did so, she noticed that the pipette she was using was just a little too short to reach inside the bottle of infected serum that she wanted to suck up. Without thinking, she tilted the bottle toward her so that the pipette would reach the fluid.

It worked, but in the process the lip of the infected bottle came in contact with her nose. After quickly putting her material into the centrifuge, she immediately scrubbed and scolded herself for being so careless. In all her long years of experience, she rarely made mistakes like this. She had to admit to herself she was scared. *What a stupid thing to do,* she thought. *How utterly stupid.* Still, accident or not, she maintained her total professional efficiency.

She completed the procedure and made her notes for her report:

> Cells were harvested, centrifuged into a pellet, fixed in glutaraldehyde, postfixed in osmium tetroxide, dehydrated, and embedded in Epon-Araldite. Sections were cut on a Porter-Blum MT-2 ultramicrotome, stained with uranyl acetate and lead citrate, and examined in a Philips EM 200 electron microscope.

What her report added up to was that the centrifuge spun the cells in test tubes until they were hard and dry. She was then able to slice them tissue-thin so that they could be stained and observed. But all this had to be done with the most detailed precision. The medical reports that were to be circulated to the scientific world later were critical. There could be no error, misunderstanding, or ambiguity.

Bob Speir took over the process from here. He mounted the specimens and got them ready for the electron microscope, which would magnify the image over 100,000 times. If a single pea were blown up this much, its diameter would cover over half the length of a football field.

Speir zeroed in the electronic lens on his object. Sonja Buckley was tense and excited as she stood by. Regardless of how much experience a virologist has, there is an undeniable thrill at a visual confrontation with the enemy.

It was there. She could see it: a fuzzy tennis ball, with black spots like obscene polka dots on its surface. There were spike-like protuberances jutting out. It was ugly, ominous. A killer mite that was dead but that seemed to be staring back at her through the lens. She felt a chill go through her.

Eight of the sinister killers were lying outside one cell. Though some were smaller than others, they were roughly of the size she had estimated. Some were nestled arrogantly inside a cell cavity, their thorny surfaces clinging to the cytoplasm of the cell, like crazy asterisks. One looked as if it were budding from the surface of a cell.

The scientific language of their report was flat and unemotional:

> Examination of pelleted cells of infected Vero cultures revealed the presence of extracellular particles of variable size and shape. The smaller particles were usually round, were surrounded by an electron-dense limiting membrane, and contained a variable number of irregularly spaced electron-dense granules [the polka dots] . . . Projections or spikes could sometimes be seen on the surface of particles and occasionally at a thickened area of the cell membrane that suggested a particle being formed by budding . . .

The last observation was important, because it provided a clue: the LCM studies in the electron microscope also showed this peculiar form of budding. More than that, they showed the same polka dots and surface spikes. The finding supported the possibility that the new African virus might be closely related to the LCM, Machupo, and Junin virus group. But whether its killing and spreading power would be more deadly than the fearsome South American viruses remained to be seen.

The pieces were falling into place with what is sometimes called scientific elegance. Wil Downs, Sonja Buckley, and Jordi Casals threw themselves into their research as if they were on the trail of a criminal.

They were, in effect. At large was a dispassionate murderer, or rather gang of murderers who were cached away in some unknown hideout, hitchhiking unseen in an unsuspecting carrier, ready to spring out at some unpredictable time or place, slipping inside a human body and taking it over until only a shell was left.

One of the most important jobs was to find and create antibodies for the new virus. Both Sonja Buckley and Jordi Casals were already involved in a joint effort to this end. Their work would be instrumental not only in assessing the possibility of developing a vaccine but also in determining whether the virus could be neutralized by the action of antibodies. If tests could be set up to check the presence of antibodies in blood samples, the extent of the disease and the localities where it would be likely to be found could be defined.

In other words, if blood tests showed that a group of Nigerian villagers had specific antibodies against the new virus, it would indicate that they had had a nonfatal form of the disease. It would also suggest that the animals in the region should be studied, bled, tested. Then perhaps the source, the all-important reservoir of the virus, could be found and ways could be developed to combat its spread. At the moment, everyone was in the dark not only about the source but about the way the virus moved from the source to the victim.

Since antibodies can be found in an animal or human that has successfully recovered from a virus disease, the Yale researchers turned for the moment to the infant mice that had been injected with the virus and were still living.

With infinite care, Jordi Casals drew the serum from his stable of baby mice, pooled it, and prepared to check it for antibodies.

Of course, even if it had developed antibodies, the serum would be of no use to Penny Pinneo; her cells had already been grossly invaded. Nor would it be of any use to future human victims. Many refinements would have to be made before that could even be considered. But in the test tube or plaque bottle it could be very revealing.

Sonja Buckley picked up the process at this point. She took the serum that Jordi Casals had drawn, sucked it up in her pipette, and mixed it with live virus. Next she put the glass container of the mixture in a bath of warm water for some thirty minutes, more or less simulating the conditions in the body. Then she drew it up in her pipette again and inoculated her healthy cell cultures.

If there were antibodies in the serum from the infant mice, the cells would remain healthy; the antibodies would completely neutralize the effect of the virus. If her carpets were riddled with plaques, there would be no antibodies working.

Her cell carpets remained whole and healthy. An animal that had survived the disease would develop antibodies that would protect it for life.

Since an antibody is nothing more than a special cell-free protein molecule, it is impossible to see it. The antibody can be tested only for what it does; it is identifiable only in the way it reacts with its antigen.

When the antibody locks into and bonds itself to a virus or other antigen, it is like fitting two specially designed mortises together. The antibody smothers or surrounds the protein jacket of the virus, clumping the antigen invaders into prison camps so they can't fan out and invade cells. Both antigen and antibody, locked in a fatal embrace, are swept unceremoniously out of the body as waste.

Jordi Casals had already set up a series of complement-fixation tests to determine the presence of antibodies in the blood. The tests enable virologists to measure more exactly the effectiveness of the antibody in reacting with the virus. They provide a clear-cut scale determined by the strength of the dilution of the infected serum under observation. In other words, the technique of titering again. The complement-fixation tests would be very important in discovering whether a safe, noninfectious virus antigen could be developed that would cause the body's immune system to create antibodies to fight off the disease, just as the yellow fever vaccine does.

Casals was continuing the exacting complement-fixation tests with serum from his unpredictable, wriggling mice. Over the years, he had grown philosophical about whether the viruses he worked with so constantly would be transmitted to him. His techniques required him to pick up his mice by the tail for frequent examinations and injections. He rationalized that if any virus was going to get at him, it would come through the dust that a mouse raised, or from its dried urine. It would not come from the tail.

He often told himself that he probably should wear a surgical mask or a respirator filter more often. It wouldn't stop a virus from going through, but it could stop the dust that might carry the virus. But he would get behind schedule and forget about it, figuring that this was an occupational hazard he had to put up with.

The complement-fixation tests continued on over the days. Basically they involved the setting up of two antigen-antibody systems that competed with each other for a very ill-defined substance in the blood called complement. Complement is another protein circulating through the blood. It is thought to be sort of a roving secondary defense against antigens in general.

Complement unites with antibody and helps the antibody to attack the antigen. The three materials—complement, antibody, and antigen—then clump together, making it possible to whisk the invading antigen from the body.

In his series of tests, Casals was trying to determine which serum from which mouse specimen had antibodies. No human was yet known to have recovered from the disease. So he could not at this time find any antibodies in human specimens. By varying the dilution of his mouse serum, he could determine the quantity of antibody.

In all these tests, so necessary for getting at the nature of the villain they were tracking, Jordi Casals was physically dealing with dynamite. His work was laborious and meticulous, especially since he had to do it without an assistant. And it was tiring. But the nature of the search lent a certain zest and excitement that overcame part of the boredom; the inherent dangers in the job overcame the rest.

The portrait of the virus was rounding out more clearly than ever. What its future would be was another matter.

The course of Penny Pinneo's illness seemed to be taking a surprising turn—for the better. Her temperature slowly dropped. After March 20 it never rose over 99°. The radio helped. She could often find a church service. She remained conscious, even if mentally dulled by both the disease and sedation. On the wall in front of her bed was a dismal picture of a city street in winter, which depressed her. It was taken down by her sister and replaced with greeting cards from many of her friends. Flowers brightened the lonely isolation room. Rose Pinneo had now been admitted as part of the team by the other nurses, and the atmosphere brightened considerably. One nurse brought a week-old kitten for the patient.

Easter came, and Penny Pinneo drew fresh hope from it, listening to the special services over the radio. Later, she wrote: "What a blessing that Christian radio program was. I listened hours each day. And the message of Easter was so real to me; the realization of what Christ had done for me. It was about the most wonderful Easter I ever had!"

On May 3, 1969, some nine weeks after Penny had entered the isolation ward, Trevor Ardill, the Sudan Interior Mission director in the States, and his wife came to pick her up and take her to their home. She still tired easily and had periods of shortness of breath. Her eyes still danced back and forth with nystagmus. She had a tendency to lean to the right when she walked. Her hearing was far from normal; there was still ringing in her ears. She had lost twenty-eight pounds and most of the hair on her head. Later, she wrote a friend: "Truly I walked physically through 'the valley of death'. But He was there."

There was a feeling of thanksgiving and relief everywhere: thousands of miles away on the Jos plateau; among the doctors and staff at Columbia Presbyterian; in the virus laboratory at Yale. What appeared to be the first patient to recover from the disease showed that it could be defeated. The problem was that no one really knew just how it had been done. There was a special optimism in Jos and Lassa, because no new cases were emerging. Perhaps, it was hoped, the crisis was a strange, agonizing fluke that could be forgotten, except for the bitter loss of friends and colleagues. At least there was some relief from the tension. But there was still the nagging question: Would it last?

The medical reports were succinct and laconic. An article by four of the doctors involved—John Frame, John Baldwin, David Gocke, and Jeanette Troup—in the *American Journal of Tropical Medicine and Health* later summarized the outbreak:

> We propose that the new disease be called *Lassa fever*, after the community where the first patient worked and presumably contacted the infection. Although this series of cases is small, certain facts in the epidemiology can be inferred. It is likely primarily a disease of some nonhuman form of animal life, and its severity suggests that it is not well adapted to the human host. It may be transmitted directly from person to person, possibly through a break in the skin. The source of the original infection is not clear, but the fact that a nurse had the first known case suggests that she, too, may

have contracted this from a patient. The incubation period appears to be from 7 to 17 days, most likely the shorter period.

Then, after noting that a patient with Lassa fever is apparently infectious for a long period of time, the report continued:

Although hitherto unreported to our knowledge, this disease is likely to be an important medical problem in the future. The fact that the incubation period allows one to be infected in Africa, then become ill with so contagious an illness a week later, and perhaps thousands of miles away, is in itself a cause of concern.

Almost certainly it has caused other deaths in northeast Nigeria. If it is indeed a disease of animals, it may become more prevalent as that populous country looks for more land to cultivate in the region of the Cameroon highlands. Investigation of this disease in the field would certainly seem in order.

We are continuing serologic investigations to determine whether in fact this is a more common disorder than we know, and whether our view of its extreme virulence may not be biased by the tragic severity in these first three cases that have come to our attention. In the meantime, here is yet another disorder to be considered in the differential diagnosis of a seriously ill patient from Africa.

When Dr. Jeanette heard the news of Penny Pinneo's recovery from John Frame, her relief was immeasurable. At least one of the three had survived. On May 14 she wrote him from Jos:

It is good to hear that Penny is well enough to have been discharged from the hospital, but I cannot imagine what kind of hospital bill the Mission is getting for her care!

I trust by this time you have received the serum samples of all the contacts and some samples from other people who may have had the same disease or a similar one. [They were all negative.] These were sent to the Virus Research Unit in Ibadan, as Dr. Graham Kemp felt it would not be difficult to transport them to New York for us.

Dr. Hamer was just here in Jos this week and gave me a copy of a more detailed case history on Miss Wine. I am enclosing a copy of this in case it may be of interest to you. He also showed me the letter he received from you and seemed to greatly appreciate your writing to him and the other Church of the Brethren Mission doctors.

She mentioned her interest in the case of one colleague who John Frame felt should return to New York for a checkup, writing that she would be "most interested to hear if you find any evidence of her having contracted 'our' virus."

Then she concluded: "Thank you for all you do for us in the Sudan Interior Mission, and especially for the good care you have given to our dear co-worker, Penny. "May the Lord bless you and guide you as you serve Him there . . . ."

Though Penny Pinneo was apparently out of danger, the scientists at Yale had their work cut out for them. Many unanswered questions still hung over the research.

Jordi Casals was working with the serum taken from her in the early stages of her illness, comparing it with that taken after she had recovered. This comparison would reveal a very important thing: the early serum should not show any antibodies; the convalescent serum should, just as the serum of the infant mice had. If antibodies showed up, he would have a human serum to work with in his tests. It would also be possible to make a crude antiserum out of it.

The practice of injecting serum containing antibodies from someone who had recovered from a virus disease into someone who had contracted the disease was an old one. It was used mainly before the techniques of modern vaccine production were perfected. It brought with it many dangers, but when there was no refined vaccine available, it was about the only technique that could be used. The benefit-risk ratio had to be weighed carefully, however. For one thing, the serum might contain hidden live virus. It had to be carefully prepared, or it could kill the patient. It might bring serum hepatitis. It might cause a complete kidney shutdown by what is known as an antigen-antibody complex, and thus kill the patient, who might have recovered otherwise.

Casals' complement-fixation tests finally revealed that

Penny Pinneo's serum now contained antibodies. Serum taken on the fourteenth day of her illness had shown no antibodies whatever; that taken on the twenty-eighth day of her illness showed complete fixation of the complement—in other words, the serum was clearly packed with Lassa virus antibodies. And they were evident in many dilutions, from 1 to 8 up to 1 to 64. This serum could be used in the lab to check whether a patient suspected of Lassa fever actually had it, or to determine if anyone had had Lassa in the past, regardless of how long ago. To use it as a vaccine or as treatment for the new fever would be risky, but possible in an extreme emergency.

With the human antibody question defined, Jordi Casals set out to find just how long the live virus hung around after clinical recovery of the victim. Tests on Penny Pinneo's serum showed that she was clear of all virus by the twenty-eighth day of illness. But this was not enough evidence to determine exactly how long a tenacious virus could survive in any living organism.

Casals asked Sonja Buckley if he could use some of her infected material for further tests in his mice. He was particularly interested in following up on urine tests. Sometimes the serum shows there is no live virus in the system, while the urine shows there are still some remaining live viruses. The virus could be hiding out in an area where it could multiply without invading the bloodstream. In the kidneys, for instance.

He doubted if his original infant mice had any virus left in them, so he felt he didn't have to take extra precautions when working with them. But collecting urine from mice is a tricky business. It has to be drawn one or two tiny drops at a time, and it takes a lot of mice to make up an adequate pool to test.

For some of his laboratory procedures, in which he had to make a broth of infected mouse brains to test, he would use an ordinary household Waring blender. This could be dangerous if any infected material were splashed up.

For the urine tests, he would go about the painfully slow job of collecting the specimens, trying to avoid the dust the mice would kick up in their cages. He had noticed that when a mouse is picked up, it becomes frightened and is likely to urinate in response. This technique facilitated the faster collection of urine.

Bob Shope, who was later to become director of the Yale Arbovirus Research Unit, was like a race horse who wasn't allowed to run. He was sure that if he took proper precautions, he would in no way endanger his children at home by doing some carefully controlled work with the Lassa virus. Semiofficially, and tacitly, he arranged with Jordi Casals to take care of his mice over a weekend when everybody was going to be away.

In the relaxed quiet of the empty lab rooms, he completed some urine tests and was startled to find that the baby mice were continuing to excrete live Lassa virus more than forty days after they had been infected. Until then, he hadn't fully realized how hazardous the new agent was. He was glad he had used forceps in handling the mice.

Further tests by Casals and Shope confirmed the tenacity of the virus. They carefully reviewed the startling results: although none of the young mice showed any signs of illness, live Lassa virus was found in their urine some forty-five days after inoculation. What's more, the mice did not show any virus in their bloodstreams, only in their urine. The tests seemed to indicate that the new virus could hide, in a rodent at least, and be distributed through the urine to anyone who was unfortunate enough to come in contact with it.

This indicated a strong similarity between the Lassa virus and its lethal South American cousins of the arenavirus group. Both the Bolivian and Argentinean hemorrhagic fevers had been documented to be borne by rodents and dispersed through their urine. The Lassa virus seemed now to be unquestionably related to the South American fever. What had been learned about the arenavirus group could be tentatively applied to Lassa.

The working hypothesis became this: the Lassa virus, like the arenavirus group, is maintained in nature in rodents, which become infected at birth. The infant rodents are able to maintain the virus without damage to themselves but can transmit it through their urine and infect humans. Of course, although this process was already fairly well established with the arenaviruses, it was still speculative as far as the Lassa virus was concerned and would have to be verified.

Meanwhile, Bob Shope was put to work trying to find out if the new Lassa virus might actually be an old familiar one in disguise. While this was highly unlikely, it was a possibility that had to be eliminated. This was done by a process called cross-reaction—a laborious procedure. Penny Pinneo's serum was tested against virus after virus, including many rare and exotic tropical strains. The names alone were formidable: Banzi; Ntaya; Spondweni; Bushbush; Wesselsbron; West Nile; Zika; Bwamba; epizootic hemorrhagic disease of deer, New Jersey; Nairobi sheep disease; Rift Valley fever; Lagos bat; Lone Star; Omsk hemorrhagic fever; Punta Toro; Silverwater; phlebotomus Neapolitan; vescular stomatitis, Indiana; Witwatersrand. There were dozens of others.

Through all the testing, the new Lassa virus stood alone and unique. A false alarm came when Penny Pinneo's serum reacted with yellow fever antigen. But this was easily explained, in that she had been inoculated with Theiler's 17-D vaccine and therefore would definitely show antibodies.

Confirming earlier suspicions, there was a very slight reaction with the LCM viruses—enough to classify Lassa as part of the same lethal group. But no relationship was found between Lassa virus and other African fevers, such as Marburg, dengue, and Congo.

Many things fell into place in grouping the Lassa virus with the LCM group: in the latter, it had been shown that children came down with the disease less violently than adults—perhaps explaining the resistance of Jordi Casals' baby mice. The possibility of Lassa virus being rodent-borne fit in with the same type of etiology, or source, as the LCM virus.

This could be especially significant in light of the burning of the bush and the great rat hunts of the wild Sudan savanna. As the savanna was burned to a stubble and the rats ran out, they were clubbed or caught by hand. When they were caught, they were frightened. When they were frightened, they urinated. When they urinated, they could spread the virus. They were often caught by children. Could the children pick up the virus from the rats, absorb it—and yet resist the disease just as the baby mice had? Could they then pass the virus along to the adult members of the compound through their urine?

All this had to be explored. It would be a massive job. Skilled manpower in Africa was scarce. So were funds. Don Carey, Graham Kemp, and others at the University of Ibadan were swamped. George Stroh of the U.S. Public Health Service had his hands full with the smallpox vaccination campaign. Depending on how the Sudan savannas are defined, they are as big or bigger than the continental United States. And no new Lassa cases had arisen. Without this, was it worth following the whole thing up in the field?

Even at Yale the question had to be weighed. The entire ongoing, broad-spectrum program of the arbovirus laboratory had been interrupted by the crisis. How much more time could be diverted to this strange virus, from a town so remote in its tiny corner of the deep interior savanna that it rarely appeared in an atlas or reference book?

Yet here was a virus that had killed two out of the first three Americans it struck. The third, by any medical calculations, should have died. There was no defense against the disease if it should break out again—only the remote possibility of using the convalescent serum of Penny Pinneo, and how much of that was there to go around?

The consensus at Yale was that the Lassa virus was too deadly to leave in the lap of the gods. More, much more, had to be found out about it because of its potential danger and potential spread.

So Yale continued to work. The Center for Disease Control in Atlanta also offered to pitch in, especially in light of Dr.

David Sencer's concern for the jet-age syndrome of epidemiologic tides springing up unexpectedly in the United States from the most remote areas in the world. Specimens were carefully prepared at Yale and shipped to Atlanta. The CDC was completing construction of a giant new "hot lab"—a maximum-security facility reminiscent of the fictional underground laboratory conjured up for *The Andromeda Strain*. When the hot lab was finished, it would be an ideal place to continue the study of Lassa fever.

Yale realized from the start the necessity for confining its Lassa virus tests to some degree. Scattered throughout the report that Jordi Casals and Sonja Buckley were preparing for the medical profession were several very revealing sentences: "For reasons of safety, animal inoculations were held to a minimum and done only in mice."

Or in the same report: "Since isolates were readily recovered from serial [serum] specimens of three of the patients, it was decided not to attempt reisolation from specimens determined to be virus-positive. This was taken in view of the hazards associated with working with the virus."

Only rarely are such sentences found in the clinical understatement that typifies articles in medical journals. Words like that are not used lightly.

Further elucidation came as Jordi Casals and Sonja Buckley went on with their tests. The Lassa virus was made up of a fatty-protein overcoat with its ugly spikes, and inside it was the coil of RNA, rather than DNA. Either RNA or DNA is responsible for the insidious work of a virus, hijacking the cell it invades. In this case, it was RNA. Its typical spherical shape could at times be squeezed into other shapes or sizes. And all through the tests it killed and killed and killed. It was not a congenial companion.

Early in June, when the warm air and sun flooded New Haven, Jordi Casals was having a bit of trouble with a hangnail. He had always been prone to them, and this one was particularly

bothersome. He stopped by the reception desk at the laboratory to ask Charlene Mousch if she had a Bandaid. She did and
provided him with one. He wrapped it around his finger and
went back to work at his bench.

In addition to his routine testing, he had to prepare a medical paper to present at a scientific meeting in Germany and was
also swamped with meetings and innumerable details of his
job. He was driving himself too hard, and he realized it. Situations like this could promote carelessness, and he promised
himself he would taper off as soon as he got back from Germany.

A few days later, again at his laboratory bench, he felt a
strange chill go through him. He ignored it and continued
working. But it persisted. Disgruntled and irritated because he
had so much work to do, he went to a lab assistant and asked
for some aspirin. He took two and went back to work. In line
with the tradition of his profession, he refused to allow himself
the luxury of imagining that his symptoms might be serious.
This would lead to constant hypochondria—a feeling to be
avoided when dealing every day with such dangerous material.

On the following day Sonja Buckley came into his lab and
saw him sitting with both a thick gray sweater and a gray tweed
jacket under his white lab coat. He was working at his mouse
tests and looked up when she entered. To Sonja, his face
looked almost as gray as his sweater. And he was shivering.

"What in the world is the matter with you?" she said.

"I have a cold."

"What are you going to do about it?" Sonja asked.

"I'm just taking aspirin," he said. "That's all."

Nearly all the women in the lab felt motherly toward Jordi
Casals. His shaggy face and quiet congeniality seemed to in-
spire it. Sonja chided him and told him to go home and rest
until it cleared up. He said he'd think about it.

Casals commuted to New Haven from New York, a sluggish
hour-and-a-half ride each way, in cars that seem to have heat in
the summer and air conditioning in the winter. On the follow-

ing day—Tuesday—he got off the train and found that his legs were hurting. He usually enjoyed walking from the station to the laboratory on College Street, especially in the welcome Connecticut spring weather. But on this morning he took a taxi.

He could barely make it through the day. The pain in his legs centered in the lower portion of both thighs. He never knew that muscle aches could be that bad. He took more aspirin and, near the end of the day, finally gave in to the pleas of his colleagues to take his notes home and work on them there for a few days.

At his New York apartment on Morningside Heights, he found some codeine in the medicine cabinet and took it. His wife and daughter were away in the country visiting his mother-in-law, and he played his condition down when he talked to them on the phone, because he didn't want to break up their visit.

He stayed home through the rest of the week, with no improvement. He had a fever. But he would not go to bed. Betty Young, the administrative assistant at the Yale laboratory, came into New York with some correspondence for him to sign and returned to New Haven that afternoon.

"You should see Jordi," she told Sonja Buckley. "He's so pale. He looks like death warmed over. I'm worried about him."

On Sunday morning, June 15, Jordi Casals decided that all this inactivity wasn't doing him any good. He could barely walk at all, but he painfully went down the elevator and walked toward the newsstand for the Sunday *Times.*

By sheer coincidence, he bumped into Ed Leifer, his personal physician and close friend. Leifer was in the Department of Medicine at the Columbia University College of Physicians and Surgeons. In addition, of course, he was associated with Columbia Presbyterian Hospital.

Leifer took one look at him and said: "What's happened to you, Jordi? You look like an old man!"

Casals mumbled something about having a cold.

"Can't you walk straighter than that? You're all bent over."

Casals confessed that he was feeling shoddy. Leifer told him to go straight home to bed and promised to drop over in the evening.

As a doctor as well as a virologist, Casals knew that he couldn't fool himself much longer. He looked in the mirror. His face was very peculiar: flushed and bloated.

When his wife and daughter came back from the country Sunday afternoon, they were horrified. His wife could only say: "My God, Jordi—what's happened to you?"

Ed Leifer came to the apartment to see him early that evening. He gave him a general bedside examination. Then he went to the phone and called an ambulance.

Jordi Casals was admitted to the isolation unit of Columbia Presbyterian Hospital within the hour, on Sunday, June 15, 1969.

Chapter Seven

Sunday, June 15, 1969, was a joyous and relaxed day for John and Veronica Frame. One daughter was back for a visit, a son had just gotten his Ph.D., there was another young graduate visiting, and they were also remembering Veronica's birthday. A generous cluster of family and friends was dropping by that evening in Forest Hills for a buffet supper. Veronica was always pleased when John relaxed; he had a tendency to work too hard and to get a little uptight about his patients. With his duties at Columbia, plus his long clinical schedule, she had to pressure him to take a little time off.

The gathering was at the height of its cordial momentum when the phone rang. Veronica answered it. It was Wil Downs calling from New York. He sounded perturbed.

She called John to the phone. She instinctively knew that something was wrong.

"John," Downs said over the phone. "I'm at Columbia Presbyterian. Jordi Casals is in isolation."

Downs continued briskly: Jordi's temperature was 104°. Blood pressure, 130 systolic and 90 diastolic. Pulse, 98. Respiration, 22. Skin flushed. He was acutely ill, there was no mistake about it. In fact, desperately ill.

It was almost unnecessary for either Downs or Frame to

mention the obvious thought on each of their minds: Lassa fever. And, of course, it was too early to tell anything.

Their thoughts were practically simultaneous about the next obvious possibility. Downs spoke about it first: "Do you know where Penny Pinneo is now?"

"I know what you're thinking of," Frame said. "It's the first thing that came to my mind."

"What kind of shape is she in?" Downs asked.

"I'm not sure," Frame said. "She's up in Rochester with her sister. About a couple of weeks ago the nystagomoid movement of the eyes dropped off, and the light-headedness has cleared up, I think. She can walk without leaning toward the right. Even her scalp hair shows some signs of coming back."

There was a pause, and Frame asked: "Do you think it would work?"

Downs thought a moment. The decision to bleed Penny Pinneo for the antibodies in her bloodstream would have to be weighed from many angles—if she were well enough to give it, and if she wanted to give it. Even under the best of circumstances, it was a risky business. "Would you feel like giving her a call?"

"Yes," Frame said. "I would. You at the hospital?"

Downs replied that he was.

"I'll try right now, and then I'll be right over to the hospital."

"Thanks, John," Downs said. They hung up.

Frame came back to the party visibly disturbed. The family could see he was worried. Finally he told them about Jordi Casals. A chill went through the room.

John went back to the phone. He tried to call Rose Pinneo in Rochester. There was no answer.

He would have to wait until morning.

On Monday, at the Columbia Presbyterian isolation unit, there was cause for alarm. Jordi Casals was acutely ill. He looked completely washed out. Like the three mission nurses, he was markedly dehydrated. His platelet count was ominous: down to about 60,000, from a minimum normal of 150,000. When these tiny red cells dropped low in the bloodstream, they fore-shadowed internal hemorrhaging, another Lassa fever symp-tom. The low white blood cell count indicated leukopenia, a clear-cut Lassa symptom at the beginning of the course of the disease. It would rise later, if it followed the same pattern. Then the ulcers on the inside of the cheeks and the throat—the buccal mucosa and the pharynx—would begin to show. There were petechiae.

Casals was sliding downhill, and rapidly.

But he was still rational. Much as he tried to look the other way, his own suspicions that he had come down with Lassa fever grew by the hour. He tried to be philosophical about it, but the slightest movement of his legs was so painful he found it hard to remain detached. He still did not like to admit that he was even sick. He kept thinking about those mice.

They had been very active in their cages behind him, and they did kick up a lot of dust, in spite of the elaborate ventila-tion system. He thought he had been careful. Maybe he should have been more careful. And then that hangnail. How could you get your work done if you were always worrying about hangnails? He didn't remember any cut in his hands. But whether it was a cut, a hangnail, or dust, nothing helped much now.

At Yale, Sonja Buckley was going over and over the situa-tion in her mind. She couldn't believe that Jordi wouldn't be coming in through the door of the laboratory, donning his white coat, sitting down at his lab bench to work.

There had always been a lot of kidding among the virolo-gists about the hazards of their work. Sonja Buckley admitted that she was scared, lots of times. Others would shrug the whole thing off and say, well, maybe it's an honorable death. Nice way to go out. For the good of society and all that stuff. Then they'd laugh about it.

He worked with all those cages of mice right behind

him, she thought. *Maybe there was an aerosol of dust in that room all the time, in spite of the negative pressure in the isolators.*

She tried to concentrate on her work, but she kept brooding. What about Jordi's funny habit of chewing on a pencil all the time? Why did he have to do that, the lovable idiot? If he checked a mouse with one hand, and that mouse had urine on it, and then he put the pencil in his mouth—who knows? And all those infected cell suspensions she had supplied him with. Had he really been careful with them? Why had he worked so many days after he wasn't feeling well? Why hadn't she forced him to go home and go to bed?

Of course he had Lassa fever now. Or did he? That was the trouble with the whole bloody business. It would take so long to find out. And when you finally did, through the slow titers and fixation tests, it could be too late to do anything—even if anything could be done. It would be at least Friday before the laboratory assays would show whether he had the Lassa virus or not. By that time he might be dead—she hesitated to use the word, even in her mind.

Her thoughts were interrupted by the arrival of Jimmy Washington, a staff assistant from New York. He brought with him the first batch of blood samples from Casals. He would be commuting back and forth with a succession of these, so that the laboratory could put all its skills and equipment to work in trying to help one of its best-loved associates.

In Rochester, New York, Penny Pinneo had been laboring through the painful process of convalescence. In the four weeks or so she had been out of the hospital, she had had alternate periods of hope and discouragement. The incessant, rapid lateral movement of her eyes seemed as if it would never stop, though it gradually did. The ringing in her ears, the deafness, the lack of balance all wore off very slowly and with uneven progress. She had frequent periods of great weakness, even faintness.

She refused to let herself worry about the loss of her hair. Either it would grow back or it wouldn't. She gained strength slowly, erratically, with innumerable setbacks. When her impatience or frustration seemed to be unbearable, she would listen to her hymns on the radio or say a silent prayer. Her sister Rose continued to read the Bible to her, because she still could not adequately focus her eyes.

Above all, she wanted to get back to work, to return to Nigeria, to continue her service at the little plateau hospital. At times she wondered whether she would ever be strong enough to do it. At other times she set her mind in stubborn determination: she would return. Nothing could stop her.

When the phone rang on Monday morning, June 16, she was pleased to hear from John Frame, then shocked at the news about Jordi Casals.

Would she, Frame asked, consider letting them take blood serum from her as a possible antiserum to give Jordi? She would not only consider it, she would take the first plane out of Rochester for New York City that afternoon. Was she up to the trip? She laughed and said: "Try and stop me."

She called her sister at work and told her the situation. Rose Pinneo had mixed feelings. She knew that Penny's serum and its antibodies would be the only possible therapy for Casals if he had Lassa fever. But she was seriously concerned about whether Penny had recovered enough from her agonizing illness to make an emergency trip at this time. And further—was she able to give her blood without severely damaging her own recovery?

With a great deal of reticence, she left the decision to Penny.

By midafternoon on Monday Penny Pinneo was aboard a 727 jet en route to New York.

Wil Downs, now commuting between New York and New Haven, was kept up to date with both the laboratory testing of Casals' specimens and his clinical progress in the hospital. It was obvious that Jordi was getting worse. But no one could be sure until the lab tests incubated and matured—a matter of several days—whether he had Lassa fever, and this was the main rub.

If he did not have Lassa and Penny Pinneo's plasma was administered, would they be exposing him to undue risks? One test had shown that Penny's serum was free of Lassa, but a series of tests was really needed. This would take days on end.

One minuscule live virus particle would be disaster. It could multiply logarithmically within hours and give Casals the disease that he might not have had in the first place. There were other, more subtle problems involved, which would be thrashed out over the days to come.

In the library of the Yale arbovirus laboratory all of Jordi Casals' colleagues gathered to try to conjure up some kind of solution to the dilemma they faced. They had received the news that Penny Pinneo was going to fly down that afternoon. This answered one part of the problem: her serum would be available, at least. But there was a risk if they did give the serum and a risk if they didn't. What's more, the ultimate responsibility for the final decision would fall on Ed Leifer at Columbia. He was personally responsible for his patient. The group at Yale could only recommend and persuade.

There wasn't a person at the meeting who wasn't almost fully convinced that Jordi Casals had Lassa fever. This included Wil Downs, Sonja Buckley, Bob Shope, and several others. But there was still that off chance that he didn't.

The speed with which the virus moved, as revealed in the other patients, did not allow much time for vacillation. Although it was always hard to pin down the exact day of the onset of the illness, especially since patients like the mission nurses and Jordi Casals were likely to keep their first subjective symptoms to themselves, the Yale doctors figured that Jordi Casals had entered Columbia Presbyterian on the sixth day of his illness.

Allowing some margin for error, Laura Wine had died

within ten days of the onset; Charlotte Shaw, within ten or eleven; Penny Pinneo reached her crisis at about the twelfth day.

Now it was seven days after the onset of Jordi Casals' sickness. At the most, there might be a two- or three-day leeway for a decision to be made, and this was just guesswork.

The hazards were thoroughly hashed over.

All the varied problems of the advisability of giving serum without an absolutely firm Lassa diagnosis were argued. In spite of the fact that the baby mice remained well after exposure to the disease, the virus lingered in their urine for weeks. The same could be true for Penny Pinneo. Serum hepatitis could develop, which on top of Casals' critical condition might be a final blow. The condition known as an immune complex could form, which could be fatal. Penny had survived on symptomatic care and treatment alone. Could Jordi Casals, without taking the serum risk?

Another very subtle possibility: Casals might have already started to manufacture his own antibodies. The Pinneo antibodies might make Jordi Casals' immune system lazy, so that it wouldn't start pumping out his own; that is, the production of his own antibodies would not be stimulated. Then, after the Pinneo antibodies had cleaned up as many of his viruses as they could, there might be some virus remaining, free to run wild in Casals' now defenseless system.

Another question: Could they wait until Friday, the first likely date that Sonja Buckley's tissue cultures would show whether or not a Lassa virus isolate was in Jordi Casals' blood?

On the other hand, doing nothing could be worse. They might just be sitting back, letting Casals sink deeper and deeper into a crisis that would kill him, just as had happened to Laura Wine and Charlotte Shaw. Further, Sonja Buckley was confident that her tests had shown that Penny Pinneo's serum was totally free of any live Lassa virus. As a precaution, the red cells of Penny Pinneo's blood would be removed by centrifuge and returned to her. The resulting clear plasma would reduce the danger of a transfusion reaction in Jordi and not drain Penny Pinneo of needed red cells.

The talk went in circles, but it finally solidified. The consensus was clear. The risk was worth taking: Jordi Casals should be given the serum with its antibodies.

If Sonja Buckley's tests could be relied on, and if the serum could be centrifuged and the red blood cells removed, the chances were that the serum could not do any harm, and it just might work.

Wil Downs went to the phone to notify Ed Leifer at Columbia.

Leifer, along with his colleagues Dave Gocke and Henry Bourne, was having his own problems at Columbia Presbyterian. As Casals' personal physician, Leifer had talked at length with John Frame about the possibility of giving Penny Pinneo's antiserum plasma. Leifer was ripped up the middle about what to do.

The danger of serum hepatitis loomed large in his mind, along with the possible antibody-antigen reaction that could cause liver or kidney shutdown. Jordi Casals, in the strange position of being both a doctor and a patient, sensed what Ed was going through. Leifer was in a much tougher position than the scientists at Yale because of his ultimate responsibility for the patient.

In spite of his pain, Jordi Casals could think clearly enough. But he was in the same position as the others: he didn't know what was the best course. He knew how terrifying Lassa fever was; he had seen his mice die in droves; he had reviewed the clinical cases of the mission nurses and studied every convulsive, racking, excruciating stage that the patients had gone through. Now the thorny microvillain was mocking him.

Frame had long conferences that day with Dave Gocke at Columbia. Gocke, a brilliant specialist in and professor of contagious diseases, had been spending a great deal of time on hepatitis. He would be a key man in deciding whether to give the serum to Casals.

Penny Pinneo had arrived in New York Monday afternoon, and now on Tuesday morning she was on her way up to Columbia for the ticklish business of giving her blood. It was important that the red cells be returned to her own system so that she would have only minimum loss of the blood elements she needed so badly in her convalescence.

Over coffee, constantly on the grill in the lab, Gocke and Leifer discussed the hepatitis problem with Frame. Gocke had developed a special test element for a hepatitis virus called AU antigen and was probably as well equipped as anyone in the country to realize the dangers involved. He was cautious but not negative. Ed Leifer was further concerned that Penny Pinneo, who had spent many years in Africa among hundreds of patients with various known and unknown fevers, might pass along an entirely unexpected disease to Jordi Casals.

Leifer had already talked to Wil Downs about the consensus of the Yale doctors. Their urging him to decide immediately to go ahead with the transfusion had made a strong impression on him, but at this point he was convinced that the time was not yet right to take the step. The fact remained that Lassa fever had not been diagnosed—could not be diagnosed until at least Friday, when the tissue cultures would bring some kind of definite evidence. Nobody envied Ed Leifer's position.

Penny Pinneo arrived, pale but as usual spirited. She had no fear, no concern for her own well-being; just a desire to get on with it.

They prepared her for the blood taking. The process she was to undergo is called plasmapheresis. It is slow and tedious. A hollow needle is put in the vein. The blood comes out in a plastic bag by gravity, very slowly. The needle is left in while intravenous fluid is maintained in the veins. The blood is centrifuged: red blood cells are whirled out of the plasma solution until they form a hard-packed mass. They are then returned to the donor in a saline solution.

About a pint of blood—500 cc, or a "unit"—is drawn off at first. If the IV, or intravenous, fluid is maintained, the vein is kept open, and the red blood cells can be returned. Then another pint can be taken.

The process takes about three hours. Penny Pinneo went through the ordeal in good spirits.

Still no decision had been made. They took the serum, stored it under refrigeration, and waited.

All through Tuesday Casals was sinking lower. Wilbur Downs came in from New Haven to see him and was shocked by his appearance and condition. Everybody's nerves were on edge at the isolation unit.

While Downs was there, Jordi's wife Lynn was permitted to don mask, gown, and surgical gloves to see her husband for a moment. She was appalled, on the verge of tears. Wil Downs, looking at her over his surgical mask, felt for her.

When her time was up, she moved automatically toward Jordi and leaned down to kiss him through her mask. Downs yelled sharply and grabbed her away. Lassa fever did not allow a margin for affection.

At Yale, Sonja Buckley was setting up her tissue cultures as fast as nature would allow them to incubate. Jimmy Washington brought her Casals' serum at least once a day, sometimes twice. She put the samples into processing as soon as they arrived. Wil Downs had come back to Yale on Tuesday afternoon, having been unsuccessful in persuading Ed Leifer to give the antibody serum. After another meeting with the staff, he phoned Leifer again, with no better results. If there were only some way to confirm that Casals had Lassa fever, the decision would be so much easier.

By Tuesday evening the situation was more ominous. Another meeting was held at Columbia's Department of Medicine. Ed Leifer was leaning toward the conclusion that there might be no choice but to give the serum, in spite of the risks. But he was still convinced he should hold off longer.

On Wednesday morning, with the news that Jordi Casals was going downhill more rapidly than ever, a major meeting was called in Room 608 of the library of the Yale arbovirus laboratory. Just before the meeting, Wil Downs put through a phone call to his colleague, Dr. Karl Johnson, a leading international virologist. Johnson was in Panama for the U.S. Public Health Service, working with the Machupo virus, which caused the deadly Bolivian hemorrhagic fever.

Downs knew that Johnson had run into a parallel crisis in Panama. People were dying like flies from the Machupo virus, and Johnson had made the painful decision to administer immune serum from patients who had recovered from the disease. It had worked in some cases; in others it did not work. But Johnson was certain of one thing: if you waited too long, the serum was useless. A patient with Machupo fever usually remained conscious until the threshold of death. Then he went into shock, there was a precipitous decline, and the whole thing was over. Once shock was reached, nothing could be done with the serum.

As Johnson listened attentively, Downs described the clinical course of Jordi Casals' sickness. He told Johnson that Penny Pinneo's blood had been drawn and centrifuged, and that the serum was clear of her red cells. He said that Jordi Casals was sinking but still conscious.

After Downs had finished, Johnson said firmly: "Wil—give that serum."

Wil Downs opened the meeting at Yale with a review of his conversation with Karl Johnson. In addition to the regular scientific staff of the arbovirus lab, Downs had invited Dr. Robert McCollum, chairman of the Department of Epidemiology at Yale and a specialist in hepatitis. Also there were Dr. Dorothy Horstmann, professor of pediatrics, epidemiology, and public health, and Dr. Gregory Tignor.

The atmosphere of the meeting was electric. Downs described Jordi Casals' condition: the continuous high fever for seven days, the ominous drop in the white blood cell count, the ulcerated throat—all the other signs.

Downs said that he was convinced Casals had Lassa fever, but that the first tissue-culture tests would probably not be in until Friday. It all boiled down again to the key question: Should the serum be given without a precise Lassa diagnosis?

The discussion could be pounded down to a series of pseudo-syllogisms:

1. They didn't know for sure that Casals had Lassa fever.
2. They knew that Penny Pinneo had had Lassa fever.
3. They knew that live virus from Lassa fever could stay around for a long time. Just how long was uncertain.
4. If Casals did not have Lassa, there was a possibility that they might give it to him by injecting the serum.

But the balance of the torturous discussion was tipped on the basis of Karl Johnson's experience: if they waited too long, it would be hopeless.

The vote was unanimous to give the serum.

Downs got on the phone immediately. He couldn't reach Ed Leifer, but he got Frame. Frame told him that Leifer had practically decided to go ahead with the serum. A test by Gocke showed that Penny Pinneo's serum was free of hepatitis at least. The ultimate decision would be made very soon. Downs was relieved but urged the necessity for speed. Frame said he'd pass the word right along.

On Wednesday night the serum was brought to Jordi Casals' bedside. There were two units of 250 cc each—half of the volume having been returned to Penny Pinneo with her red cells. The hazards were on the minds of everybody—including Jordi, who knew as much as anyone about the dangers.

The serum began going into Casals' veins drop by drop. The slower it went in, the less danger there was of any sudden reaction.

All through the night the drops of serum from Penny Pinneo, someone Casals had never met, went into his bloodstream, as the medical team watched and waited.

The next morning, Thursday, there was little change. Jordi's mind was wandering a bit, and he didn't always make sense in what he said. His throat was worse. The electrocardiogram showed the beginning of a cardiac problem. There was at least no sign of a liver or kidney shutdown. The high temperature continued.

Hanging over everybody at Yale and Columbia throughout the day was the question: Have we done the right thing?

The following morning, Friday, Sonja Buckley entered the laboratory before anyone else. After getting the news that Jordi had survived the night, she went straight to her tissue cultures.

She almost dreaded to look, for they were now certain to show whether he actually had Lassa virus or not.

If the tissue cultures failed to show a virus, it would mean that Jordi had been exposed to a potentially dangerous serum for nothing. If the cultures showed positive for Lassa, at least she could have the comfort of knowing they had done everything medically possible to try to forestall the ravages of the disease. She took a deep breath, went to the plaque trays, pulled the bottles out, and examined them. Every cell carpet in the bottles had come down with the overwhelming cytopathic effects—the ravages of Lassa virus.

Her computations showed that he had 10,000 Lassa virus particles for every milliliter of blood serum.

But not all the results were in yet. Jordi was hanging on clinically. Which direction would he go?

The answer came that morning. Jordi Casals took a definite turn for the better.

The medical report from the team of Columbia doctors later put it laconically:

During the 24 hours after administration of immune plasma the temperature fell to normal and improvement in well-being was noted. During the next few days, the patient was again febrile, but to a range of only 101° to 102°F; following this, there was continuing improvement. He became afebrile [no fever] on the 11th hospital day and remained so . . .

The relief at Yale and Columbia was indescribable. Casals continued to improve. Bob Shope, visiting him at the hospital, used an expression that Jordi Casals claims he will remember to his dying day. Shope said: "Jordi, we were very frightened."

Scientists don't use that word often.

The joy at Jordi's gradual recovery was tempered by the implications of his coming down with the disease by laboratory contact with the virus. There were now four confirmed cases of Americans who had been stricken by Lassa. Half had died.

This created a serious problem to public health, especially in the jet age. Further studies at Yale revealed that the virus remained in Casals' throat washings for at least fifteen days. This was an extremely long time for a death-dealing agent to hang on.

On hearing the news about Jordi, officials of the U.S. Public Health Service in New York called John Frame on the phone.

They were very concerned. It was one thing for a mission nurse to contract Lassa fever in Africa. It was another thing for the disease to be transported to and contracted in the United States. The implications were serious. Who was going to be next? What precautions could be taken? Would it move out of the hospital and virus laboratory and into the streets?

Frame joined in the Public Health Service's concern. They discussed what should be done in detail. Together they made up a hastily improvised procedure to be put into effect immediately at Kennedy and other international airports.

The plan amounted to an epidemiologic dragnet. All public health officers at the airports would question any travelers returning from Nigeria in detail about their recent medical history. Had they had any fever in the past few months? Any recent illness? If so, what nature? How long had they been in Nigeria? Had any members of their family been ill?

If there were any indication whatever of illness, the traveler would be required to contact John Frame through the Public Health Service immediately. Arrangements would be made with Columbia Presbyterian Hospital to put the traveler in the isolation unit for an immediate and thorough examination.

In addition, the U.S. Public Health Service sent out an alert bulletin to all its officers throughout the country to be on the lookout for anything resembling Lassa fever.

John Frame drew up a succinct summary of the disease for the benefit of doctors who might be confronting it for the first time. It read in part:

> Lassa fever is a newly discovered viral disease from West Africa. Morphologically, morphogenetically, and clinically, the agent resembles Machupo virus, the agent of Bolivian hemorrhagic fever . . .
>
> Though there is an apparent immunological relationship, the two viruses are distinct entities . . .
>
> Lassa virus was first isolated from acute sera of three missionary nurses from Nigeria. Two of these nurses died in their illness. Subsequently, it was isolated from the blood of a virologist working with the disease . . .
>
> When the disease first occurred, we predicted that it would prove to be a disease of lower animals, that it must have been present, though not recognized, for a long time, and that it might prove to be widespread across Africa . . .
>
> The first prediction, that it would be found a disease of lower animals, has not been confirmed as yet. Certain epidemiological data suggest that it is a disease in mice, and other viruses of this group, Machupo, LCM, and Junin among them, are in fact diseases of mice or rodents . . .
>
> In all early cases at various stages of infection, yellow fever, malaria, typhoid, or typhus have been considered as a diagnosis. In some cases streptococcal throat infections have been suspected. Many mission societies have histories of illnesses and deaths among missionaries that may well be examples of Lassa fever . . .

The bulletin went on to describe the classical course of the disease in detail. Onset, gradual to sudden. Muscle aches, malaise, and weakness. Leukopenia, or drop in the white blood cell count. Moderately elevated fever. Sore throat on the third to fifth day. Throat and mouth ulcers with yellow centers and red halos. Abdominal discomfort and tenderness along the rib cage. Mild swollen glands. Petechial, macular rash on the body. Bleeding under the skin. Swelling of neck and face, caused by swollen glands or edema—fluid in the tissues. Some mental disturbance and inability to concentrate. On or about the ninth day a fall in blood pressure. In fatal cases, coma, shock, and death on about the eleventh day of illness. The bulletin added that specific diagnosis could be made only by virologists in the laboratory.

A major outbreak in the United States was considered unlikely, but the Public Health Service had to be ready for it. Doctors were asked to check for Lassa in any patient who showed up with an unusual fever, whether he had been to Nigeria or not. The Center for Disease Control of the Public Health Service in Atlanta joined in the alert and prepared to start work on its study of the specimens supplied by Yale.

All international travelers coming to the United States, from Africa or anywhere else, receive a small yellow card with red typeface when they are cleared through immigration and customs at airports and docks. It is headlined: "Health Alert Notice." On one side it is addressed to the traveler and says:

> Keep this card in your wallet or purse 6 weeks. If you become ill during this period, give this card to your physician and advise him of your recent travel outside the United States.
>
> You may have been exposed to a communicable disease before arriving in the United States. If so, a knowledge of the possibility of exposure abroad will help your physician arrive more quickly at a diagnosis.

On the reverse side is a message to the doctor, telling him that the person presenting the card has recently been abroad and may have been exposed to a communicable disease not usually present in the United States. It names some of the diseases—yellow fever, plague, cholera, and others—and advises him to get in touch with the CDC in Atlanta immediately by phone.

More and more, with the advent of the 747 jumbo jets, the card is becoming crucial. In the case of Lassa fever, there was a feeling among those who knew its virulence that the card might be more important than ever. What the future held was anybody's guess.

Jordi Casals' progress continued to be amazingly good.

He eventually met Penny Pinneo. He saw what he described as a charming little lady come up to him and say: "So you are Dr. Casals?"

It was reminiscent of Stanley meeting Livingston, except they were meeting through a viral wilderness even more frightening than the African jungles of the two British explorers.

To Penny Pinneo, Casals was "very charming." He gave her a sterling silver key ring with a simple phrase engraved on it: "Bless you." Penny Pinneo accepted it, and her eyes filled with tears. Because of the antibodies now in their systems, they were two people who never had to fear Lassa fever again.

The convalescence for Jordi Casals, as for Penny Pinneo, was slow but steady. The follow-up blood specimens, throat washings, and urine were packed with Lassa. The live virus held on stubbornly in the specimens through the seventeenth day of illness, near the end of June.

Jordi Casals chafed under the duress of his isolation, but he was so grateful that he was ashamed of himself for feeling so. Finally, the specimens showed no live Lassa virus in his system. After a two-week precautionary waiting period, during which several additional tests were taken, he was released from the hospital. It was the thirty-sixth day of his illness. Later, Yale would advise him of the results of the final tests as a matter of routine.

Jordi, his wife, and his daughter went up to Vermont in the warm and delicious sun of a New England July to recuperate. The air of the Green Mountains, the evergreens, the charm of the little village where they stayed were invigorating and therapeutic. But shortly after he arrived in Vermont, he got an urgent phone call from the Yale virus laboratory.

The tests from his last few days in the hospital had just been analyzed. His urine was found to still contain live Lassa virus.

He was to be very careful, to keep absolutely clean, to have no contacts with anyone. He must leave his family immediately and return to Yale for additional tests.

At the height of his thanksgiving, Jordi Casals found himself an enemy of society.

Chapter Eight

In that June of 1969 an uneasy calm settled over the Jos plateau. There was still the feeling on the part of many that something was going to happen, but nobody knew quite what it would be. People went about their everyday routines as usual, and not much was said.

John and Esther Hamer were packing to go home. Their long tour of duty in Lassa was coming to an end, and they faced the departure with mixed feelings. The savanna had gotten in their blood; so had the tribespeople and the village of Lassa. They would miss the jagged Cameroon highlands on the horizon, the glorious blossoming of brilliant color when the rainy season turned the brindle, thirsty bush grass to a lush emerald green.

They would miss Von and Elsie Hall, miss the clean, swift brightness of an African dawn and the warm, soft smile of a Nigerian midwife as she successfully completed serving a childbirth. There would be a strange nostalgia for the little wood-burning stove, the black cement bathtub that scratched their skin, the mosquito canopy over the bed, the scarlet mantle of the flamboyant trees, and the twisted ugliness of the upside-down monkey bread trees. They would even miss that moment each evening at ten when all the light bulbs in the house slowly dimmed, like the house lights in a theater, as the gasoline generator was shut off.

Von and Elsie Hall would be the only Americans left at Lassa station; no new doctor had yet been found to replace John Hamer. Ngamariju Mamza, the supervisor of the nursing staff, would be taking over the medical duties. His long years of apprenticeship had made him almost as qualified as a full doctor—even more qualified in the strange twists and turns of tropical diseases.

It was a sad farewell when the Hamers got into their fully packed Land Rover, went past the fields of Guinea corn, and disappeared around a bend in the now muddy ruts of the tracks to Michika on the main road.

They had heard about Jordi Casals being stricken with Lassa fever over the mission radio and were shocked that the disease that seemed to have begun with Laura Wine had now reached all the way to the United States. In Lassa the only thing that seemed to be left of the disease was a bitter and tragic memory.

At Jos there was also comparative calm, considering the constant pressure of everyday work on the hospital staff. The outpatient department, a breezeway and cement floor protected only by a roof, continued to be jammed with Nigerians, young and old, waiting patiently for their turn at examination, their faces filled with a majestic sadness of great dignity.

Gladys Tuck, the head outpatient nurse, would be up at six to get breakfast—mostly hot cereal, toast, and coffee—for her two daughters and her husband Bill, the mechanic who kept the Sudan Interior Mission planes flying so consistently. At seven she would get into her uniform and then spend an entire half-hour praying and reading the Bible. "This is a precious time," she told a friend, "and one I need before getting involved with the activities at the hospital."

At 7:50 she would arrive at the outpatient pavilion. There were usually more than 200 patients already lined up. But before the medical work began, an evangelist from the Sudan Interior Mission would conduct a ten-minute service. Some of the strained and tired faces would light up at this; others would look glum and indifferent, or even scowl. There were many Muslims in the area, and this was not their faith. Some would get up and walk out on the service, returning when the last reedy voice had trailed off on the final hymn.

But prayer was an integral part of the hospital. It could not be escaped. While the pavilion service was being conducted for the patients, the graduate medical staff and the clerical staff held their own prayer meeting in a different area, praying for the needs of their patients or their own need, as they expressed it, "to live in Jesus Christ as we work."

There would consistently be four or five children running temperatures up to 105°. Nurses would promptly whisk them off for a cool bath and an aspirin to bring the temperature down, then bring them back for examination, diagnoses, and whatever treatment might be needed. There were laboratory tests to be assigned, results to be studied and acted on. Just in the normal routine, the pace was demanding. When a crisis arose, it became overwhelming.

By six in the evening Gladys Tuck was usually exhausted. But promptly at 9:30 she would begin another half-hour of Bible reading and prayer with her family. "It is wonderful," she would say, without reticence, "in the day-by-day work to experience God's help as He gives wisdom in diagnosis, as He gives patience in teaching students, as He gives opportunities to tell of Jesus Christ's ability to change us."

In spite of some smoldering resentment in Jos town against the mixing of medicine and liturgy, no one faulted the brisk, competent treatment that the hospital staff offered, and especially the selfless devotion of the mission nurses. They would follow up patients who had been dismissed, visit them at their homes, bring presents to their families with a joy that might seem to some outsiders as just a bit short of hysteria. But for most patients, the joy was therapeutic.

Dolores Rohe reflected the mood of the entire nursing staff

—a mood not always shared by all of the patients—when she wrote in her journal:

> I love this walk to the hospital. It is only a third of a mile; sometimes in the middle of a hot day it seems much longer! However, in the stillness of the morning it is just beautiful. It is time to think, to pray, and a time to be thankful. This morning, the sun looks like a big moon as it hangs over the city—the harmattan causing it to look a bit hazy. Now, during the dry season, everything is dry except the trees. The mango trees are especially green and lovely all year long, for their roots go deep. This reminds me of the Psalmist who says that he who delights and meditates in Your world day and night will be like a tree that is planted by a river, for then its life will be useful and beautiful and useful to behold.

The route took her past the paramedical training school, so essential to the work of the hospital, and past some of the huts in the compound.

> As I pass the six little round mud huts with their thatched roofs, I think of thousands who live in homes like these out here—people who are very dear to Your heart. A few yards further on, I pass our school for the training of dispensers. The dormitory is alive with activity, for the sixty to seventy fellows must have their breakfast and be ready for prayers by 7:30. Dear Lord, bless these young people today in their classes, their studies, and their practical work in the outpatient department, the operating room, the general ward, and the laboratory. They have so much to learn in such a short time. Help them most of all to learn about You.

The strength of such convictions would soon be put in a crucible that an ordinary hospital might have found too overwhelming to handle.

At the University of Ibadan, Don Carey and his colleagues were waiting uneasily for the yellow fever outbreak, but there wasn't much they could do without any firm reports.

The work at the Ibadan virus lab continued at an even keel, with Graham Kemp steeped in his work on African hedgehogs and Don Carey getting more and more bogged down with administrative duties. Soon to arrive was Akinyele Fabiyi, the Nigerian virus researcher who had gone to America to study at Syracuse University, the University of Washington, and finally the University of Pennsylvania, where he took his Ph.D.

Dr. Ottis Causey, chief of the Ibadan virus lab for the Rockefeller Foundation, was getting ready to return to the United States permanently. While Carey had been grooming himself to take over the reins of the lab when Dr. Causey left, Fabiyi was being groomed to take over when Carey would leave, a few years later. This was the inevitable trend in the tide of Nigeria's independence, and most felt it was a healthy one. As head of the only virus laboratory between Senegal and East Africa, Fabiyi would be taking on an enormous burden when the Americans and the Rockefeller Foundation officials were phased out.

Life on the university campus at Ibadan could be pleasant enough at times, and neither the Kemp nor the Carey families bristled under it, except when emergencies struck.

Even though the tragic civil war was going full strength in the east-central and southeastern regions of Nigeria, there was a surprisingly good supply of food in the stores and no great hardship on that score. Occasionally, the Ibadan Film Society would show movies at one of the university halls—anything from an old Czech art film to a documentary. There would be PTA meetings, teas for the faculty wives, a few academic cocktail parties, and even a bazaar thrown by the American Women's Club in Ibadan. "The setting—with American women and their hairdos and men in their Bermudas—could just as easily have been a Wellesley, Mass., church bazaar," Don Carey wrote his family.

Like so many other virologists, Carey, Causey, Kemp, and Fabiyi had their own special philosophies about the microenemies of man they dealt with every day.

Fabiyi, his Nigerian philosophy tempered and polished by

Western education, put it succinctly: "I'm not afraid when we have to bring a risky, hazardous virus into the lab. I just hope and pray, and I don't think about it."

This philosophy would also be coming to a test in the near future.

At the CDC virus laboratory in Atlanta, researchers also were working on the Lassa virus. Virologist Brian Henderson was glad the new $2.5 million hot lab had been completed by the time the first specimens containing the Lassa virus had arrived from Yale. The complex maximum-security lab had only recently been dedicated, and the Lassa virus was its first assignment.

Specimens were untouched by human hands; they were fed into the lab on conveyor belts through long tunnels, and nothing came out without being automatically sterilized or incinerated. Even the air emerging from the building, known as 5A, was incinerated.

The researchers stood outside isolators—large steel section tanks with wide, thick glass windows for full visibility. In the windows were steel-framed portholes, with arm-length rubber gloves. The scientist placed his arms in the gloves and worked with the animal or tissue culture on the conveyor assembly line.

The building had special air locks, air-flow systems, filters, and incinerators. Anyone entering the inner chamber of the lab, which was surrounded by the isolator work docks, had to change his clothes in a special room, don disposable garments, and on leaving expose himself to ultraviolet light and shower.

Bob Shope had shipped the first live virus specimens from Yale to Atlanta. The shipment had been too precarious to send except by special messenger, and Shope had written the Atlanta virologists:

> John Carley has kindly consented to hand-carry from the Yale Arbovirus Research Unit to you the Nigerian virus we discussed on the phone.

The material is wet-frozen as supplied by Dr. Buckley. It is the second Vero passage fluid of patient Lily [Penny] Pinneo, bled on 2/25/69. This is the prototype virus which has had 3 prior human passes [in Nigeria] by contact infection among mission nurses.

He went on to describe the strength of the titers of the fluid, including the titer of the plaque-forming ability. The titer was ominously high, which put Atlanta immediately on the alert about handling the specimens in the hot lab.

Since then, Yale had been continuing its studies along with those of the CDC, although Yale did not have the elaborate protection facilities of the hot lab. Care and caution had been redoubled, however, after what had befallen Jordi Casals. But the question remained: Would care and caution be enough?

On his emergency return from Vermont, Casals was immediately put through new tests at Yale, with emphasis on the urine specimens. A virus that could survive in urine long after it had been neutralized by the antibodies in the bloodstream would have to be watched with great alertness.

Casals continued to recuperate well, and the viruses did not return. Within a few weeks he was back at his laboratory, more determined than ever to get at the enemy that continued to defy the most elaborate equipment and best brains that modern science could bring to bear against it.

There would be a double confirmation on the tests now, with CDC's elegant facilities available to match and compare the studies. Casals was interested in following up the puzzle of why baby mice seemed to be so resistant to the bug, in contrast to adult mice.

A favorite technique of virologists in exploring this sort of question is to make a soup of mice brains and then use the fluid to challenge test serum in the various complement-fixation and neutralization tests. Such a procedure would give Casals more detailed information on the behavior of this contemptuous virus aggressor. He could work with more vigor and less caution now. He had nothing to fear. His antibodies would be —or should be—total protection forever.

Meanwhile, John Frame was carrying on the battle from his end of the phalanx in New York. Frame had a hunch—he seemed to have many good ones along this line—that Lassa fever antibodies were not confined to Nigeria but might well be found in the blood of missionaries who had recovered from fever of unknown origin further to the west, in Guinea, Liberia, or Sierra Leone: all part of the Guinea savanna and at the same time part of the ill-defined Sudan. Through a missionary in Sierra Leone, he learned of a case of "typhus" there in 1965 that sounded like Lassa fever in disguise. He began following the case up, along with several others in West Africa, all of them to the west of Nigeria.

Frame also began a campaign to assemble some equipment for the Sudan Interior Mission doctors in Jos to have on hand if another outbreak occurred: a centrifuge, for instance, and plasmapheresis equipment in case they had to separate serum in an emergency, as had been done with Penny Pinneo when Jordi Casals faced his crisis.

The outlook for gaining solid, articulate information was now greatly enhanced by the availability of the clearly identified serum of the victims, against which any suspected serum could be matched by complement-fixation tests.

With Yale, the CDC, and Frame settling down into a quiet, determined campaign, the weeks went by swiftly and turned into months.

In Rochester, New York, Penny Pinneo was chafing at the bit to get back to work in Nigeria. She was immune now, just like Casals, and could serve without danger if the disease should break out again. She could help in the research with impunity, visiting villages and drawing blood with no fear of personal contagion. Although she was growing stronger, however, her health still would not permit her to return. She had gained back some of the twenty-eight pounds she had lost. Her scalp hair was also growing back, a great psychological boost, if nothing else. The only thing that still remained of consequence, aside from occasional weakness, was the ringing in her ears and some difficulty with hearing.

All through the summer it was hot in New York, New Haven, Rochester, and Atlanta; it was hotter on the Jos plateau, and rainy too.

By September several of the mission hospitals on the plateau were recording a number of patient admissions with febrile illnesses of a vague sort. The lack of specific diagnostic facilities, as usual, made diagnosis difficult.

At the Sudan Interior Mission's Evangel Hospital, Dr. Jeanette Troup and Dr. Hal White seemed to be getting their usual run of infectious hepatitis cases and were watching them carefully in line with the yellow fever possibility.

In mid-September of 1969 a young Hausa woman by the name of Tamalama Hansetu Sale told her husband Mallam the joyous news that they were about to have a baby. Mallam Sale was a skilled man and therefore reasonably prosperous. He was a mechanic for the M. S. Tawas Company of Nigeria, Ltd., on Queens Barracks Road in Lagos. He and his family lived in one of the labyrinthian compounds in Lagos, and each morning Mallam walked to work to repair the motors of the huge Mercedes diesel lorries that jam the main roads of Nigeria every day. He was also a Hausa, born in the neighboring republic of Mali, but had been raised in Nigeria, in Jos town on the plateau.

By ancient Hausa custom, an expectant mother must return to her own family compound many weeks before the child is born and remain for forty days afterward. Here she is tendered the love and care of both midwife and family until she is considered well enough to go about her own affairs.

Tamalama's family lived up on the plateau in Bassa—a town near Jos that had no relation to Lassa whatever except for the rhyme. Although he would have to lose five days of work to take Tamalama from Lagos up to the plateau by train, Mallam Sale had no other choice under the stringent Hausa custom. They gathered their three-year-old daughter and possessions for Tamalama's several-month stay and took the two-day train ride to Jos.

The village of Bassa, like Lassa, is isolated and remote, although not too far from Miango, where Charlotte Shaw lay buried. Tamalama's arrival at Bassa was one of great happiness, for Nigerian families never leave their villages in mind and spirit, regardless of how far away they move. Tamalama's red mud-brick hut, with its thatched roof and raised clay bed, was ready for her, and from then on she would be pampered without letup by her family. There would be special highly spiced gruels prepared for her, fortified with potash. She would be given more than her usual share of meat. There is a Hausa proverb: "Meat is like a stranger; it only comes occasionally." For the pregnant woman, this does not apply.

Mallam Sale was not idle during his brief stay in Bassa. He bought firewood and corn stalks to last through the long period of postnatal care for Tamalama. For forty days after the baby was born, she would be given a special Nigerian rubdown with chediya or runhu tree leaves dipped in boiling water. Her vagina would be spared. A warm douche would suffice.

After Mallam completed his husbandly duties and said his good-bys, he returned to Lagos and his Mercedes trucks. Tamalama Sale settled down for her two-month wait for the baby to arrive.

The lull that Dr. Jeanette Troup and Dr. Hal White had been experiencing at the Sudan Interior Mission hospital in Jos over the past months was abruptly broken on October 23 by the appearance of what seemed to be several yellow fever cases. As the senior doctor, Jeanette Troup lost little time in getting on the mission shortwave radio to report these events to both Don

Carey at Ibadan and the UN World Health Organization office in Lagos.

Dr. Jeanette's ability for coolness in the face of crisis were well known by the medical and public health profession in Nigeria. She never jumped to a conclusion or spread a hasty panic signal.

Later that Thursday afternoon Don Carey got a telephone call from Dr. Desmond Nugent, the World Health Organization representative in Nigeria, who also had received Dr. Troup's radio message. Since the World Health Organization could not intervene actively without the express invitation of the Nigerian government, it was agreed that Don Carey would make an immediate and direct investigation of the situation on the Jos plateau and recommend further steps if there was an epidemic.

Carey was conferring with Graham Kemp and Vern Lee, an entomologist on the staff, in a matter of moments. They hastily pulled together their equipment that evening: liquid nitrogen cannisters for refrigerating specimens, syringes, test tubes, containers. They fueled and prepared two vehicles, Kemp's tired Peugeot and a Land Rover. They left Ibadan at nine the next morning, Friday, October 24. As Carey noted in his journal, the day was clear, the journey dusty, the roads poor.

They drove all day, moving further into the plateau highland, where the trees become scarcer and the savanna spreads out to wide horizons. The tin roofs of the villages near Ibadan gave way to the conical thatched roofs of the round clay huts. Debris from old accidents as well as new ones was strewn along the road. The drip castles of the red anthills, up to fifteen feet high, towered above the trucks and cars. Cattle, killed by passing trucks, lay blood-smeared and disembowled on the road, with the enormous African buzzards swarming over them. Herdsmen walked along, their hands gripped to a cattle prod across the shoulders, their arms hanging down like clothes on a line. And, of course, there was either the red laterite dust or wallowing mud to contend with. When the halfway village of Bida loomed ahead at the end of the long day on the road, it was a welcome sight.

Carey, Kemp, and Lee checked in at the Government Catering Rest House at Bida, a cluster of white bungalows reeking with the ghosts of colonial days. At one time the scattered rest houses were the only hostelries in which to stay in reasonable comfort, with their tile floors, huge slow-turning ceiling fans, and verandas where British officers once sat to swap stories and where engineers of a tin-mining company or district officers could shoot a game of snooker under the light of Tilly lamps.

The three men registered, simply by checking their names off on a large blackboard, ordered some local Nigerian beer, and tried to bathe. There was a severe water shortage, only thimblefuls of water were available. Then there was dinner at the ancient mission-type dining room table, with a mildewed tablecloth and the choice of either a British- or Nigerian-style dinner. They chose the British: shredded boiled lamb, thin beef broth, spinach, odd sweet-tasting bread. At the table was the usual clientele—Iranian hydraulic engineers, Egyptian educators, British agronomists, Nigerian state bureaucrats, German tse-tse fly researchers, Italian road construction engineers —a strange and interesting cross-section of the most unlikely people.

They retired early to their rooms in the bungalows, separate from the main rest house building, where single beds, made like scrawny four-posters, held up the inevitable thick mosquito netting. Sometimes, there would be spiders and scorpions to share the room.

On Saturday morning they were off not long after dawn on another punishing twelve-hour drive in the blistering heat or the mud. They drove past precariously leaning buses, each labeled with a title across the cab: "Faith and Charity"; "Envy No Man"; "Little Drops of Water." Ironically, there would be a sign here and there along the route: "Road Safety Week." There were tribesmen with their heavy scars; trucks parked on the road, over a blind hill, with the drivers sleeping underneath them in the shade; helmeted soldiers with tommy guns; and finally Jos.

They went to the Hill Station Rest House—a most delightful rest station, altitude 4,000 feet, high on the hill at the end of Rest House Road in Jos. It had been the center of the colonial subculture and still maintained the traditions of the past in the face of changing times. The rooms were restful, the food excellent, the bar amply supplied. The view, sweeping across the high plateau, was breathtaking.

Early the next morning Carey, Kemp, and Lee showed up at the long white cement bungalow blocks of the Sudan Interior Mission's Evangel Hospital. Within moments they were closeted with Jeanette Troup and Hal White in the medical office just off the outpatient veranda.

The situation had grown worse in just the two days it had taken to drive to Jos. Reports were pouring in from the Vom Christian Hospital, fifteen miles from Jos. People were dying at an incredibly high rate.

The Ibadan team went immediately to the Sudan Interior Mission ward with the two mission doctors. There the disease was revealing itself in all its horror. A twenty-year-old Nigerian was in his bed. At the moment they arrived he spewed out a stream of black vomit—the coffee-ground-like sediment typical of the fever—that indicated blood was leaking uncontrolled in the viscera. He was in the throes of maniacal agitation, screaming, thrashing, spreading horror and panic among the other patients. The ward assistants could barely hold him down. Within the hour he was dead. Others were also deathly ill but quieter. An odd fish odor emanated from some. Every organ in the body was attacked. Most of the patients were hemorrhaging internally.

It was Sunday, and the Ministry of Health offices in Jos were closed. Carey and his team collected all the information they could. Five other plateau hospitals were reporting deaths with the symptoms of yellow fever, and the upswing in cases was now clearly evident.

Carey and his colleagues formed plans quickly. For the next four days they would visit hospitals and dispensaries out in the bush. The objective was to collect as much material for yellow fever virus isolation as possible. It would be rushed by missionary aircraft to Ibadan, where Causey and Fabiyi and the staff would begin isolation tests at once. If yellow fever virus were revealed, as expected, the Ibadan group would organize the fastest possible campaign to fight the outbreak and retard its spread among a population—about a million in the area—that had not been inoculated against it.

The three men from Ibadan fanned out in the Rover and station wagon to the Vom Christian Hospital and the bush dispensaries. The extent of the suffering was much greater than they expected. Patients at Vom were approaching a 60 percent death rate. The smell, the heat, the panic in the wards when the maniacal stage of the disease struck the victims were almost too much to bear.

While Kemp and Carey drew blood specimens from the victims, Lee was out in the bush on the trail of every mosquito he could catch. Because he did not have the time to set up an elaborate mosquito-trapping system, he used himself as bait, soliciting any other volunteers who would join him. On Monday evening, just before dark, he stationed himself in a swampy area, stripped to the waist, and waited for the "crepuscular biter with a predeliction for the forest canopy," as the textbooks put it. There were no forest canopies here, but there were trees and swampy places. These would be his targets.

A mosquito would hover, then land on his arm. He would wait a moment to be sure the mosquito was settling down to inject its deadly needle into his skin. Then, just before it happened, he would expertly clamp a flat-bottomed glass tube over the insect, wiggle it slightly, and shake the mosquito down into the tube. He would then seal the tube with a Monel wire-mesh cap. He was careful not to let the insect bite. Any mosquito containing blood would be discarded from the laboratory testing, because Lee had been vaccinated with Max Theiler's 17-D strain, which would automatically neutralize any virus within the mosquito. At the bottom of each tube was a dampened piece of blotting paper to keep the insect alive until it reached the laboratory.

The fatality rate in Jos and Vom continued to climb. At the Vom Christian Hospital six patients died within a week of admission, with symptoms of jaundice, hemorrhage, and kidney damage. Another eleven patients died almost at the moment they were admitted, some collapsing in the arms of nurses and doctors, spilling the hideous black vomit over the hospital workers and the floor of the waiting room. A fifty-year-old man, his eyes deep yellow, staggered into the hospital shaking with chills and fever. He reported that his entire village, fifteen miles away, was filled with "people turning yellow."

The same picture was taking shape in the medical stations across the plateau. In an informal tally, Carey and his team counted forty deaths in the two hospitals at Jos and at Vom. The fatality rate had now climbed to over 60 percent in the hospital cases alone. How much more was going on in the bush villages?

Carey and Kemp got the first specimens off by air to Ibadan, where Bob Shope had arrived from Yale to buttress the fight.

By Wednesday the Ibadan field team had collected and iced blood specimens from fifty victims, shipping them back to Ibadan as fast as the Sudan Interior Mission could schedule flights. On Friday morning the virus team packed the Land Rover and Peugeot and took off, exhausted, for the two-day trek back to Ibadan. By the time the trio got back to Ibadan on Friday night, the lab tests had already confirmed the isolation of yellow fever virus.

Carey and Kemp spent the rest of the weekend, night and day, in the university laboratory, following up the other specimens. The results showed there was no question about it: the plateau was reeling from what seemed to be an unprecedented epidemic of yellow fever. If their preliminary estimates held up, it would be the biggest or second-biggest outbreak in African history. Only a handful of men at Ibadan were equipped to handle the epidemiologic part of the situation—and they were on the brink of exhaustion. Only a few hospitals were available on the plateau for medical help, and their supplies were dwindling as the fatigue of their staffs rose.

Carey arranged a meeting with officials of the World Health Organization in Lagos and the Nigerian Ministry of Health, then took off on a Nigerian Airways plane for Lagos, still exhausted from his Jos trip.

At the meeting he reviewed the tragic situation on the plateau. The only hope lay in an immediate mass inoculation program. Both the government officials and the WHO staff agreed that expert assistance should be called in from the United Nations agency without delay.

But it was wartime, which meant endless red tape to get even a visa application considered.

Carey flew back to Ibadan, with the 15,000 doses of yellow fever vaccine that had been available in Lagos. Bob Shope, on his way from Yale to Ibadan, had picked up 20,000 doses at Dakar, supplied by the United Nations WHO agency. This made a total of 35,000 doses—still a drop in the bucket in the face of the present epidemic. The lowest estimate at the moment was 100,000 cases on the plateau, and the number was climbing.

Dakar had another million doses available, at 5 cents a dose. The U.S. Agency for International Development also had a supply available—but at the staggering price of 20 cents a dose. Perhaps USAID could be persuaded to supply it as a donation.

There were priorities to set: Who would get the vaccine first? Probably health personnel, because they would have to work directly with the diseased. Then people who performed essential services, cases of direct contact, schoolchildren, and members of the armed forces. The demand would be over-whelming, the supply short, the logistics bewildering in the vastness of the land and the remoteness of the villages.

Then there was the problem of mosquito control. What insecticides were available, and how fast could they be put into use?

Taking only a few brief moments to see his family, Don Carey boarded another Nigerian Airways plane the next morning and headed for Jos. He carried with him the 25,000 doses of yellow fever vaccine and 2,000 syringes with needles.

At Jos, he went immediately to the head of the Ministry of Health of the Benue Plateau State. The ministry had sent out about a dozen people to the villages in the last forty-eight hours. The 25,000 doses Carey brought with him were pitifully few in light of the estimates they arrived at: at least a *million* doses were needed.

The other problem was to get more of the high-speed jet injectors that were being used for the smallpox campaign. They could be switched over for the yellow fever emergency, but the Benue Plateau State, of which Jos is the capital, had only eight injectors, four of them without nozzles.

Vaccinations were to begin the next morning. But the rural health teams had no experience with the injectors and would have to have a training course before they started out for the bush. This was a regrettable but necessary delay. There was no sense in puncturing arms unless the dose could be effective.

At nightfall Graham Kemp pulled into the Hill Station Rest House at Jos in his station wagon. With him were Bob Shope from the Yale laboratory and Vern Lee. Lee had had trouble trying to find adult mosquitoes of the *Aedes* species, always suspect as prime yellow fever vectors. He was now particularly interested in finding the breeding places of the *Aedes aegypti* mosquito, which was nearly always a villain in passing the disease.

He had found a few of the species *Aedes Simpsoni* in the

axils of coconut yam plants growing near villages and huts. Perhaps these would be a clue; it was too early to tell.

Kemp and Shope joined Carey and went over to the Sudan Interior Mission hospital. Dr. Jeanette was not there at the moment. But when they arrived a fulminating case was rushed into the emergency room, along with another less violently ill case.

On Thursday morning, November 6, Kemp, Shope, and Carey set off for the bush to the town of Du, accompanied by an interpreter. They had picked up syringes and needles from the Ministry of Health office. They were after blood samples, as many as they could get. It was the only way they could gain a clear idea of the actual number of people stricken by the raging epidemic.

Getting blood samples from a remote bush village involves a special technique. The first step is to persuade the local chief. Without his help the situation is hopeless. When the chief is found, the palaver begins. And it can go on interminably. Many villages have what is called palaver houses, for just such a purpose. There are amenities to observe, regardless of the crisis at hand. The ceremonies can go on, with palm wine and kolanuts, while valuable time is lost.

Chief Davov of Du was no exception. He wasn't enthusiastic about letting three Americans puncture scores of his people with needles, especially when they weren't bringing vaccine at the moment. They were only testing. Finally, he gave reluctant, provisional approval.

There was a small clinic in the village, and Graham Kemp, who was a genius in "going out to get some bloods," began persuading the hapless patients there to let him stick needles in them. In spite of his proven charm, he had difficulty in persuading more than a handful.

Carey and Shope were no more successful. In one hour they had only six specimens of blood, and it seemed as if the job would drag out to hopeless lengths.

They finally came up with an idea that helped. They would give the blood donors yellow slips of paper that would entitle them to high priority when the vaccinating team arrived. The pace increased, but slowly. They wanted at least 150 specimens. They were nowhere near approaching that at the end of the second hour. The chief hung about, asking them if each patient were the last one to be bled. The tribesmen, sensing the reluctance of the chief, became increasingly nervous and tense, but always with the warm, deep shyness and courtesy found in most Nigerians.

Carey, Shope, and Kemp were already tired, and they were even more frustrated by the lack of progress. Finally, a schoolmaster arrived, bringing a group of schoolchildren to the clinic. By this time, the vaccinating team with its limited supply of jet guns had also arrived. They began inoculating those who had already given blood. The donors were waving their yellow slips for attention now, and the pace picked up for both bleeders and inoculators.

The method used was simple and fast. The blood was drawn up into the syringe, placed in a wooden box, and left there to clot. Later, it would be put in the refrigerator for return to Ibadan for testing.

By midday, in the broiling heat, they had more than 180 samples. By now the chief was putting his foot down in earnest, and the bleeding ended abruptly—over quota but lacking in adult male samples. Most of the men were at work in the fields. The deficiency would have to be made up later. The sweating virus hunters climbed wearily into their vehicles and headed back to Jos.

At the Sudan Interior Mission hospital, Dr. Jeanette reported three more yellow fever deaths. Liver samples were taken and prepared on ice for the trip back to Ibadan. With Dr. Jeanette, Carey worked out a plan for a clinical study of the cases pouring into the hospital. The nursing staff, as well as the doctors, was already so overtaxed that any additional work, however slight, would be a burden. But it had to be done.

Without stopping to rest, Carey, Kemp, and Shope went to the Roman Catholic hospital and set up similar procedures in the crowded wards. Back at the hotel they met Vern Lee, just returning from another mosquito hunt. He was elated because he had caught over 200 adult *Aedes africanus* mosquitoes, prime suspects as disease vectors.

During dinner at the hotel, they met two doctors from USAID. The federal team had arrived in a Dodge power wagon and was already making plans for a mass vaccination on the plateau. The doctors brought the heartening news that the U.S. government had agreed to supply a million yellow fever vaccine doses—a godsend. But a million doses do not inject themselves. Just how long the yellow fever teams could keep going without falling over was the question.

Back at Yale, the pursuit of the Lassa virus continued. There was little the Yale researchers could do directly for their fellow virologists on the distant yellow fever scene. It was strange and tragic that another disease had settled in the very place where Lassa fever had struck. It seemed almost as if fate were venting its wrath on that surpassingly beautiful plateau.

But Thanksgiving was coming to Connecticut, and a welcome respite from the grim search at the Yale arbovirus laboratory was in sight.

Jordi Casals set aside his work on mouse brains and finished up several jobs on the Wednesday before Thanksgiving, glad to have a letup in the routine. He was practically recovered, but he tired more easily than before. He closed up shop and went down the hall toward the elevators. On the way down, he said hello to Juan Roman, a young lab technician who, with his wife, was working on research on other projects. Roman was planning to take his wife down to York, Pennsylvania, for a family visit. They wished each other a happy holiday and went their separate ways.

Juan Roman picked up his wife at Sonja Buckley's laboratory, where she was being trained as an assistant in tissue cultures. Juan had had trouble sleeping the night before, and his wife asked him how he felt now. He told her that he thought he had a touch of the flu but that he wasn't going to let it spoil the Thanksgiving fun. The couple took off for Pennsylvania cheerfully enough, and for the most part the virus laboratory was closed for the long weekend.

On Monday the lab reopened for business as usual. Sonja Buckley was a little curious when neither Juan Roman nor his wife showed up by lunchtime, but she figured there may have been a traffic delay somewhere.

She was just getting ready to go to lunch when the phone rang.

It was a doctor from York, Pennsylvania, a relative of the Romans.

Juan, it seemed, was sicker than he first thought. He had been feeling miserable driving down to York and had come to see him on arriving there. The doctor had forbidden him to make the trip back to New Haven. It was probably some kind of mild virus infection, and he wanted to keep Juan confined in bed a day or two longer.

Sonja Buckley told him that she'd pass the word along to Wil Downs, and that she was terribly sorry to hear Juan was ill. Of course it would be all right at the laboratory, and she said to tell Juan to forget everything and concentrate on getting well.

She hung up, and for a fleeting moment the thought crossed her mind: *Could this possibly be Lassa fever?* But she immediately dismissed it, chiding herself for being paranoid.

Juan's job had nothing to do with the Lassa virus; he worked in an entirely separate lab, down the hall from Jordi Casals. On top of that, the doctor on the phone was not alarmed about Juan's condition.

You simply cannot go through life in this business worrying all the time, she told herself. *It could drive you up the wall and out of your mind.*

She put on her coat and went out to lunch.

Chapter Nine

Juan Roman did not improve. Yet he did not appear to be critically ill. The symptoms were not marked but faintly suggested typhus or typhoid or even rabies. As a precaution, he was admitted to the hospital in York, and a blood specimen was sent to a virus laboratory in Philadelphia for further checking. Through a mixup, it was thought the test was for rabies only. If it were rabies, a disease that develops slowly, speed was not the most critical point; careful analysis was. The laboratory put the specimen in the freezer to be tested later in the regular procedures.

By the end of the week Juan Roman and his wife had still not shown up at Yale for work. But Sonja Buckley was sure she would have heard if anything critical had developed.

A call finally came from York, but not until the following week. The news was not good. Juan Roman's condition was very puzzling, and Jordi Casals was immediately notified.

Casals checked into the specific type of research Juan Roman had been involved in and found he had been working on Eastern equine encephalitis. None of his work had been connected in any way with Lassa fever, and at least that was reassuring. Still, Casals decided that a blood test should be made to be absolutely certain he had not somehow been contaminated with it. Casals notified the York doctors that he would come down on Saturday, review the case, and bring back a blood specimen to Yale.

In the short time between the phone call and Casals' arrival at the hospital, Juan Roman's condition worsened precipitously. He was in critical condition.

His symptoms looked very much like typhus. There could be no Lassa diagnosis for another four or five days at best, and even if it were positive the doctors would need time to go through the elaborate checks and double-checks before trying to give him Lassa fever antibodies.

Casals took the blood sample from Roman and hurried back to Yale. He and Sonja Buckley put the serum into tissue cultures and mice.

But nothing that came out of the tests would be of any use. Within two days Juan Roman was dead.

A few days later the results of the tests were determined. Juan Roman's system was riddled with Lassa virus, and Lassa virus alone.

The news stunned everybody involved, from Roman's grieving family to the medical staffs on the remote Jos plateau. Of the five Americans who had come down with the disease, three had died. Only a miracle had seemed to save the other two. The exact channel of infection was impossible to trace in this case. Juan Roman had never touched anything that had anything to do with the Lassa virus. He had never entered Jordi Casals' special isolation room.

The atmosphere in the Yale Arbovirus Research Unit was one of total shock and fear. A sword hung over everyone who worked there, everyone who entered.

The action was swift and unequivocal. All research at Yale involving the live Lassa virus was to stop immediately. All live Lassa specimens were to be shipped to the CDC hot lab in Atlanta. All remaining materials and equipment used in the live Lassa virus research were to be immediately incinerated or thoroughly sterilized. Any worker in any part of the laboratory was to report the first sign of any illness, regardless of how minor or how trivial it seemed. Bulletins were sent from Yale to medical and public health officials throughout the world. No new specimens suspected of harboring Lassa virus would be accepted at Yale.

The Philadelphia virus lab that had received Juan Roman's serum for testing went into near panic when it heard the news of Lassa. Lab technicians scurried to the freezer, seized the unopened serum, and incinerated it.

The CDC hot lab in Atlanta would redouble its efforts now, since it would be the only laboratory in the world to follow the research. This would put a heavy load on Bob Kissling, chief of the virology section; James Mason, his deputy; Brian Henderson, who headed the arbovirus unit; and the rest of the staff. It was hard to find anyone who envied their job.

Yale researchers would be able to continue some tests, using only killed virus and immune serum. This would be limiting, but they still could play an important part in future research.

It took several weeks for the Lassa story to break in the nation's press. When it did, it was a bombshell. For the restrained and cautious *New York Times,* there was a four-column headline on page one: "New Fever Virus So Deadly That Research Halts." Written by veteran newsman Lawrence K. Altman, the article reviewed briefly the bloody history of the saga. There was a four-column spread of pictures on the front page, including shots of Downs, Casals, Buckley, and the electron microscope photo of the thorny, vicious Lassa virus itself.

"American doctors have discovered a virus so virulent that they have stopped their research into its mysteries," the story began. Then it went on to tell about Juan Roman, the laboratory worker who died with no known contact with the virus.

The *Times* story ended by saying: "The researchers say they believe there is no threat now to anyone associated with these cases . . ."

But no reporter or researcher could anticipate what was smoldering on the Jos plateau in Nigeria, which was still reeling under the mountainous yellow fever epidemic.

So many yellow fever patients were coming into the Sudan Interior Mission hospital at Jos that Don Carey left the visceratome in anticipation of the inevitable new deaths that would
follow. The visceratome is an instrument for slicing the liver
and other vital organs after an autopsy, to prepare tissue slides
for microscopic examination.

Graham Kemp, Vern Lee, and George Stroh had been
working without respite, along with the other teams sent to the
plateau to administer vaccine, take blood samples, or track
down and destroy mosquitoes.

In mid-December, just when it seemed that the medical
teams in the bush and in the hospitals could endure no longer,
the cases began falling off as rapidly as they had appeared.

Don Carey, back in Ibadan now, began pulling together the
mass of information from his staff: from Troup and White at
the Sudan Interior Mission hospital, from the Vom hospital,
from the Ministry of Health, from the World Health Organization, and all the others.

Summarizing the material for the *Bulletin of the World
Health Organization,* he wrote:

> The Virus Research Laboratory of the University of Iba-
> dan, Nigeria, was notified on 23 October 1969 that cases of
> suspected yellow fever had occurred in the Jos area. The
> diagnosis was confirmed by virus isolation, and the existence
> of a widespread outbreak on the Jos plateau and adjacent
> areas was established. This was the first recognized epidemic
> of yellow fever in Nigeria since 1953 . . . The case fatality
> ratio for hospitalized patients was approximately 40 percent
> . . . It is estimated that up to 100,000 cases of yellow fever
> may have occurred during the epidemic . . .
>
> The epidemic reached a peak at a time when the rainfall
> was rapidly declining and temperatures falling. Indeed the
> drying up of potential habitats for mosquito larvae in No-
> vember greatly hampered the search for a vector . . .
>
> It is believed that these climatic factors were principally
> responsible for the rapid termination of the epidemic by De-
> cember 1969 . . .
>
> The establishment of a massive program of immuniza-
> tion, in which approximately 20 percent of the plateau popu-

lation were given 17-D vaccine, may have served as a barrier to the reintroduction of yellow fever . . .

The death rate had dropped in the final tally, but it was still appalling, with forty patients out of every hundred dying. The Ibadan team never did definitely identify the mosquito, but certain evidence pointed toward the *Aedes luteocephalus*.

At the Sudan Interior Mission hospital the nurses, ward cleaners, and doctors were relieved from the daily struggle to help the victims of the disease. Dr. Jeanette and Hal White went on with business as usual, exhausting enough in itself. The mission nurses, both expatriate and Nigerian, scurried about the wards with amazing resilience.

Life went back to normal. The cooking fires of the families in the hospital compound reeked with the brawny odor of Nigerian food. It would be brought in to the patients by worried mothers or wives, who sometimes slipped a potion or concoction from the ju-ju man in the food to buttress the efforts of modern pharmacology. There would be balls or paste from bullrush millet, locust bean cakes, or spicy porridge made from millet or Guinea corn. Special efforts would be taken to feed the sick with stew made from scarce chicken, salt, locust beans, baobab leaves, okra, and groundnut oil.

Christmas would soon be arriving, and paper cutouts of holly wreaths would appear on the hospital walls. In both the hospital and missionary homes, thorn trees would be brought inside and lavishly decorated with cutouts and bonbons. At the Hill Station Rest House the pink gins, swizzles, and stout would be accompanied by black tie and glittering evening dresses.

A new calm had arrived in Jos town and at the Sudan Interior Mission hospital. For this, the exhausted staff was grateful.

A month earlier, in mid-November, at the plateau village of Bassa, twenty miles from Jos, Tamalama Hansetu Sale had given birth to a son. With the appropriate Hausa ceremony, the midwife of the village had severed the umbilical cord, compressed the wound with warm water, washed the child seven times with warm water and soap, and put antimony in his eyes. The placenta was buried behind the hut and covered with a rock, the cord to follow later when it atrophied.

The grandmother had dipped the runhu tree leaves in the boiling water, applying them painfully to the new mother's body. Slightly cooled warm water was poured directly into the vagina. Warm palm oil followed, over the entire body. Tobacco flowers were rubbed on Tamalama's teeth. Her breasts were massaged to make milk come. Seven days later the child's feet were rubbed with mother's milk, so that when the blistering dry season came the trails would not burn his feet. Then the gifts arrived—calabashes full of kolanuts, groundnuts, sweetmeats, goat meat, hot peppers, palm wine, Guinea corn beer. All night, the drumming ceremony would go on, as constant and unrelenting for births as it was for deaths.

The boy was proudly named Mohammed Kabiro, and the tribal marks were carved into his face.

Tamalama was proud and happy when she could get up and strap the baby to her back and show him off in the village. Like all Nigerian mothers, she liked to feel his warmth and softness on her back, even when his hot urine soaked the back of her dress.

On Christmas day the Christians in the village prepared a parade with drums and chanting. Tamalama looked forward to seeing it, but when she tried to get up she felt ill and was burning with fever. Her three-year-old daughter, Hauwau, would go to the parade with the family; Tamalama would have to remain in bed.

It wasn't long before her family realized that she was very sick. With the help of her brother and family, she boarded a crowded bus for Jos, taking Hauwau and the new baby with her, the baby strapped to her aching back.

She entered the Sudan Interior Mission's Evangel Hospital on the last day of December.

There is a long-standing superstition among many of the

plateau tribes, Muslims and pagans alike, that the correct name and address of a patient should not be given on entering a hospital. For when the patient is cured and returns home, the evil spirits of the disease cannot then follow him and plague him again. Tamalama believed in this custom. Thus her brother gave the hospital a fictitious name and village in registering her.

Tamalama was critically ill, with a high fever and severe pulmonary involvement that left her coughing and gasping for breath. She was placed in a corner bed of A Ward. Near her was a window where the prevailing breeze would come into the room to bring some comfort in the stifling heat.

Dr. Jeanette could find nothing specific to pin her patient's condition to. At least, she was sure, this was not a new yellow fever case. She was thankful for that. Another outbreak like the one that had just ended would be an inconceivable burden for the exhausted staff. Dr. Jeanette ordered aspirin to bring the fever down and antibiotics to fight the unknown infection, as well as the usual precaution for malaria, Aralen.

Tamalama remained in the hospital for ten days. There were times when it looked as if she would not pull through, but she eventually got her strength back and was dismissed. Her specific disease remained undiagnosed.

She returned to Bassa with her two small children, weak and emaciated. She had been so sick she could remember practically nothing about her stay in the hospital.

Within three days of her arrival at the family compound, her mother and both her children came down with searing fevers.

Her mother and baby boy gradually recovered. Hauwau, her three-year-old daughter, died within a few days.

All the cases remained undiagnosed and unreported to the Sudan Interior Mission hospital.

The new year of 1970 brought new hope to the mission in Jos. The long, cruel war in the south looked as if it might be ending any day. New cases, anxiously watched as they entered the hospital, showed no more signs of yellow fever.

The break gave Dr. David Christensen a chance for a brief vacation, and his workload fell on the two remaining doctors, Jeanette Troup and Hal White. But they could cope, as they had before. Both were known for their sinew and ebullience—and for their calmness in the face of emergencies.

But what was to happen began so slowly that awareness was not immediate, even in the face of the many ominous signs. A crisis, in the last analysis, is not a sudden thing. It grows out of minutiae, out of an accumulation of cellular events that mass and collect and then seem to sweep over everything in an overwhelming wave. When the wave hits, it comes more as a surprise than a shock, more as a puzzlement in retrospect.

Shortly after the then anonymous Tamalama Sale was dismissed from the hospital, there appeared to be two new cases with the vague but serious symptoms that Tamalama had recovered from. One, a thirty-three-year-old Nigerian woman, newly admitted, had been taking care of a child in A Ward during the time that Tamalama lay in her corner bed. The other, a thirty-one-year-old Nigerian woman, had been a patient in A Ward during most of the time that Tamalama was there. The only difference between their symptoms and those of Tamalama was that they did not have the hacking cough and the pneumonia-like syndrome that Tamalama had developed.

Both of the patients were administered the same symptomatic treatment that had been reasonably successful with Tamalama. Both were very sick.

Within four days the thirty-three-year-old Nigerian woman was dead. Her face and neck were swollen. She had had a severe sore throat, and there were patches on the palate and tonsillar pillars surrounded by erythematous borders. The fever had been high. The white blood cell count had dropped and then soared at the end. There had been petechiae, shock, coma, and death.

Meanwhile, three more patients had been admitted with similar symptoms. One of them was an eighteen-year-old Nigerian named Adikitoi, a ward cleaner in the hospital who hoped someday to be a male nurse. He was a favorite among the nurses, conscientious and always cheerful.

Dr. Jeanette and Hal White each knew what was on the other's mind, but they hesitated to talk about it. They simply could not believe that Lassa fever had returned. They could easily have jumped to that conclusion when the yellow fever epidemic first broke out. So many symptoms were similar. But they had to admit that these new cases could not be diagnosed as yellow fever or any of the conventional diseases, and the symptoms were strikingly like those that had come to Jos with the three mission nurses almost exactly a year ago.

The two doctors left nothing to chance. They immediately put serum specimens in the refrigerator to send to Ibadan for study as soon as they could complete a report on the cases and analyze their own laboratory findings. Meanwhile, more cases were hospitalized, among them Adung, another ward cleaner, age forty-one; Raphael Adeyemi, the twenty-five-year-old chief dispenser at the hospital; and Maigari, age thirty-five, a male scrub nurse. With four of the staff stricken, the question in the minds of the others was inevitable: Who would be next?

There had now accumulated in sweeping suddenness a total of twelve suspicious cases, all of them seriously ill, with several running temperatures over 104°.

Emphasis was put on the same type of treatment given Tamalama, because she had survived and because there had been only one undiagnosed death. So far, the other patients seemed to be holding up, sick as they were. Dr. Jeanette and Hal White pushed ahead with their own laboratory tests, as they continued to collect serum to forward to Don Carey at the University of Ibadan at the end of the week. Nothing specific was showing up in the hospital's own limited tests, but the conviction that an unknown virus was sweeping through the hospital grew with each day.

On Wednesday night, January 21, the usual prayer meeting took place, and the atmosphere among the mission staff was tense. The speaker of the evening, either by intent or coincidence, opened the meeting by reading from Psalm 91.

"He that dwelleth in the secret place of the Most High shall abide under the shadow of the Almighty," the reading began. "I will say of the Lord, He is my refuge and my fortress: my God; in Him will I trust."

Then the reader continued: "Thou shalt not be afraid for the terror by night; nor for the arrow that flieth by day; nor for the pestilence that walketh in darkness."

Whether the words were heartening or frightening, they could not have been more appropriate for the mood of the meeting. It was taking place in the hall of the former Bingham Memorial Hospital, whose facilities had been transferred to the Evangel Hospital's new wing. It was in this building where Laura Wine and Charlotte Shaw had died, where Penny Pinneo had first been admitted with the disease. Now, almost a year later, the possibility of the dreaded Lassa fever loomed again.

Dr. Jeanette had been asked to say a few words. She spoke briefly, but her words carried much weight.

She said that she had always found comfort in the Psalm 91, that it gave her strength in the face of crisis and spiritual nourishment in the face of the tragedies she confronted daily in her work. She reassured the staff members that everything possible was being done for their co-workers who were sick, as well as for the other patients.

Then she said: "We should all bear in mind that nothing can come to a child of God, except that it passes through God's heart of love first. With the Lord, there can be no such thing as spiritual harm."

To Ivy Hanna, the peppery little dietician of the hospital who took care of all the patients whose families could not cook the proper type of food for special diets, the two brief sentences were unforgettable in the face of her fears. To others, Dr. Jeanette's calm, gracious, and gentle dignity brought renewed courage.

The following Sunday morning before dawn, Joseph, the night nurse on duty, was beginning to worry about Maigari. He was on his hospital bed, having difficulty in breathing, but strong enough to sit up in spite of it. A few hours before, a friend had asked Maigari how he felt, and he had replied: "Not too bad. Just haven't quite been feeling well."

But now he could not sleep. He was in pain and panicky with his desperate gasping for breath. Joseph watched him silently, trying to give him some comfort. Suddenly, just after dawn, Maigari tried to get out of bed. Joseph reached for him, and Maigari collapsed into his arms. Joseph called for help over the hospital intercom. A short time later Maigari was dead.

Head nurse Dolores Rohe, responding to the summons, found that it was too late to do anything. Dolores, who had lived through many crises with the Nigerian scrub nurse, found herself racked with silent sobs.

She left the bedside and went out of the ward, into the hospital compound. The African morning was lush and beautiful, the bougainvillaea and poinsettia spilling over with color. She covered her eyes for a moment in silence. Then behind her she heard someone crying. She turned quickly to look. It was Dr. Jeanette, who had declared Maigari officially dead. She was leaning against the wall, trying to choke back tears.

Neither of them spoke. They walked together in silence to the hospital office, to make out the official reports.

There was Bible study that Sunday night. Everyone was there—the nursing staff, Dr. Jeanette. There was little to say.

Near the end of the meeting a breathless messenger arrived from the hospital. He carried a note from Hal White, who was on duty there. Adung, the ward cleaner, the first of the hospital staff to enter as a patient, was dead.

There was a stunned silence at the meeting. Then Dr. Jeanette burst into tears and openly wept. In moments she regained her composure. An autopsy would be held that evening on Maigari. She would arrange to have a plane take all specimens, blood and tissue, to the University of Ibadan with an accompanying letter.

The meeting ended with a prayer for those they loved who had died so swiftly and so tragically. Dr. Jeanette prayed briefly and repeated her thought earlier in the week: "Nothing happens to us unless it passes through the Lord's hands first."

She left the meeting to set up the autopsy.

Transferring from her international flight at Kano, a Nigerian city an hour's flight from Jos, Dorothy Davis knew nothing about what was brewing at the Sudan Interior Mission hospital. She was anxious to return after a year's sabbatical, was rested and refreshed after her long odyssey with Penny Pinneo. She looked forward to seeing her fellow nurses. The reunions when long-time friends returned were always joyous. It was almost a ritual for all the available staff to turn out at the Jos airport and greet a returning colleague with uninhibited enthusiasm. But at the Jos airport there was not the usual group from the mission to greet her plane. Joan Potter, the executive officer of the hospital, was there. The minute she saw her Dorothy Davis knew something was wrong.

"Dr. Jeanette told me to say how badly she felt about not meeting your plane," Joan Potter said. "But she has to do an autopsy."

During the drive back to the mission, Dorothy gathered the story together from Joan Potter. It was 1969 all over again, but even worse—although no one could be sure it was Lassa yet. The specimens were being flown to Ibadan in the morning. Only then would they know. In the meantime, they could do nothing but work and pray. Dorothy would be needed more than ever now, to help take some of the burden off the overworked staff. In spite of the growing terror and fear, no one had flinched from his job.

Dorothy Davis listened in silence. She thought: *I was lucky last year. Maybe this time it will be me.*

In the operating room there was total silence as Dr. Jeanette made the first incision in the body of Maigari. In the recent past he had been standing by the table, handing instruments, sponges, sutures—anything needed by the surgeons as they worked. Now he was dead, and on the table himself.

Outwardly, Dr. Jeanette was completely calm and professional again. The scalpel moved down through the chest, exposing the rib cage, then down to the abdomen to get at the viscera. The chest was wide open, and Dr. Jeanette carefully began to pull the ribs apart. She pushed the scalpel in to free one of the ribs, and as she did so the scalpel slipped. It sliced cleanly through the rubber glove and into the finger of her other hand. Blood spurted from the wound.

Quickly, she jerked her hand out of the bloody chest cavity, went over to the scrub sink, and removed her slashed rubber glove. She ran water freely over the cut, which was a nasty one. Then she let it bleed profusely for a few moments, scrubbed it with surgical soap, and flooded it with antiseptic. She bound it carefully with gauze, put on a new rubber glove, then went back to the autopsy.

The job was finished in about an hour. The organs were sliced with the viscerotome; the tissue specimens were made ready to be sent to Ibadan in the morning.

Hal White, finished with his rounds in the ward, stopped by the operating room to see if he could help. But the job was finished. Dr. Jeanette was alone in the room.

She said to him: "Hal, I've been out here in the Sudan for sixteen years. I've made an awful lot of stupid mistakes in that time. The Lord has had to cover them up for me. And I just made another one."

She held up her bandaged finger. White tried to reassure her. She asked him not to tell anybody about it. "This is no time to alarm the staff," she said.

As she moved out of the operating room toward her office, she added: "Guess we'd better get on with the job, Hal."

They assembled the specimens in plugged tubes and jars, checked the labeling carefully, and put them into a large thermos jug on wet ice. It was a grim job. In the wake of the two deaths, there was little conversation. Whatever fear and terror they had were unspoken. They left instructions for inoculating the staff with gamma globulin, in as high a dosage according to weight as possible.

Then they methodically pulled out all the records and studied them. There was enough variance in the symptoms, among both the recent patients and the three nurse victims of the previous year, to hold off on a definite conclusion that it was Lassa virus. But there were also enough signs to indicate that it very well might be. Without confirmation from Ibadan, everything was guesswork. They finished their work long after midnight.

The next morning Dr. Jeanette sat down at her typewriter to write to Don Carey at Ibadan. There was a mass of data in front of her. A Sudan Interior Mission plane was leaving late that morning, and she would send both the specimens and the letter with the pilot. She had some difficulty in typing because of her bandaged finger, which was sore.

She sealed the letter, packed the thermos of specimens very carefully, and gave the material to a courier to take to the Jos airport. Then she cleaned up her desk and got ready to go out in the wards. As she was about to leave, Joan Potter came into her office, gravely concerned.

Adikitoi, the second ward cleaner to be felled with the new disease, was slipping badly. It was doubtful that he would live through the day.

Around four that afternoon the package and letter from Dr. Jeanette arrived at Don Carey's office in the virus laboratory at the University of Ibadan. He opened the letter quickly, knowing that Jeanette Troup was not the sort to send inconsequential messages. It read:

Dear Dr. Carey:

We have something going here again!!! We don't know what it is that we have, but we have a suspicion that you may be able to help us find out what it is!—for we strongly suspect a virus. Our first case was admitted on 18 Jan., and we have now a total of 12 cases (possibly 2 others) who have presented almost the same clinical picture. Four of these people have died (the 2 noted as possible cases also died but were unsuspected as being this at the time).

She went on with a long, detailed clinical picture, including the results of their own laboratory tests. Then:

Treatment given has been primarily symptomatic: IV fluids as indicated; antibiotics tried—penicillin, sulfa, tetracycline, chloramphenicol—all apparently had no effect on the course of the disease . . .

Our fatal cases were 2 women and 2 men. Two deaths were quite sudden, but the patients were seriously ill. One other patient was semicomatose or comatose for 12 hours before death. The 2 men were members of our hospital staff (and we have 2 more of our staff in the hospital with the same thing now, one is improving, and one is still serious). It does not seem likely that they contracted the illness from hospital patients; one of them was a "floor boy" in the wards, the other scrubbed with us in surgery . . .

After a detailed description of the post-mortem examination, the letter continued:

No patients have lived long enough to get paired sera [serum from the first stage of the disease and from the convalescent stage, so the growth of antibodies could be traced] to send you, so we are sending along the first specimens, and hope we will be able to send more taken from these patients at weekly intervals.

These cases are a bit reminiscent of another virus-caused epidemic we saw just about a year ago [Lassa virus]. And some of the features of the disease are a bit suggestive of yellow fever, but there is no obvious jaundice in any of them.

We shall keep the sera from this epidemic separate from other sera we send you. I hope it is all right to send you the autopsy specimens for examination as well for this particular case; I thought it might be helpful to fill out the picture.

Thanks for your recent letter. The yellow fever book is at the post office and will be collected in a day or so. Received also the preliminary report regarding the yellow fever research.

A letter from Dr. Frame in N.Y. sounded hopeful that money would be forthcoming for the research [virus] project for Nigeria he has proposed—you perhaps have heard about this.

We shall be anxious for any word from you in regard to our present urgent problem. If you have any advice regarding specimens or tests which should be done or treatment, or perhaps information as to diagnosis, you could phone through the Sudan Interior Mission in Yaba, and they can contact us by radio. Thanks so much for your help.

Sincerely yours,
J. M. Troup, M.D.

The letter, with its matter-of-fact style, was typical. Dr. Jeanette made no mention of her uncontrollable tears, her deep concern about herself and the staff. She made no mention of slicing open her finger and exposing it to body fluids that might contain deadly virus. There were no panicky pleas for help, no reflection of her own fatigue and exhaustion.

The first thing Don Carey did on finishing the letter was to take the specimens to the freezer. He put them in a separate compartment, away from all other material. He issued strict orders that no one was to touch or open the container except himself.

The understatement of the letter did not fool him one minute. He knew Dr. Jeanette well. He was alarmed and frightened. He immediately cabled the news to Yale, asking if it were possible to send an air shipment of two units of Jordi Casals' own serum with its antibodies as quickly as possible. He also asked if Casals could be freed to come to Nigeria immediately. Casals was the only Lassa-immune scientist and doctor anywhere in the world.

He took out the specimens from the freezer. Then he

locked himself in a private laboratory with Graham Kemp and began setting up tissue cultures. They worked halfway through the night. They would not take the risk of inoculating the serum into mice. If it were Lassa, tissue cultures would be dangerous enough.

The anxiety of waiting for the results to come in from the Ibadan tests was equaled only by the tension created by the new cases arriving at the Jos hospital, all with the same ominous symptoms.

The list had now grown to nineteen. Of them, ten had already died, a fatality rate of over 50 percent. Adikitoi, after a brief rally, was sinking again. At 9:30 P.M. on January 29 he died.

Three of the four staff members who had been stricken were now dead. Raphael, the fourth, was struggling against all the symptoms that had felled his colleagues. Every night Dolores Rohe would go to his bedside and pray with him. He would say: "I've been waiting for you so we can both have devotions together." Dolores did not tell him of the deaths of his friends. In his condition, she did not think he could bear it.

At the funeral services Dr. Jeanette sang a hymn, her voice strong in spite of her tension. Most of the others were weeping. Afterward, the traditional drummers began with their mournful tribute, which seemed to blend with the Christian service. Death brought its own strange ecumenism.

Dr. Jeanette drove back to the hospital with Joan Potter and Dolores Rohe. The doctor was more upset than the others had ever seen her. "We don't have anyone to call on for help," Dr. Jeanette was saying. "Except Ibadan and Yale, and they are miles away. It's so overwhelming when we have to be our own experts!"

Joan Potter tried to reassure her, reminding her that even if she were the greatest surgeon in the world she alone could not hold the key to life and death in her hands.

Dr. Jeanette replied: "I'm thankful I can look to the Lord for wisdom. He can override everything."

It was this basic philosophy, the nurses and doctors claimed, that enabled them to go into the wards each day, exposing themselves to countless assaults of disease-laden dust, contaminated materials, blood, sputum, and excreta. One patient, seized with uncontrollable coughing when Hal White examined his throat, jet-propelled bloody sputum directly into White's mouth. Another nurse was soaked with sudden vomit. Hal White later said that, although he was distressed, he never felt fear. There was too much to be done. There were no facilities for real isolation. The staff was too small and overburdened to follow complex isolation procedures if there had been.

In addition, there was a water shortage. There was barely enough trickle to wash hands, let alone bathe. The doctors and nurses rationed the water so they could wash their hands as frequently as possible, without bringing the water pressure to a standstill.

The prayer meetings were among the few things that brought them comfort; they also tried to keep up some semblance of a social life. Dr. Jeanette sang and spoke again at the next prayer meeting. She repeated her conviction that the Lord could override anything, that it was up to the staff to utilize everything that modern science could provide and then leave the rest to the Lord. She told her colleagues: "What if the Lord should decide to take me away by a virus, for example? It is His will that decides this, not mine."

At the time she made this statement, no one other than Hal White was aware that she had cut her finger while doing the autopsy on Maigari. She had explained her bandaged finger to the staff as a slight scratch. But now the others sensed something. Did Dr. Jeanette have strong forebodings that something was going to happen to her? If she did, she didn't show them. She had gone ahead with the second autopsy, marking and sending a second shipment of specimens to the University of Ibadan.

Her letter of January 31 to Don Carey, which accompanied the new specimens, retained a calm demeanor:

Dear Dr. Carey:

Thank you for your note acknowledging receipt of the last lot of specimens. Later in the day that I sent them to you I realized I hadn't sent the autopsy specimens I wrote about in the letter, so I am sending them to you now.

We have had 2 more deaths since I wrote you, one of which was another of our workers, a ward helper, and I was able to do a post-mortem examination on him. So you will receive specimens from both autopsies.

There are also specimens from the other patient who has died—the blood being taken from the heart immediately after death.

We still have 6 surviving patients so hope to get more serums at weekly intervals; one of the survivors is still in a critical condition (and I thought several days ago would already die).

The deaths I have observed seem to be perhaps due to heart failure—marked dyspnea, tachycardia, terminally hypotension. This is how the 2 deaths from Lassa virus impressed me [Laura Wine and Charlotte Shaw, from the previous year].

The yellow fever book has been collected from the post office. Thanks.

Sincerely yours,
J. M. Troup, M.D.

At Ibadan, Don Carey was hampered by the fact that he had not yet received the killed Lassa virus antigen from Yale. Without the antigen, he could not match the new agent against it to confirm the specific diagnosis.

His cell cultures, however, had already come down with plaques, an indication that the first specimens received from Dr. Jeanette definitely had a lethal effect that was the result of a cytopathic agent—a virus.

His frustration was great because more people were dying.

No one knew exactly what they were dying of, and everyone involved was left with nothing but a horrifying suspicion.

Other matters also were demanding Don Carey's attention.
His wife Barbara began to develop aches and fever. Trying not
to alarm her, he drew some blood and brought it to the laboratory. On the heels of the ending of the Nigerian civil war, stu-
dent riots broke out on the University of Ibadan campus. Gates
were locked, buildings seized, classes disrupted, demonstrations
staged. It became touch and go as to whether Carey would be
able to get to the laboratory to check the progress of the specimens. Things returned to normal in a few days, however, and
Barbara recovered quickly from her fever. But the killed Lassa
antigen and Jordi Casals' immune serum had still not arrived.

In New York news of the crisis was fragmentary, most of it
coming through Don Carey, relayed via Yale. John Frame was
continuing doggedly with his research back through the past
decade, because he was convinced that Lassa was not new: only
newly recognized. If his contention was correct, he was sure
that he would eventually discover antibodies in the serum of
missionaries in many other parts of West Africa. He was especially interested in one case from Guinea, on the west coast of
Africa north and west of Nigeria.

Among the blood specimens he had collected, even before
Laura Wine had come down with the disease, was that of a sixty-
two-year-old missionary by the name of Carrie Moore. She
had been sick with a fever in 1965 and had barely survived.
After the tests at Yale were under way, her blood had been
tested and found to have a generous supply of Lassa antibodies,
indicating that she had suffered from Lassa fever while in
Guinea. Writing to a mission nurse in Sierra Leone, he asked
her to keep a weather eye out for unknown fevers and to forward specimens from suspicious cases to him. He included a
sharp warning in his letter, however.

"If you are doing anything with blood at all, please be very
careful," he wrote. "Two people in the laboratory at Yale be-

came infected in their experiments, and one died. Even though most such illnesses will not be Lassa fever, there may be other viruses still unknown among your patients."

Like those at Ibadan, Yale, and the CDC in Atlanta, Frame was intent on trying to find the root source of the disease, which remained one of the most important, if not the most important, mystery to solve. Several paragraphs in a letter he received from Carrie Moore, which described her living conditions in Guinea in 1965, intrigued him greatly in this regard:

> I lived in an old mud-brick building that had evolved through the years into a house. It was always mouse-infested. I killed them with traps and rat poison, but they came in from the field around us. I should have had a cat, but I disliked leaving pets behind when I left the station for annual conferences, etc.
>
> The mice loved all the books and papers in my office, next to the bedroom, and I sometimes found mouse dirt on my desk, papers, etc. I know that I must have touched it a number of times, in cleaning up. They also ran, at night, over the rough kitchen tables, though we kept things scrupulously put away.
>
> About those mice again: One time, I remember a student-houseboy was daily setting up a trap in the attic, and we kept count. When it got to be over thirty, I said: "Jean, let's not count any more!"

What interested Frame was that this anecdote could contribute to the rodent-borne theory of Lassa, even though it still couldn't clinch it. And the case further suggested that Sierra Leone might well be put on the alert list. Four similar cases from Guinea also suggested the virus was not confined.

It wasn't long before Frame got further, though fragmentary, news through Yale. Even though Lassa had not been confirmed, the picture in the Sudan Interior Mission hospital looked dark indeed. The fatality rate of ten patients out of twenty made it seem evident to Frame that the disease would have to be Lassa, or a virus similar to it. There are just not likely to be that many undiagnosed tropical diseases that could travel from person to person and cause such a high fatality rate in such a short time. Other diseases that approach this potency have to travel by means of a mosquito.

In talking with Yale again, Frame was relieved to hear that Jordi Casals was rushing two units of his own serum, plus killed Lassa virus, to Ibadan. Casals was also trying to get a Nigerian visa.

In light of this, John Frame redoubled his efforts, with the help of the CDC, in assembling plasma materials such as a centrifuge and plasmapheresis equipment to forward to Jos. If the mission doctors had any recovered cases, they would then be able to prepare their own plasma, as tricky a business as that was.

At the same time, he was having his own trouble with a sore throat, which did not help his wife Veronica's equilibrium. Fortunately, it developed no further. But everyone who was privy to the news that a new outbreak might be developing, whether in Africa, New Haven, New York, or Atlanta, suffered the same syndrome: a sore throat, a chill, a backache, any symptom of the flu was a red flag that loomed far out of proportion to the symptom itself.

As soon as Penny Pinneo, still in Rochester, got word about the possible new Lassa outbreak, she called John Frame and pleaded with him to certify her so she could return to Jos as an immune medical worker.

Knowing that she had still not gained back her strength, that she still had buzzing in her ears and trouble with her hearing, he was hesitant. But she argued that she was the only nurse available who could not be harmed by the disease if it were Lassa. She could bring her own plasma to Jos. She could also get blood samples and safely help in field research.

Her arguments were not without effect. Frame told her he would give her another examination if she could persuade the mission to let her go back to her former post.

No one in America could hear and see and smell the acrid course the new outbreak was taking at the Sudan Interior Mission hospital in Jos. But there was one encouraging note, even if a slim one. Raphael, the twenty-five-year-old chief dispenser of the hospital, miraculously continued to improve.

This brought an inordinate sense of relief to the staff. Even though, almost to a man, they committed their fate to their Lord, they could not help but have great foreboding, with three out of four of their good friends on the staff dead. Nearly all the nurses came down with sore throats during that time. Each symptom that developed brought an unspoken dread. In spite of all the apprehension, however, staff members claimed that a peace and calm came to them from their faith and enabled them to go on. It was the symbol of their subculture, and it gained the admiration of outsiders, even those who could not share the same conviction.

In Jos town, the terror had now grown to monstrous proportions. Meetings were canceled. Social engagements dwindled. Business trips were postponed. Air traffic into the city was thinned to a trickle. The American and British embassies forbade any of their staff to enter the town. The University of Ibadan banned travel to Jos, making an exception only for virus lab personnel. A pall swept in over the plateau like the harmattan, worse even than during the yellow fever outbreak. That disease had *known* dimensions; there was a vaccine for it that was effective. The new killer—whether Lassa or not—was an unknown with no respect for any known treatment.

Travelers would speed through the town, rolling windows up regardless of the heat. One driver asked directions by shouting through closed windows, drenched with sweat. The water —what there was of it—was boiled for nearly an hour, rather than the usual twenty minutes. Then it was filtered twice, instead of once, through porcelain filters. Great caution was taken in avoiding mice or any rodents. Anyone coming down with the flu was convinced he had Lassa and became a social outcast.

Jos was a beseiged city.

The mission community clung firmly to its faith. "We know that God can heal and help the doctors find a solution" was a communal rallying point. "It is God's will that counts, no matter what the circumstances." The mission workers were either envied for their steadfastness or scoffed at for their naïveté, depending on the point of view of the outsider.

Raphael continued to improve. Hal White, after making his usual rounds, looking in throat after throat, dodging the spray from the coughing, washing his hands after each patient as much as the water supply would allow, dropped by to see him at the end of the day.

White was amazed to find that Raphael's fever had dropped to a comfortable 99°, after a steady run over the days at blistering temperatures. His rally seemed firm and holding. As the first staff worker to survive, would Raphael signal an end to the tragedies that had been ravaging the wards?

As he was ready to leave, White noticed a glass bottle containing a strange liquid on the table beside Raphael's bed. White asked him what it was. Raphael was a little embarrassed to answer, but he did: it was a concoction that a friend had brought him from his tribal ju-ju man, a preparation of herbs and roots and bark that was indefinable. It had tasted terrible, but he had taken it because he felt that nothing else in modern medicine was helping and it wouldn't hurt him to try. Whether it had had anything to do with his apparent recovery, he did not know.

The liquid was a strange purple color, with a dark varnish-red sediment at the bottom. Contrary to common opinion, medical doctors do not scoff at the work of the medicine men. Many modern pharmacological drugs have been adapted from tribal medicines. Modern tranquilizers were used for centuries as native medicine in India. One of the most effective adjuncts to anesthesia, curare, came from the poison darts of Brazilian Indians. Quinine came from tribal herbs. And there were many others.

The problem was that experiment could be very risky. Whether or not the strange mixture had played a part in Raphael's survival, Hal White could not take the responsibility of going outside the bounds of rational therapy. Further exploration of this and other concoctions was being carried on extensively in laboratories all over the world.

Even with Raphael's rally, there was no reason for optimism. By the first week in February a total of twenty-one cases of the fever had been counted; eleven of them were dead. Four new cases were admitted. Two more may or may not have died, because they were taken away by grieving relatives and never heard from again.

But the hospital workers, nurses and doctors alike, would not let themselves succumb to despair. Some continued to play a little tennis. Others brought food, tea, or hot chocolate to one another's diggings on the hospital compound for a social get-together.

Late one afternoon Joan Potter, the executive officer of the hospital, cycled back to the compound from a game of tennis. She met Dr. Jeanette by the compound gate. Cheerful and resilient still, Dr. Jeanette said: "Why don't we pool our supper tonight and try to have a pleasant time? We could check over our stamp collections, and I might even play the accordion for a change!" Both were inveterate philatelists.

At Dr. Jeanette's quarters they cooked chicken and okra, blended it with rice and gravy, and had an enjoyable dinner. They avoided any conversation about the disease, the hospital, and their deep concern about the outbreak.

Dr. Jeanette got out her accordion and was about to play a few of her favorite hymns when she noticed that Joan Potter seemed to be feeling ill. Joan protested that she felt all right, perhaps just a little dizzy. Then she almost seemed to black out. Dr. Jeanette put her to bed in her quarters, insisting on staying with her until she felt better. Joan was too weak to protest.

She stayed at Dr. Jeanette's for two days. Although she began to feel better, she was still weak on Tuesday evening, February 3. Dr. Jeanette came home that evening, examined her, and found that she seemed to be out of the woods. But now Joan Potter was beginning to be concerned about Dr. Jeanette. She was definitely not her usual energetic self. She looked pale and drawn, and was very uncommunicative.

Finally, Dr. Jeanette lay down on the sofa to rest. She said, very softly: "Joan, I think I'd better ask you to leave now. You're much better, and I think it would be good for you to go home and just rest there a couple of more days."

Joan was aware that something was wrong with Dr. Jeanette, but she did not want to make an issue of it. She quietly gathered together her things and left. By the time she got to the door, Dr. Jeanette was asleep on the sofa.

Dr. Jeanette woke up later that evening to go to bed. She was shivering; she had a severe chill. Her muscles ached all over, and her back was particularly painful. The next morning the aching of the muscles—myalgia—had increased. She felt feverish. She got up, dressed, and made the rounds of the wards —but only reading and checking the charts. She avoided going near any patients and avoided most of her colleagues. Then she went back home and rested.

The next morning she talked to head nurse Dolores Rohe by intrahospital telephone. "I've got a slight fever, a touch of the flu, Dolores," she said. "I don't want to spread anything around. I'll be right here for telephone consultation at any time. Would you tell Hal White I won't be making the rounds and thank him for me?"

Dr. Jeanette did not show up for her usual cup of hot chocolate with Joan Potter on Saturday afternoon. Joan went to see her on Sunday morning. Dr. Jeanette was lying on the bed, fully clothed, resting. She had just made the early-morning rounds and again had looked at the charts, but avoided contact with the patients. She was reluctant to talk about how she felt.

Joan prepared a Sunday midday meal, but Dr. Jeanette hardly touched it. She insisted that she would be all right, that she had a slight fever but it was nothing to worry about. Over her protests, Joan called Hal White.

White arrived quickly and took her temperature. It was

over 102°. Her throat was so sore she could hardly swallow. White strongly advised her to go to the hospital. Dr. Jeanette protested that whatever she had, she did not want to spread it around. When Joan Potter offered to take care of her in her quarters, Hal White reluctantly agreed.

But two days later, when he came to see her, her temperature had risen to nearly 104° and she vomited while he was there. He insisted that she let him drive her to the hospital in his car.

On Tuesday evening, February 10, she was put in a private room. Dr. White ordered that no one was to enter her room without full cap, gown, and mask.

It was the closest thing to an isolation unit that could be improvised.

Chapter Ten

In Rochester, New York, Penny Pinneo finally got word from the Sudan Interior Mission that she would be permitted to return to Nigeria. Although no one in the States knew how critical the situation was, it was obvious from the fragmentary information from Jos that the situation was not good. The news of Dr. Jeanette's illness had not yet reached the Sudan Interior Mission's New York office, or Yale or Columbia.

The problem for Penny Pinneo, in addition to her lingering physical weakness, was to get a visa. Every possible avenue was explored. But with the chaotic political situation in Nigeria, nothing could be done to expedite the process. Nonetheless, she carefully packed her few possessions and made arrangements to have three units of her blood drawn and packaged. Then she waited impatiently.

In New Haven, Jordi Casals was facing the same visa problem. He had already been bled, and his serum had been centrifuged and packed on ice. The killed Lassa virus specimens, which were essential in pinning down the Lassa diagnosis, were also ready and packed. He hoped to be able to take the critical materials with him, as Penny Pinneo planned to do, rather than risk sending them by ordinary air shipment. But the waiting seemed endless. If his visa was not cleared shortly, there would be no other choice than to take that risk. With communications so sparse and disjointed, Yale still wasn't aware of the extent of the emergency.

In New York, John Frame was running into similar problems. He sent several cables to Jos but got no reply.

Meanwhile, the press picked up the Lassa story again as a result of a talk Frame gave to the New York Society of Tropical Medicine. Frame said nothing about the current crisis, because he had no clear information about it. The press stories covered only the previous Lassa history and gave no hint of what was going on in Nigeria at the time.

Frame continued working with the CDC in Atlanta to get the plasmapheresis equipment lined up so that Penny Pinneo could take it with her to Jos along with her own serum.

In the CDC hot lab in Atlanta, Brian Henderson was waiting for serum to arrive from Don Carey in Ibadan and was extending his tests on the material supplied by Yale from the previous outbreak. He was also testing John Frame's older specimens to check the geographic extent of the disease.

At the University of Ibadan, Don Carey and his staff were waiting for both the Casals serum and the killed Lassa antigen from Yale. They were cautiously trying to grow their own live virus for complement-fixation tests, but this was a slow and dangerous process in light of the facilities of their laboratory. They were less equipped than Yale to handle such a job, and Yale had already ceased operations because of the danger.

At Jos, the news of Dr. Jeanette's illness spread through the mission and through the town with the speed of light. Hal White, now in charge of her case, added the requirement of rubber gloves in addition to masks and gowns for anyone who worked on the case or entered Dr. Jeanette's room.

On her bed in the new Bingham Ward of the Sudan Interior Mission hospital, Dr. Jeanette realized she probably had Lassa. She asked Hal White personally to handle her case and left all the decisions to him. "This is the Lord's will," she told him. "I know you will do everything possible."

Dr. White, however, preferred to discuss everything he was doing in the way of treatment with her. She did not object.

He gave her tetracycline, aspirin, and intravenous fluids. There was not much else anyone could do. He went through and seemingly futile tests for typhoid O and H, paratyphoid A and B, *Brucella arbortus*—undulant fever—and other diseases that could be analyzed in the hospital laboratory. All the tests were negative.

On February 11, the second day after she had been admitted, she complained of greatly increased malaise. Her skin became very flushed. Then the red patches in the throat and tonsillar pillars appeared, followed by the erythematous halos. Her white blood cell count dropped precipitously. Later, petechiae were to appear. She was markedly depressed.

The hospital workers were stunned with disbelief. Still, they held fast to the belief that God was in control, and they prayed for a miracle. About half the victims had died and half had lived since the disease had struck barely a month before. Couldn't Dr. Jeanette just as easily be one who lived rather than one who died? Only Hal White knew that she had cut her finger with the scalpel. Dr. Jeanette had pleaded with him not to let the word get out; it could only cause panic.

Her thoughts of the earlier prayer meeting lingered in the minds of many: *What if God does decide to take us home by means of a virus? It is His will. There can be no spiritual harm. In His will, there is peace.* It brought a strange combination of both comfort and distress. Did Dr. Jeanette know then that she was going to die? Or would the Lord now perform a miracle and let her live?

Dolores Rohe, donning mask, gown, and rubber gloves, read the Bible to her every day. Dr. Jeanette was muted and distant, however. Dolores felt that the doctor did not want to be a burden to anyone. "I love to be read to," Dr. Jeanette told her. "But isn't there something else you'd rather do? I'm not very good company."

Dolores could feel the tears coming to her eyes as she read.

She was glad to have the coverage of the mask. It concealed at least part of her grief. *In Dr. Jeanette's suffering, she is thinking only of other people,* Dolores thought as she read.

Joan Potter worked, visited, watched, waited for any hopeful signs that might be showing. One evening she left the room, took down her mask, leaned against the hospital wall and burst into tears. Hal White, on his way to Dr. Jeanette's room, asked her if his patient was worse. "No," Joan told him. "It's just me."

That same evening, a former Nigerian patient at the hospital came to Dr. Jeanette's room and begged Hal White to see her. He gave the woman a gown, mask, and gloves, and she entered the room. She brought with her a bottle of an herb solution from her tribal medicine man, and pleaded with Dr. Jeanette to take some. Dr. Jeanette reached out and took her hand, then picked up the bottle and touched it to her lips without drinking. She could barely swallow as it was, but she was touched by the love and tenderness expressed.

The nurses took turns in caring for her, twenty-four hours a day. Comfort, a tall, handsome Nigerian nurse, was at her bedside every chance she could get. She bathed her, tended her, fed her. One time, Dr. Jeanette mustered a smile and said: "Comfort, if I don't get well, it won't be because you didn't take wonderful care of me."

Dr. David Christensen, now back in Jos, joined Hal White in many conferences about what steps to take next. Although there were times when Dr. Jeanette seemed to rally, her course went steadily downhill. They gave serious thought to sending her to Ibadan, and messages were exchanged with Don Carey in this regard. But there was little that could be done until the Lassa antigen arrived with Casals to clinch or disprove the Lassa hypothesis. Sending her to New York was out of the question. When Penny Pinneo had been flown there, no one knew or could guess at the nature and extent of Lassa fever. Since it was now suspected, no one would think of risking other people's lives, as had been done in innocence before.

With the fragmentary communication system, it was not clear at Jos what the situation was with Jordi Casals and Penny Pinneo. The question of administering their immune plasma with its Lassa antibodies was now becoming a crucial point. Jos knew nothing about the visa struggle that both Casals and Pinneo were experiencing.

At Yale, a cable from Don Carey in Ibadan finally got through, stating that Dr. Jeanette was seriously ill and that Lassa fever seemed highly likely but was unconfirmed. Within minutes Jordi Casals was on his way to Kennedy Airport with two units of his own serum and the Lassa antigen that he had hoped to bring to Ibadan in person. He could not go with it, because his visa had still not been cleared.

There was a major problem: in the hurried communications back and forth, the Yale doctors had gotten the impression that Dr. Jeanette was being transferred to Ibadan and would not be in Jos when the serum was likely to arrive. They thought that it would be safer and surer to send it to Ibadan in any case, because of the better air service there.

On Sunday, February 15, the Lassa antigen and Casals' immune plasma arrived at Ibadan by special USAID courier. Carey immediately set up a test with the antigen to confirm or discard the Lassa virus theory. No news was heard from Jos on Dr. Jeanette's condition.

On the same day, though he was unaware of the arrival of the immune plasma, Hal White decided that the only thing to do was to get Dr. Jeanette to Ibadan by Sudan Interior Mission plane. But quite unexpectedly, her temperature dropped from 103° to completely normal. Dr. White felt a surge of relief, and talked it over with Dr. Jeanette.

Under the circumstances, it looked as if the trip to Ibadan would be unnecessary, and she agreed with him. The dramatic temperature drop forestalled an idea that he and Dave Christensen had discussed in detail: the possibility of giving Dr. Jeanette plasma from Raphael, who was now well on the way to recovery. Dr. Fom, the bustling Jos physician, also joined them in conference. They discussed the pros and cons of the critical step at length, just as had been done at Yale with Jordi Casals.

They kept going back to the idea of sending Dr. Jeanette and Raphael to Ibadan together. There was proper equipment there, including a refrigerated centrifuge, which would enable them to extract the red blood cells from the serum cleanly. But the antibodies, if any, in Raphael's blood had not even been confirmed. They would be working completely in the dark, and they realized it. A kidney shutdown under these conditions would be highly likely. The introduction of live Lassa virus was equally possible.

The drop in temperature came at a fortuitous time. It seemed that Hal White had been spared one of the most anguished decisions he had ever faced. As he went to bed Sunday night, he prayed for wisdom and guidance and gave thanks for the sudden change in the course of the fever. The strain was showing heavily, both on him and on Dave Christensen. Their faces were tired, gray, haggard.

In the morning he checked the intravenous feeding, because he had been having trouble with it. Every time he injected a needle of any kind into Dr. Jeanette, blood would ooze and continue to do so. To maintain the intravenous flow, he had been forced to do a cutdown—slicing into her arm and bringing the vein directly to the surface. Blood continued to ooze from this and any other location where an intramuscular injection had been made.

After adjusting the intravenous apparatus as well as he could, he took Dr. Jeanette's temperature. It had dropped as precipitously as it had risen: down to an alarming 94.6°. This was critically below normal and most disturbing. Her urine output was distressingly low. Her white blood cell count had soared, jumping from 3,000 to over 11,000—one of the most baffling of the Lassa fever signs.

There was no question that again the decision about the serum had to be faced. He tried to get in touch with Ibadan but was unsuccessful. He still knew nothing of the Casals serum.

In the hospital library he met with Dave Christensen and

Dr. Fom. Dr. Carl Myers from the local Baptist mission joined them. On the table were medical textbooks that had been studied and restudied over the past days, none of them offering any clue. They agreed that there would be a greater risk in not giving Dr. Jeanette Raphael's serum than in giving it. But it would have to be done immediately. There was no time to send the two to Ibadan.

They discussed the ways they could collect the serum without the proper equipment. Their only choice was to take as much blood as they dared from the still-weak Raphael and let the red blood cells settle simply by gravity. Then they would draw off the straw-colored serum by a large spinal needle. They would have to inject it carefully, because Dr. Jeanette bled every time she was stuck. Her sheets were covered with small puddles of blood.

The decision made, Hal White went to her room in his mask and gown and told her about their plans. She weakly agreed: "You're the doctor, Hal."

As the refrigerated red blood cells settled out of Raphael's serum—without the benefit of centrifuge—Hal White reflected on his decision. He was aware that he might have talked the other doctors into agreeing to giving the serum. Yet if he had decided not to give it, he would have felt the same anguish, the same concern.

He changed over the needle from the intravenous fluid bottle to the bottle containing Raphael's serum. They had been able to get about 150 cc of serum—about a third of a pint—out of the 300 cc of blood they had drawn. He pulled the vein to the surface with his hand, put the new needle in, and tied it in place.

Then, along with the entire mission staff, he waited.

It wasn't until Tuesday, the day after Hal White's decision, that Don Carey was able to get his preliminary results from the Yale material. There was no question: the serum tested showed clearly the presence of Lassa virus antibodies. This was confirmed by a definitive test the next day. There was indeed an outbreak of Lassa fever in Jos. He immediately cabled Yale and New York: "Several convalescent sera fixed complement in the presence of Lassa antigen."

Then he tried to get through by either radio or telephone to Jos.

On Wednesday, as the mission staff continued to pray, Hal White greeted Comfort in Dr. Jeanette's room. The tall Nigerian nurse was in tears. The night had not been good. Dr. Jeanette's progress had gone steadily downhill. Her blood pressure had dropped. She was giving out practically no urine. Her white blood cell count rose even higher, to 37,000.

At 1 P.M. she was given 10,000 units of heparin intravenously, along with intramuscular Vitamin K. She still responded to her name and was able to take sips of water. Her respiration became labored, and external cardiac massage was attempted.

By late afternoon it was obvious that she could not last much longer. She was still conscious. She held out her hand, and took Comfort's in it. "You've done everything for me, Comfort," she said. "God bless you." In the last minutes she held on to the nurse's large, strong hand. Comfort's face mask was wet with tears.

At 4:30 P.M. on Wednesday, February 18, Dr. Jeanette's hand relaxed its hold on Comfort's. She was dead.

Over and over, the thought went through Hal White's mind: *Maybe I killed her. But she might have died anyway. I know we did everything in our power—and we left the rest to God.*

The message from Don Carey confirming Lassa fever finally got through. It added to both the sadness and the terror in Jos. The doctors met again in the hospital library and discussed the advisability of doing an autopsy.

They were very frank about their decision. Lassa fever had

definitely been confirmed, so there was little if anything to be gained by another post-mortem. Two autopsies had already been done in the recent outbreak. No new information would be forthcoming. Another autopsy could pave the way for another death. The dangers far outweighed any benefits. All four doctors—Hal White, Dave Christensen, Dr. Myers, and Dr. Fom—voted unanimously against it. Their decision was received with gratitude by the entire medical staff. There is a time in medical science when rational fear is a healthy thing.

The same applied to Don Carey at the virus laboratory in Ibadan. Except for the Jos emergency, he would have immediately sent all specimens unopened to the hot lab in Atlanta. He had taken great risks in doing the preliminary testing himself. With the disease confirmed, he forwarded one specimen of everything in a special frozen airtight container to Brian Henderson at the CDC in Atlanta. It would be opened again only behind the sealed isolator compartments of the maximum-security lab.

Without further delay, Carey and Kemp burned all the remaining tissue cultures and boiled all equipment that had been used. One single test tube or Roux bottle dropped on the floor could be disaster.

Back at the Sudan Interior Mission hospital, everything possible was also burned or sterilized. The total number of cases that had entered the hospital now came to twenty-three. More than half of them had died. Some of the cases, especially those involving children, were quite mild. Of the serious cases, 75 percent had died. Because of the strangeness and suddenness of the disease, no one knew how many had died in the bush without diagnosis or the benefit of hospitalization.

Dr. Jeanette was buried at Miango, next to the grave of Charlotte Shaw, before a stunned and grief-stricken mission staff. *The Lord has taken her home,* Dolores Rohe thought. *It is His will. Amen.*

From the graveside came the words of part of Psalm 91: "He that dwelleth in the secret place of the Most High shall abide under the shadow of the Almighty. I will say of the Lord, He is my refuge and my fortress: my   God; in Him will I trust."

In a sad anticlimax, the visas for Jordi Casals and Penny Pinneo came through in the latter part of February, just before Penny Pinneo received the news of Dr. Jeanette's death. Her first reaction was one of utter disbelief, then deep remorse. But quickly, the remorse shifted to determination. She could now return to the Jos plateau, armed and equipped to fight the virus, immune from it, and bringing her own plasma and equipment to do the job.

She reached New York City on February 26, to the accompaniment of a five-column headline in *The New York Times*: "Nurse Goes to Nigeria with Plasma to Fight Lassa Fever Virus." Just a few days before, the *Times* had run another headline: "Spread of Deadly Viral Fever Is Suspected in Nigeria."

John Frame gave her a final checkup and a hesitant approval to undertake the trip. If it weren't for the emergency situation in Jos, he told her, he'd recommend extending her medical leave. She was not in the best condition to undertake such a trip. After he checked over both the plasmapheresis equipment and the packaging of her plasma, he handed her a letter he had prepared for her:

> *To Whom It May Concern:*
>
> Miss Penny Pinneo, a nurse of the Sudan Interior Mission, is returning to her place of service in Jos, Nigeria. She is bringing with her three units of human blood plasma as well as some other equipment to help in the control of a viral disorder in Jos.
>
> Please assist her in every way possible to deliver this life-giving plasma to Jos, where it is very much needed.
>
> John D. Frame, M.D.

With her package, baggage, and letter in tow, Penny boarded the BOAC flight to London. Here she would change planes for Kano and then take the mission plane to Jos. Her sorrow at the loss of Dr. Jeanette was deep and distressing. She found a verse that brought her some consolation, and repeated it in her mind as the plane flew over the Atlantic: *Except a corn of wheat fall into the ground and die, it brings forth much fruit.*

Two days later she arrived at Jos. She was met with a warm but subdued welcome from the mission staff, still reeling under the impact of the tragedies. There were tears and embraces. In her arms she clutched a carton, marked "Perishable: Refrigerated Material." There was comfort in realizing that a carefully prepared serum was now available in Jos, though precious little of it. There was deep regret that it had not arrived in time for Dr. Jeanette.

Jordi Casals arrived in Ibadan two days after Penny Pinneo reached Jos. A barrage of cables had preceded the event. But coinciding with the arrival of both immune medical workers was a decline in the cases of Lassa fever, which ironically began disappearing as mysteriously as they first appeared. Only two new cases entered the Sudan Interior Mission hospital after Dr. Jeanette's death, children of eight and six—and their cases were relatively mild. The vicious, spiky virus seemed to have emerged, brought havoc in its wake, and then gone back into hiding.

Hal White, deeply saddened by the death of his colleague, wrote a news bulletin for distribution to mission personnel to try to clarify the bewildering maze of events of the past weeks. Mission families all through West Africa were anxious and confused. He wrote:

> The Lassa virus has been much discussed in recent weeks. It has been reported over the BBC and the Voice of America, and written up in *Time, Newsweek, The New York Times,* the *London Telegraph,* and other publications . . .
> Work at Yale on the virus has been suspended because of its deadly nature. However, the CDC in Atlanta has begun research in their maximum-security laboratory . . .
> Dr. Jeanette Troup cared for many of these patients and

performed autopsies on two who died. During one of these autopsies, she received a cut on her finger. Ten days later she developed symptoms, and after 14 days of illness she went to be with the Lord on 18 February . . .

Despite plasma and other measures, the Lord saw fit to take Dr. Jeanette home. She knew what the possible outcome would be. Yet she was certain that anything that came to her must first come through God's hand. The same is true for us . . .

We do not know the mode of transmission as yet, but the epidemic seems to be subsiding. We will keep you informed of any new developments that might affect you as part of our mission family.

We have appreciated your prayers and encouragement during these past difficult weeks. We ask that you continue to pray for all who work here at the Jos medical center.

There was hardly anyone involved with the crisis who didn't think at one time or another that he was coming down with it. There was also another thought: *I've got to get away from here.* But no one took such a step.

In Ibadan, Don Carey's wife Barbara came down again with suspicious symptoms, vomited, and lost five pounds. But she recovered. Don Carey, having taken great risks in working with the live virus of the second wave at Jos, came down with a sore throat, along with his daughter Blythe.

There was considerable anxiety about a laboratory infection, with the memory of Jordi Casals and Juan Roman fresh in everyone's mind. But Carey recovered in time to meet Casals at the plane. The question was: Should *anyone* attempt to work with this deadly virus except in a maximum-security laboratory? And was it safe even there?

There was a killer extant. A killer whose habit of going into hiding made it all the more dangerous. No one knew where or when it might attack again—either in West Africa or in the United States. The virus was so devious, it even disguised the key cases involved, and researchers couldn't tell exactly where the initial case picked up the virus, or from what animal.

224 John G. Fuller

The problem was that the cases in both waves of Lassa fever seemed to be *hospital-transmitted*. A single case had obviously arrived at the hospital in both instances. Then it mowed down patient after patient, even those who had had no direct contact. But where did that initial case—the index case—get it? The answer to that question would reveal the ultimate source. And if the ultimate source were known, some intelligent battle plan could be worked out to fight the virus.

Where, for instance, did Laura Wine contract the disease? From the bats in her attic? From another patient in the obstetric ward, where she worked most of the time? If so, which patient? Everyone had been too busy trying to save lives to do a proper research job. The problem called for a specialist with special equipment—a long, dangerous, painstaking task that might lead nowhere.

Why did some people get the disease and some who had equally close contact fail to get it? Dr. John Hamer and his wife Esther, for instance. Dorothy Davis. Hal White. Dolores Rohe. Comfort. Joan Potter. All the others who risked their lives daily taking care of the dying. Yellow fever was different. The vaccination was incredibly effective. Lassa fever would remain out of reach of an effective vaccine unless its whole history could be revealed and studied.

The key in March 1970 lay in two things: first, finding the index case that had started the awesome chain of death; second, finding the reservoir in nature that had transmitted the virus to the index case.

There were a number of questions to be answered: Did the hospital cases have anything in common that would reveal where they had picked it up on the outside? Did most of the patients come from a certain neighborhood or village? If so, what was the environment? What animals were lurking in their neighborhoods or homes?

Meticulous study and analysis would have to be carried out. There was neither the time nor the manpower available for it, but Don Carey, Graham Kemp, and Jordi Casals intended to go after it anyway, with an assist from Penny Pinneo.

In addition to his own immune plasma and the killed Lassa antigen, Jordi Casals had brought with him respirators—filter masks. While a virus could go through a respirator like an all-American fullback through a high school line, the mask would at least stop the dust that the virus might hitchhike on. Since the amount of dust that can be inhaled on the Jos plateau in the dry season is prodigious, any method of reducing the aerosol made sense.

The final tests that Carey completed at the University of Ibadan lab, before shipping out the perilous specimens to Atlanta, showed that three serum pairs were "found to give unequivocal rises of antibody titer against Lassa virus." Carey had tested the blood of three patients. Each patient had blood samples taken at the beginning of the disease and later after he recovered from the disease. The samples taken early in the progress showed no Lassa antibodies. The samples taken later, during convalescence, showed Lassa antibodies in each patient.

The matched pairs of specimens proved without doubt that all three patients had recently suffered from Lassa fever, and clinched the diagnosis. If antibodies had shown up in the specimens taken early in the course of the disease, as well as in the later specimens, it would mean that all the patients had had Lassa some other time in the past. It would not clearly identify the disease with the current outbreak. This was a very important fact, and Carey had notified officials at the Ministry of Health in Lagos so they could send out warnings regarding the disease.

All sorts of quarantines were considered, but none of them proved practicable. Efforts were now centered on finding the index case, bleeding tribesmen in the area to see if they had antibodies (which would indicate the extent of the disease in a geographic area), and trapping as many animals as possible to see which might be acting as reservoirs for the virus.

The Ministry of Health officials were not happy about the virus being named after Lassa, the village where it was first recognized. Later, they were to petition the UN World Health Organization to change the name. But by that time the name Lassa was indelibly stamped in the medical and scientific professions. It would join the place names throughout the world that have been unfortunate enough to be identified with virus diseases: St. Louis encephalitis, Rocky Mountain spotted fever, Bolivian hemorrhagic fever, Venezuelan equine encephalitis, London and Hong Kong flu, Marburg virus disease, and others.

On Monday evening, March 2, Carey, Kemp, and Casals carefully packed their equipment and materials and prepared to drive to Jos.

Writing her family in the States two days later, Barbara Carey reported:

> Yesterday morning at 10, Don, Graham Kemp, and Dr. Casals, who had arrived here the day before from the States, took off in our new Ford bus for Jos. They planned to stay in Bida last night and get to Jos today. Don has been very eager to get up there to trace down the cases of Lassa fever and had decided last week that even if Dr. Casals didn't come, he would go on Saturday. Then on Friday they received word that he would arrive on Sunday, so of course he waited for him to get here.
>
> On Sunday evening while at the Causeys, visiting with Dr. Casals (plus the Kemps and Lees, who were also there), they decided that it would be a good idea for Graham Kemp to go along too, to collect animals . . .
>
> Don has assured me that there is no more risk in his going up there than going out on the highway in a car. There haven't been any new cases in a week or so, and in any case if there is any risk to be taken, Dr. Casals can do it as he is immune . . .

The problem that Barbara Carey failed to consider was that with an agent like Lassa, it was hard to tell just where the areas of risk lay, since no one knew where the virus was hiding.

The ride to Bida, the halfway stop to Jos, was the usual hot, dusty, chaotic trek. At the Government Catering Rest House at Bida, there was little water and no room. A generous Britisher in a room with three beds let Kemp and Casals share it, while Carey dragged out his safari cot and set it up on the bungalow veranda. They were able to salvage three buckets of water for a bath.

At Jos, the Hill Station Rest House was full, but they again managed to land one room for the three of them. Their arrival brought a tremendous boost in morale to the beleaguered hospital staff. The mission workers felt that they had not been deserted, that there were others who would risk exposure to the hazards they had been enduring for so many weeks.

Jordi Casals greeted Penny Pinneo as a long-lost friend; it was the first time he had seen her since their brief meeting in New York. He found her delightful and friendly, her face all smiles and contagiously cheerful in the somber setting of the hospital.

"All the people at Jos seem to give so much of themselves and expect nothing back," Casals said later. "They are an extremely dedicated lot. Don't know how they do it. And Penny Pinneo speaks Hausa as if she were a fellow tribesman. This was a big help in the research."

Hal White and Penny Pinneo, along with the Benue Plateau State Ministry of Health, had already begun trying to unravel the structure of the epidemic. The figures at the time showed a total of twenty-three cases. Thirteen had died—over half. January was the heaviest month. Eighteen victims had come in then, and eleven of them had died—over 60 percent. Since it was the biggest single cluster, the consensus of the medical and scientific staff was that through these patients the wellspring of the disease might be traced.

George Stroh and Graham Kemp, both tenacious as bird dogs, sat down with the Sudan Interior Mission staff and began to look for clues to some common experience shared by the first eighteen patients.

At this time no one associated the disease with Tamalama Hansetu Sale. She had entered and left the hospital under a false name, and her case lay buried under dozens of others.

The records showed that the first person to come down with symptoms clearly identifiable as Lassa was the thirty-three-year-old woman who had taken care of a child in A Ward during the last three days of December, and also on January 5 through January 9. She had entered the hospital on January 16 and had died within a few days. From then on, the cases mounted rapidly, with the first seventeen patients reporting the onset of the disease between January 15 and January 22. The three hospital workers who died before Dr. Jeanette— plus Raphael, the only one to survive—had entered the hospital by January 22.

But beyond the hospital scene, what else was there in common among the first patients to come down with the disease? Slowly, a picture began to emerge. Many of the patients lived in an area of Jos along Kazaure Street, a highly significant geographic cluster that gave the researchers a lead.

Kemp and Stroh, neither of them immune, were off to Kazaure Street almost as soon as they could get their equipment packed. They drove down Rest House Road, through the center of town, past the supermarket and then on past the traditional market with its open stalls. Dodging the pedestrians who crowded the sides of the road, they turned on to Kazaure Street.

They studied the dusty environment, the houses, the people. They checked the garbage, the living conditions, the sanitary facilities. These were neither better nor worse than those in many parts of Jos. They were looking for something different in the area. They set traps for mice, rats, and other animals. The sun was too hot to wear the respirators that Jordi Casals had brought; it was almost impossible to breathe with them. They were thinking about only one thing: Where was the virus hiding?

In their traps a few days later they found such rats and exotic animals as *Mus musculus, Mus menutoides, Rattus rattus,* and *Crocidura.* They would have to wait for the CDC in Atlanta to announce the results on these, although Carey decided that they would do some restricted testing on their return to Ibadan.

Meanwhile, they turned their attention elsewhere, because there seemed to be no coherent picture as far as the Kazaure Street theory was concerned. They slowly reached the conclusion that there must be some other common denominator than a simple geographic area of Jos.

They questioned the surviving patients about get-togethers, parties, picnics, marketplaces, religious ceremonies—anything that might have drawn this unlucky group together.

By the end of the first week they had gotten nowhere. But at least there were no more new cases of Lassa coming in. The fact that many of the patients had deliberately given false addresses frustrated much of their effort. For those they could locate, Carey and his team fanned out to the compounds, persuading, cajoling, begging the neighbors and other members of the family to let them draw blood. Jordi Casals concentrated on the wives and children of fatal cases; fifty-five of them were bled in two days.

Within the week Carey and Casals packed up the animals and blood specimens and headed back to Ibadan. They agreed on two obvious and urgent needs: extensive blood surveys in the Jos-Vom area and extensive trapping of mice and rats in both the households and the fields so that the organs and urine could be tested for the presence of the virus.

Graham Kemp remained behind in Jos to continue work with George Stroh and Penny Pinneo. Kemp's Canadian blood was boiling at the many loose ends. Before the index case, whoever that was, there *had* to be something that had started the whole thing off. He tracked down every fact he could find about the twenty-three patients: When were they admitted to the hospital? Who visited them there and when? Who was in contact with whom? What happened before a patient got to the hospital, and what happened after he returned home?

It soon became clear that the one and only thing the patients had in common was the Sudan Interior Mission hospital. But further than that, many of them had been in A Ward. Many visitors had come to the ward to see their ailing friends and relatives. Kemp and Stroh and Penny Pinneo began cataloging the flow of patients and visitors and staff in meticulous detail. In addition, they took into consideration the urinals, the laundry, the food and the people who prepared it, the locations of the patients' beds, the routines of the nursing and cleaning staff. Then they went back through all the hospital records again. They still had not found a single case that could have infected directly or indirectly all the primary patients in the outbreak.

Those who were stricken among the hospital staff were easy to trace. Their infection had to come from contact with the patients they were exposed to in their daily routine.

But there were white lies to deal with. Raphael, the one hospital worker to survive the disease, claimed that he never went near A Ward. Later, Kemp discovered that he was a favorite friend of one of the night nurses, and that he slipped over to the ward in the early hours of the morning to give a hand in the routine.

Finally, they began looking through the records of former patients who might have had symptoms that could be associated with Lassa fever, and Kemp came across Tamalama's case history. There were enough signs to warrant marking the case suspect. Since she had left the hospital at least a week before the first confirmed case of Lassa had been admitted, she wasn't the most promising lead, but was worth considering. He drew an elaborate chart and tried to determine what relationship, if any, she had with the other cases involved.

At first it looked hopeless, except for the hospital staff

workers who might have been in contact with her. He took the fatal cases first and tried to find some relationship between the onset of their illness and Tamalama's stay in the hospital. The first woman who died, he noted, had been taking care of a child in A Ward for several days in December and early January, when Tamalama had been seriously ill in the same ward. She had been exposed to Tamalama for at least five days. Another case, a twenty-six-year-old woman who had died in February, was found to have been a visitor to A Ward early in January. A third case, a thirty-five-year-old woman, had also been taking care of a child in A Ward while Tamalama lay sick in her bed. A fourth case who died was a friend of the first case and had visited A Ward early in January. As Kemp went over the reports, he began to sense a clear pattern: the first seventeen cases had been patients, workers, or visitors at the hospital when Tamalama was under treatment. Only two patients could not be pinned down exactly on this score, one of them being impossible to locate and the other claiming to have visited only the outpatient pavilion while Tamalama was in the hospital.

Most important, Kemp discovered that Tamalama's bed was in a corner of the ward where the prevailing wind swept over her toward the other patients. Further, her sickness was accompanied by a hacking cough that could have produced a constant aerosol to be carried across the ward by the breeze.

But if the theory were true, what about the cases that followed the first seventeen? Kemp began to study the information concerning them. He numbered the cases in the order in which they reported the onset of the disease before coming to the hospital. He discovered that Case 17 was the husband of Case 2. That Case 20 was the nephew of Cases 14 and 21 and also the brother of Cases 23 and 24. That Case 21 was the husband of Case 14. Case 14 was the aunt of Cases 20, 23, and 24.

But most interesting was a finding that resulted from more medical detective work: Case 15 was the brother of Tamalama, who had brought her to the hospital and had taken care of her much of the time. No one had known where he came from. He too, had registered under a fictitious name.

What evolved in theory was that Tamalama had brought Lassa fever into the hospital—from where was still a question mark—and passed it on to many patients, who in turn passed it on to their families and friends as milder secondary infections.

The theory was elegant, but to confirm it, Kemp would have to locate Tamalama and take her blood to see if it contained Lassa antibodies. If it did, Kemp would then trap every animal in her village with hair or feathers and bleed everyone in the village he could get his hands on. He would be on a sure track of the virus hideout.

The problem was: Who and where was Tamalama?

Kemp returned temporarily to Ibadan and ran ads in the Jos newspaper appealing for help in locating her. Finally, a lead came in. Someone thought that Tamalama might be the wife of a truck driver known as King of the Railroad. The woman was supposed to be in Bauchi, some 600 miles from Ibadan, on the other side of Jos. Her name, the informant thought, was something like Soulé, but there was no guarantee of this.

Kemp decided that the 1,200 mile round trip might be worth it. He would meet Don Carey in Jos on the return trip and was so confident that he could crack the mystery that he told Carey to bring a big red ribbon to tie up the package. He took off in his Peugeot station wagon again. It was a punishing three-day trip to Bauchi. When he got there, no one seemed to know of a woman named Soulé who was married to a truck driver, but by an incredible stroke of luck he was referred to a woman named Sale.

He found her in her family compound, grinding millet and startled to be greeted by a stranger. Yes, she had been married to Mallam Sale, of Lagos. She was now divorced. She did not know his address or where he worked. But she had never been in the hospital at Jos, nor did she know whether he had another wife. This was all the information she cared to share.

In addition to being hot, tired, and dust-bitten, Kemp was thwarted and baffled. He had put too much faith in his hunch, he realized that. Nigeria was a big country, the largest in Africa, with a population of nearly 60 million. Lagos, the sprawling capital, had a population of some half a million in the city proper alone. All he had to go on was the name of a man called Sale, otherwise known as King of the Railroad.

This, he figured, was no time to quit. He only regretted the remark about the big red ribbon. The solution looked a long way off. They had made a good start, regardless, and the entire team had survived the Jos survey without coming down with Lassa. They could be thankful for that.

As he drove back toward Jos, he was already making plans to go to Lagos and find the King of the Railroad, just how he didn't know. The Lassa virus had become a sworn enemy, and he was not going to let it get away with any more murders.

Chapter Eleven

There is a saying in Hausa "Bayan wuya sai dadi," which simply means: "After the storm comes calm." It does not of course say how long the calm will last.

In Jos, the month of March continued calmly and quietly. Although the immune serum of Jordi Casals and Penny Pinneo was safely packed in the small freezer, there had been no need to use it. The medical staff at the Sudan Interior Mission hospital was still dazed by the double impact of the yellow fever and Lassa outbreaks. It was almost like a scorched company of fireman poking through the gutted frame of a building after a disastrous fire.

With the epidemiologic team gone, Penny Pinneo went about her chores with incredible zest. Like Graham Kemp and the others, she had declared an all-out war on the enemy virus. She had given blood five times since her recovery, and she was ready and willing to do it again in spite of her frequent shaky spells.

She was also busy taking blood samples from the local population. The more specimens she could get for the CDC hot lab, the greater the chance of tracking down the virus. She visited and revisited relatives and neighbors of those who had been stricken, going out into the bush almost daily to take "bloods."

There was stubborn resistance to overcome. One patient who had recovered refused to give his blood as possible antiserum, even though his wife and child had died from the disease. He would give blood only if a relative came down with it. Others refused for religious reasons. Penny Pinneo worked and cajoled and finally persuaded most of them to help build up the plasma bank in case of another outbreak.

She was distressed at the number of families who were left without support as the result of the disease and tried to do everything she could to help them. One widow was left with eight children to support, and Penny Pinneo gave her work to do and as much food as she could spare from her own kitchen. She wrote to John Frame to keep him up to date, in line with his efforts to get more medical equipment for the hospital:

Dear Dr. Frame:

It has taken me much longer than I have wished to write to you, but doing this Lassa research, keeping up with it day by day, has taken up all my time!

It has been exciting working with the virology team and I have thoroughly enjoyed it . . . The mornings have been taken up with conferences, studying charts, the P.M.'s with visits to the compounds to get stories of contacts, rats and mice from the compounds. Then in the evenings, I'm organizing all that has been discussed during the day—in my own brain, planning for the next day. It's taken a lot of study!

It has seemed useless to send you details as yet, for we have been adding cases, taking out cases, juggling them, since the data changes as we get more information. But soon we'll be getting the cases in order, and I'll send you more information.

Investigations have revealed some amazing stories. Hadija was caring for her four-month-old child on A Ward during two admissions in early January and the child was discharged. Hadija became ill January 11, was admitted January 23, and died January 26 at the hospital. Her husband became ill January 17, was admitted January 24, and discharged January 26. The baby, Fatima, died January 29. A friend of theirs who works in a tin mine had been visiting them on weekends. He became ill and died at the Vom hospital. The symptoms of all these are of Lassa fever. So the poor father has lost his wife, child, and friend from Lassa fever, and had it himself.

Sincerely in Christ,
Penny Pinneo

P.S. Healthwise, I've been doing quite well, considering the number of hours I'm working. But I can't help working this much while the research is going on. After another week I trust I'll be able to slow down. I've become fatigued occasionally, severely so two times since I've returned. There have been dull headaches, light-headedness, increased ringing in my ears with fatigue, occasional chest tightening. I've had to take a sedative each night for insomnia. Occasionally with that I'm wakeful and tired the next morning. Recently, I've become more weepy at times.

Her weepiness was understandable. Dr. Jeanette had been among her closest friends. Maigari she had loved and worked with. The two ward cleaners who died were among her favorite people. And just as she was beginning to regain her equilibrium, a wave of meningitis patients began swarming into the hospital.

Some time after that, she noticed that Dave Christensen was looking very pale and drawn. He had always been a strong, imposing young doctor, active and buoyant. Within a day he was in bed with a high fever, sore throat, and marked malaise. The fever would not go down. Tension again began to build at the hospital. He was put in a makeshift isolation ward. Penny Pinneo took a blood specimen to the airport and personally flew to Ibadan with it.

Don Carey opened the virus laboratory and set up the serum for testing. In an emergency like this, rules had to be broken. They could not wait for the long trip to the CDC hot lab: by that time Christensen could be dead.

While he waited for the results of the tests at Ibadan, Hal White faced another anguished decision. This time, however, he had a reliable antiserum prepared with the best modern equipment at Columbia.

When it looked as if Christensen was about to reach an irreversible crisis, the decision was made. He was given the immune plasma under carefully controlled conditions. The tests that would confirm Lassa fever had not come through, and, as in the case of Dr. Jeanette, the decision rested on an assessment of the symptoms alone.

Slowly, Christensen began to recover. Later, the tests showed that he had not had Lassa fever, but administration of the immune serum proved that it alone was not harmful. This established a very important point: well-prepared serum could be given when Lassa was apparent, without harm to the patient, even if the complement-fixation tests showed later that he did not have the disease. But the supply of antiserum was meager indeed. If a major outbreak occurred, it would be exhausted quickly.

In preparing an official report, the epidemiologic team under Don Carey summed up its opinion for the Ministry of Health and for general publication in the medical world:

> Because of its case fatality rate of approximately 50 percent, a lack of understanding of the mode of transmission, and ignorance of the reservoir, Lassa fever looms as an awesome, newly recognized disease of tropical Africa.
>
> Further studies are in progress to define the extent and prevalence of human infection, to elucidate the reservoir, and to detect new cases of illness should they occur.

In New York, John Frame remained convinced that one of the secrets of forecasting new Lassa fever outbreaks lay in the study of past cases that had escaped the attention of doctors or that had been diagnosed as something else. He still feared that a sudden outbreak might occur west of Nigeria and pressed his program to collect blood specimens from Sierra Leone, Guinea, Liberia, and other West African countries.

With the help of Jordi Casals and the Yale Arbovirus Research Unit, he extended his random sampling to include eighty sub-Sahara African hospitals, which would send blood specimens to the CDC for analysis to determine if Lassa antibodies could be found in any considerable percentage of them. The presence of antibodies would indicate those areas where a sudden outbreak might occur.

There was, of course, a firm clue, with Carrie Moore's 1965 blood specimen from Guinea showing Lassa antibodies. Since her mission in Guinea was 1,500 miles west of Lassa, the disease obviously was far from confined. Further, there were those mice that had overrun Carrie Moore's house, leaving their urine drops dispersed about it. Frame was able to get a series of small grants, and he would extend his program to getting rodent specimens in addition to blood samples.

The latter had now mounted to over 700 specimens, of which only five showed Lassa antibodies. But four of these were from Guinea, indicating that it might be a focal point for the disease. Frame figured that an outbreak might suddenly arise there, or in the neighboring West African countries of Sierra Leone, Liberia, Mali, Upper Volta, and the Ivory Coast.

He also noted that the West African missionaries whose blood showed Lassa antibodies had not been stricken with the disease as severely as those on the Jos plateau. In November 1970 he told a group of virologists in San Francisco that Guinea might be a good place to find a milder form of the virus. But since the sensitive political situation in Guinea might make it difficult for virologists to enter there, he suggested Sierra Leone as a good substitute for the search. It was important, because a less virulent form of the disease could serve as a starting point toward the long, arduous job of developing an effective vaccine.

Bob Kissling and Brian Henderson continued their tests in the Atlanta hot lab with extreme care. Even with the gas-tight chamber system, no one ever really felt safe when working with live Lassa virus. Just before the hot lab had been put into active use, and fortunately before any Lassa specimens were opened, it was decided to test just how effective the gas-tight chambers were with a harmless smoke bomb. If there were any cracks or leaks anywhere in the system, they would become evident with such a test. Inside the lab itself the chambers held perfectly, no smoke leaked out anywhere. But several floors above the hot lab smoke began seeping out of the electrical wall receptacles, to the astonishment of the laboratory workers there. There were some raw nerves until the situation was corrected. People and equipment are fallible, and Lassa left little room for fallibility. None of the materials arriving from Africa were opened outside those chambers; none ever left the hot lab except by incineration.

In their report Henderson and Kissling concluded:

> Lassa virus was isolated from specimens collected from 12 or 13 patients involved in an epidemic of Lassa fever which occurred in Jos during 1970.
>
> Sero-epidemiological studies indicate that Lassa virus infection occurs over a wide area of western Africa extending at least from Guinea to Nigeria.

With a gargantuan area such as this, the location of a new outbreak would be anybody's guess.

The CDC intensified its alert on any sick travelers arriving from Nigeria. Dr. James Mason, deputy director of the Atlanta center, indicated that the strict hospital isolation procedure would be put into use for any such cases.

In reviewing the history of African diseases, Bob Kissling, the chief virologist, felt very strongly that an epidemic that had decimated several large population centers in sub-Sahara Africa fifteen years before the Jos outbreak might very well have been Lassa fever. The mortality rates had run up to 60 percent. As in so many other instances, the disease was thought to have been typhus, but no proper virus isolation tests had been carried out.

Meanwhile, Graham Kemp was intent on locating the index case in the recent Jos outbreak—a woman who might be married to a truck driver in Lagos named Sale, also known as King of the Railroad. He was trying to get more information before plunging into the Lagos labyrinth but was not making much progress. The city directory and phone book were useless. Only a handful of private individuals have phones in Lagos. So he sent out inquiries to contacts in the area and continued his work at the Ibadan laboratory.

The summer slipped by with everything quiet on the savanna and plateau. Results from more tests trickled in from the CDC. Many of the human specimens showed Lassa antibodies, but the rodents and other animals remained negative.

Kemp continued to hunt and trap animals of every size and description, but his frustration was growing. One of the problems was that Nigerians, whose natural charm is appealing, often are reluctant to give information directly. On one occasion, in eastern Nigeria, Kemp was trying to discover how many of the local population made rats a regular part of their diet. The answers he got were universally negative; he assumed they felt it was beneath their stature to admit to such a practice. After passing out the highly prized kolanuts, he began showing pictures of various rodents in a book, in order to see if the villagers could identify them. He reached a picture of a native African rat, and one of the villagers called out impulsively: "Oh, that's delicious!"

If only he could find the index case, he would at least be able to narrow down the animal hunt to a more limited area. His attempts to get further information on the King of the Railroad had thus far been fruitless. Finally, however, he received a clue, insubstantial as it was. He was told that the Hausa term for King of the Railroad also meant King of the Motor Park. Since a motor park might be a logical place for a truck driver, he could start his investigation in that area. It was already fall; he decided to wait no longer.

Kemp persuaded a herdsman he knew in Ibadan to join

him on the trip to Lagos. Ibrahim was a gentle man, a Fulani shepherd from the north who knew both a Fulani dialect and Hausa. Kemp knew him well and could trust him. He had him dress in his finest robes, and Kemp himself dressed more formally than usual. He even tried to clean up his Peugeot. Good dress, a car, and especially a gold tooth will elicit more information from status-conscious Nigerians than a battery of questions. Unfortunately, Kemp lacked the gold tooth.

In Lagos, Kemp stayed at the Ford Foundation Rest House; his herdsman stayed with a friend who, by coincidence, lived only a few houses away. They roamed through the dusty streets of Lagos in search of motor parks. These were little more than large outdoor parking lots for semitrailer trucks, where the drivers congregated between trips to drink beer and palm wine, smoke hash, and gather ju-ju man trinkets for the next trip to the north country.

After a full day of asking truckmen if they knew of a driver named Sale, who was also possibly known as King of the Motor Park, they returned to their diggings in discouragement. No one seemed to know anything about their quarry.

That evening, Ibrahim introduced Kemp to a friend from the neighborhood, a member of the national police who was on leave. He was a knowledgeable man and knew Lagos well. He told them that there were a large number of Hausa trucking concerns in northern Lagos, and that this might be a good area to look. When he offered to help, Kemp hired him on the spot.

Ibrahim had been somewhat timid in his inquiries; the federal policeman was more aggressive and familiar with investigative routine. The whole approach in a search like this among the gentle Hausa people requires a rare combination of softness and firmness.

The subject is never approached directly. A long period of jokes, stories, gossip is necessary before the direct questions are asked, and these are then slid in as if they were second thoughts. The combination of the timid Fulani herdsman and the authoritative Hausa policeman might work very well,

Kemp thought. He wanted above all to avoid that point when the person being questioned suddenly says: "Shikina!" This is the Hausa word meaning "Finished"; "Washed up"; "No more." It can come in a conversation for the most mercurial of reasons, and at that point the inquirer might as well pack up and go home.

Armed with pockets full of kolanuts, the trio took off to cruise the area of the northern motor parks. Kolanuts are a welcome gift in Nigeria. They keep down hunger and provide a bit of a stimulation. The taste is bitter, the texture brittle. Kemp liked to chew them himself.

Lagos is not the most fragrant or clean city in the world. The noise, traffic, dust, dirt, crowds, and smells begin to grate on the nerves very quickly. Kemp kept his cool as they went from motor park to motor park, with no results. Toward the end of the hot afternoon, when Lagos was beginning to taste most acrid, they finally located a driver who knew of a man called King of the Motor Park. Kemp was delighted. They swamped their informer with kolanuts and made their way on his directions to the Fawaz Trucking Company, only a few minutes away. The motor park was a confused conglomeration of big semitrailers in various stages of repair. They went straight to the boss, another must in the interrogation procedure, and spent nearly half an hour in small talk with him. Gingerly, Kemp steered his balanced team of interpreters into asking the boss if he had a truck driver by the name of Sale, known as King of the Motor Park.

He did. But Sale wasn't a truck driver, he was a mechanic. The truck company boss led them to a big Mercedes diesel lorry, where the King of the Motor Park's hind end was sticking out of the motor. It didn't take long to find out he was from Jos, and that his wife was from Bassa, a town near Jos.

When Kemp tried to explain through his interpreters that he wanted to draw blood from his wife, the picture changed. A massive supply of kolanuts failed to help. Just why did Kemp want his wife's blood? What was the matter with her? How did he know it was safe? Did Kemp realize this was a Muslim fasting period, and that his wife was already weakened as a result? What good could come of it? She had already been sick—almost a year ago. She wanted to forget about it. So did he.

It was a tough job to argue through two interpreters, and Kemp was hard put. Mallam Sale was suspicious as well as reluctant. How did Kemp find out about his wife? How did he know Kemp was a scientist?

Kemp tried to explain the importance of his wife's blood. How she was the most critical case, because if they could find out how widespread Lassa fever was in her home village, they could find the cause of the killer disease and begin to deal with it. After more kolanuts and more general chatter, Mallam Sale finally agreed to let Kemp see his wife and get the blood specimen. But he couldn't do it now, because his boss had him on working hours.

Kemp knew better than to let this chance go. He went to the boss, paid him an amount equal to Mallam Sale's lost time, and got permission for Mallam to leave work.

Mallam's little one-room house was within walking distance of the motor park. By this time Mallam had warmed up a little, and Kemp was relieved. He was afraid of dropping the ball at this moment, when he was so near to completing the job.

The house was dark, with baked-clay walls and a corrugated iron roof, part of a long row of houses in a rather shabby section of Lagos. Tamalama Hansetu Sale was in the small house, her dark eyes shy and a little fearful at the incursion of three strange men. Kemp went about persuading her to let him take a little blood, showing her the Vacutainer, how it worked, what it did, and assuring her she would feel very little pain when he used it. She was not willing to let him do it. Kemp then turned toward Mallam, seeking his support.

Surprisingly, Mallam backed him up. He directed Tamalama to let him take the blood. When she balked again, Kemp was relieved to find Mallam insisting that she go ahead with it. Kemp assured her he would not take much blood, although he knew he had to get 10 cc, which was a considerable amount. Taking it would probably lead Tamalama to the feeling that she was being bled to death.

He decided to fall back a few moments, talk longer, and try to get her more relaxed. When the atmosphere softened after about five minutes, he gently took her arm and put the needle in it. She winced and began backing off from him. Kemp kept moving toward her as she moved away, holding the needle in her arm precariously. Mallam kept telling her to keep still. Kemp watched nervously as the blood came out into the tube, very slowly. He was sweating and trying to keep a smile on his face.

Before he had even 5 cc, Tamalama called out: "Shikina! Shikina! Shikina!" Mallam looked worried. Tamalama kept backing away, Kemp following her. The tube reached 8 cc, and Tamalama shrank into a corner, yanking her arm so hard that Kemp was afraid of injuring her. He quickly extracted the needle. He had just about enough of the specimen. He felt lucky to have that.

Aware that he would probably hear the call "Shikina" from both Tamalama and Mallam at any moment, he now pressed for information about her earlier illness. Slowly the vital information came out. They talked for nearly half an hour before they cried "Shikina."

From the information, he would plan his new strategy. It would involve the long, slow job of bleeding her neighbors in Bassa and trapping as many animals with hair or feathers as possible.

When he returned to Ibadan, he wrote up his report:

Armed with one Hausa man, whom I have known as a herdsman at the University of Ibadan for some years, and another Hausa man, an off-duty Nigerian policeman who is resident in Lagos, and a good supply of kolanuts, we attempted to trace the index case of Lassa fever in the Sudan Interior Mission hospital in Jos.

Tamalama did not go anywhere away from Bassa in the three-week period prior to her illness. She did not go to a naming ceremony, a party, or a market.

Tamalama apparently does not know small insect bats which might have been in the thatch of her compound roof. She only knows the larger fruit bats which eat mangoes. It was not mango season during her incubation phase.

There are dogs in the compound but they never enter the house. There are rats in the house—small gray ones. The boys trap them frequently in the house. Tamalama never touches the rats to throw them out. The boys do this. Tamalama never touches the traps either.

A cat is allowed in the house. It frequently catches rats in the house and in the bush and carries them back to the house.

Tamalama does not eat rats cooked or raw, nor does she eat bats cooked or raw. Most Hausa people deny this but many do so, particularly in the poorer areas.

Tamalama did have many visitors come to greet her when she returned to Bassa from Lagos. She says they were from "all over."

Kemp was a true bird dog; the big question was: Would his tenacity pay off?

Kemp realized that too. Over the past months he had worn out himself and his Peugeot tires driving thousands of miles across Nigeria. He still wasn't sure how much nearer he was to the solution than when he started. Tamalama's blood had not yet been tested. If it turned out not to have Lassa antibodies, he would have spent innumerable man-hours tracking down a red herring. If it did, his job would just be beginning.

Kemp waited for the results of the tests. When the news came, it was almost an anticlimax. Tamalama's blood was full of Lassa antibodies. She could be assumed to be the index case. The careful piecing together and charting of the cases in the Sudan Interior Mission hospital had borne fruit. Would the long, grueling job to come at Bassa also bear fruit?

That remained to be seen.

Shortly after receiving the test results, Kemp set out for the punishing trip to Bassa. He was armed with dozens of Vacutainers for more bloodletting, animal traps for his hair-and-feathers campaign, and several pounds of kolanuts. He was confident that he would crack the mystery of the animal reservoir of the Lassa virus this time.

He stopped at Jos to pick up George Stroh, and at dawn the next morning the two of them drove to Bassa.

They were after blood specimens first, and they would not be satisfied until they got every possible man, woman, and child in the village. If Tamalama had gotten her infection there, the blood fields of the villagers should be rich in Lassa antibodies. If they were rich in antibodies, the rodents and other animals might well be rich in live Lassa virus. At least that is what Kemp and Stroh felt should be the case.

They didn't want to leave anything to chance. They allowed two full days just to exchange pleasantries and to get acquainted with the local chief. They buttressed the kolanuts with undressed skin mats, a goat, millet balls made from spiced millet mashed up with tamarind juice, calabashes of rice, onions, and locust bean cakes. They met Tamalama's parents and explained to them what they needed to do. Each night they drove back to Jos, then out again early in the morning.

On the third day they left before dawn, having already made arrangements with the chief and the villagers to draw blood early in the morning. It was very cold on the plateau. All the villagers were wearing their long Hausa robes in an attempt to keep warm.

The first recruits came up to the crude table improvised for the occasion. But they were so cold that it was impossible to raise the veins enough to get the Vacutainer needle into them. Kemp was getting worried. This was no time to strike out, and a second chance would be hard to come by. He made a brave attempt on the first two volunteers and succeeded only in getting them to scream with pain. The rest of the recruits, waiting their turn, began to get restless and uneasy. There were about seventy-five of them, and if he failed on the first few, he sensed that the project would be doomed.

He talked it over with George Stroh, and they came up with the idea of getting them to do calisthenics. This alone was a difficult thing to explain in Hausa.

The volunteers listened patiently and eventually began to catch on to the idea. The long, flowing robes were not particularly advantageous for the exercise drill, and again the veins failed to rise. By now the restlessness was turning into sullen rebellion. Finally, Kemp got the seventy-five people together and told them to follow him as he jogged. They fell in line and began jogging; with their long robes flapping in the breeze, they looked like a bunch of Halloweeners. Before long everybody was laughing, Kemp and Stroh included. After about half a mile of heavy jogging, Kemp called a halt and went back to the tables for a third try.

It worked. The veins stood out easily on the sweating black arms, and before the morning was over they had more than seventy precious blood specimens. They returned to Jos and shipped the specimens to the CDC hot lab in Atlanta.

But the job was just beginning. Stroh and Kemp returned, hired local hunters, set traps, and began collecting animals and birds from the village, filling the Peugeot station wagon each night with the corpses, tagging them, wrapping them, packing them in ice, and sending them off to Atlanta.

The job extended over many weeks. Kemp and Stroh worked and waited patiently for the results of the blood tests to come back from Atlanta.

When the news came through, there was cause for modest elation: there were antibodies in many of Tamalama's fellow townsmen, indicating local infection with subclinical symptoms, symptoms so mild they had gone unnoticed. But unfortunately the source of the virus remained a total mystery. None of the animals trapped and hunted in the area showed any signs of Lassa.

Frustration abounded. The medical journal article written by the entire scientific team, including the Benue Plateau State Ministry of Health officers R. F. Addy and A. L. Fom, reflected a quiet despair:

> The nature, then, of the peculiar circumstances that permitted a single patient to serve as the source of infection for 16 others *is still unresolved.* In one respect, the [index]

illness did differ from most: there was severe pulmonary in-volvement. The original diagnosis had, in fact, been pneu-monia.

[The index case] was, moreover, placed in a corner bed on A Ward across which a prevailing breeze blew to the rest of the ward. Such a combination of factors could favor the airborne spread of virus, but *there is no firm basis for any conclusion.* [Italics added.]

The article, appearing in the *Transactions of the Royal Society of Tropical Medicine and Hygiene,* was tantalizing to the medical world, which had been hoping that a breakthrough would be made in the battle against the virus. No doctor had any illusions about the probability that the virus could attack again without warning, either in or out of Africa.

But the lull that followed the heavy outbreak at Jos contin-ued for many months. In the meantime, Don Carey went all the way back to Lassa, bled many local people, captured more animals, and came up with the now familiar results: many of the human specimens showed Lassa antibodies; none of the an-imal specimens showed any presence of the virus.

Speculation turned again to the mahogany rat. But further trapping would have to await full assessment of the animal specimens that had now piled up on the overloaded hot lab staff in Atlanta. Kemp and others had collected an aggregate of 1,500 to 2,000 specimens. The facilities of the Atlanta lab simply were not large enough to handle this flow, especially under the slow and painstaking conditions of working through the gas-tight portholes in the modular cabinets.

As month after month went by with no sign of a Lassa out-break, the research relaxed somewhat. There were those, how-ever, who distrusted the calm, among them John Frame in New York and Brian Henderson in Atlanta. Frame, with his own particular form of bird dogging, was keeping up with his random sampling from missions all over West Africa. He also issued a bulletin to all West African medical mission stations, briefing them on the disease and alerting them to its dangers.

Brian Henderson was spending a great deal of time in the hot lab assaying Frame's specimens and was able to draw some conclusions. In preparing his notes for a medical journal article, he wrote:

> The mission station at Telekoro, Guinea, appears to be a particularly favorable environment for infection with this virus. It is of interest that the three adults from this station with antibody had an unusual and prolonged illness previously. None of the other members of the station complained of a similar illness.

Chapter Twelve

Not far from the Telekoro mission station in Guinea is the village of Zorzor. It is just over the Guinea border, in the jungle rain forests of Liberia. The two countries hug Sierra Leone, and all three are splashed by the Atlantic Ocean. To the east, Liberia and Guinea share a common border with the Ivory Coast.

Early in March 1972 Esther Bacon, a mission nurse in the Curran Lutheran Hospital at Zorzor, was going about her routine duties in the obstetric ward. She had been working in the interior of Liberia for over thirty years and was considered a legend in her own time. A graduate of the Johns Hopkins School of Nursing, she had also taught tropical medicine to many aspiring young doctors at the Columbia medical school, who came to West Africa to learn more about exotic diseases.

Miss Bacon had arrived in Zorzor in the early 1940s and had had to walk fifteen miles just to get to the mission base. It was said that she never slept, working day and night, delivering babies, tending both infants and mothers with generous care. She would never hesitate to go out into the jungle in the middle of the night on horseback to get a maternity patient and carry her back to the hospital. Like many nurses in the tropics, she would do her own Caesareans. She was eccentric but beloved by all those who worked with her.

In spite of her stamina, she was having some trouble with her varicose veins, which had a tendency to develop into open sores on her legs. An affliction that would slow some people down considerably, it never kept her from going about her duties in the obstetric ward.

On this March night Esther Bacon faced a rather nasty case that needed immediate attention. A pregnant Liberian woman was in the process of aborting twins. After seeing the case through, she went about doing a dilation and curettage. In the process, the blood from the woman's uterus spilled over the varicose vein sores on her legs. She completed the job, then washed herself thoroughly, and thought nothing more about it.

Nurse Bacon kept a close eye on her sick maternity patient, because the abortion was complicated by what seemed to be influenza symptoms. They included fever, vomiting, sore throat, weakness, aching, and difficulty in swallowing. But the patient began to improve, was able to sit up and eat—and very generously shared her food and cup with a patient near her who was without relatives to cook her food. Soon she was dismissed and went back to her village.

It wasn't long before the patient with whom she had shared her food came down with the same symptoms. Another Caesarean patient in a nearby bed followed suit. Esther Bacon, who was taking care of all these cases, also began to show signs of serious illness and was forced to go to bed, much against her will.

Within ten days the first patient was dead. The Caesarean case died shortly thereafter. Esther Bacon's condition was grave, but with remarkable tenacity she continued to hold on.

Unfortunately, Dr. Paul Mertens, the senior medical man at the Zorzor Lutheran Hospital, had not received John Frame's warning bulletin. But he had happened across a medical journal article and a 1970 *Time* magazine article that described Lassa fever in some detail.

He looked the articles up and was struck with the similarities in his own hospital. He immediately got on the radio to contact Dr. Robert Patton, a USAID officer in Monrovia, the capital of Liberia. Patton in turn made phone contact with the CDC in Atlanta.

Within hours an alert was out, and plans were made to rush in assistance from both the United States and Nigeria.

Something serious was happening within a few miles of where Frame and Henderson had pinpointed a potential disaster area several months before.

Almost before Dr. Paul Mertens could assemble and pack the blood specimens of the first cases, six more nurses were stricken with the disease. With Esther Bacon's case, this made a total of seven medical workers alone. Four other patients were riddled with the same symptoms, and there seemed little doubt that they pointed to Lassa.

Esther Bacon's condition was deteriorating rapidly. Mertens made plans to get a missionary plane to ship her to the town of Phebe, Liberia, where better hospital facilities were available. The whole grotesque picture was that of Lassa and Jos all over again.

Mertens sent a note with the pilot to Frank Keller, head of the Phebe hospital, indicating that he was not sure what was going on but that he strongly suspected Lassa. He told him that the CDC was summoning help from Nigeria—help that would include, he was sure, a shipment of immune plasma from either Ibadan or Jos, where the precious fluid was stockpiled.

But it was already too late for Esther Bacon. Shortly after she arrived in Phebe she went into shock. Within hours she was dead.

Before the hospital had time to recover, another Zorzor medical worker, newly arrived in Phebe, also died. The toll had now mounted to four deaths, and as usual no one knew the direction the disease was going to take.

In Ibadan, Tom Monath, a CDC virologist on loan to the university, was in the process of packing his household goods to return with his family to the United States when a cable arrived from the U.S. State Department's international health office. The Liberian government had joined the CDC in asking for help in the crisis, so the request for epidemiologists and equipment had come through official channels. Monath was just finishing up two years of yellow fever work, and he and his wife were looking forward to returning to Atlanta. But fast and sudden changes were an accepted part of his job. He began assembling his equipment, gathering the sterile and disposable Vacutainers he would need in Liberia. He knew he could count on Randy Moser, the CDC smallpox eradication man in the Liberian capital of Monrovia, to supply the necessary iced containers to preserve the specimen shipments to Atlanta. He said good-by to his family and caught the first plane to Monrovia.

In New York, John Frame was quietly having dinner when the phone rang. It was a call from a ham radio operator who informed him that he had Penny Pinneo on his wireless from Africa and would try to patch the call in for a three-way conversation.

It worked. Penny told Frame that she was on her way from Jos to Liberia to help with what looked like an outbreak of Lassa. It had come just about in the spot he had predicted. Frame was almost startled by the uncanny accuracy of the forecast, and he began wondering about the ramifications if this succession of outbreaks continued.

Also in New York, Jordi Casals was resting in his Morningside Heights apartment after a hard week's work at the New Haven laboratory. It was Sunday, and his wife, who worked as a part-time secretary for the Lutheran Church, returned from the morning service to tell him that the church had received a message from one of its missions in Liberia that some strange things were happening in Zorzor. The city was in the midst of some harrowing epidemic. Casals immediately called Frame, who filled him in on what he knew, and together they notified other health agencies, including the UN World Heath Organization, headquartered in Geneva.

The CDC in Atlanta had already gone into action, notifying Ibadan and instructing its personnel in Liberia to meet Tom Monath and Penny Pinneo when they arrived with immune serum.

Monath and Pinneo had taken the same flight from Nigeria, and Randy Moser, the smallpox eradication officer, was there to meet them when they touched down in Monrovia. They flew on to the Zorzor airstrip, some one hundred miles northeast, in the Lutheran mission's Cessna four-seater.

Monath had an uncanny feeling on arriving at Zorzor. The entire ambience of the mission and the hospital was subdued, depressed. Another patient had just died, and it was becoming impossible to get enough staff to work in the improvised isolation ward. For all practical purposes, the hospital was closed for everything except suspected Lassa cases. Monath sat down with Dr. Paul Mertens and other members of the staff and worked out a plan of attack. They would follow generally the same procedure carried out in Jos. The emphasis would be on finding the index case and trapping animals in the area.

In the village of Zorzor the reaction was much the same as it had been in Jos. Travelers driving through the town rolled up their windows, regardless of the steaming rain forest heat. Truckmen refused to unload their supplies, remaining in their cabs while the townspeople unloaded the goods themselves. Peace Corps volunteers were recalled from the area. The cases now totaled eleven, with four dead. Fatality rate: 36 percent.

Then the news arrived from Atlanta: the specimens clearly confirmed Lassa fever infection. Tom Monath and Penny Pinneo got busy on the now familiar routine of collecting animals and getting "bloods." Monath hired twenty village hunters and with their help set traps every night. Each morning he picked up about fifteen or twenty rodents. In addition, he set out fine-meshed nylon nets, which bagged five or ten bats each night. Some were big fruit bats, which lived on bananas, with an eighteen-inch wingspread. They were vicious-looking creatures, with pointed teeth and eyes that glared out at him through the mesh of the net. He had to extract them with meticulous care. In eight nights of trapping he collected a total of 164 rodents and bats.

At an improvised laboratory set up in Esther Bacon's house, Monath went about extracting blood from the hearts of the bats and rats. He then cut the animals open, snipped out sections of the internal organs, and packed them in tinned iced containers for shipment to Atlanta. He used all available precautions: mask, gown, and rubber gloves.

No more cases of Lassa showed up, and the outbreak at Zorzor died down almost as quickly as it had arisen. The virus went back into hiding, leaving no clues as to its hideout. His work in Liberia done, Tom Monath arranged to meet his family at Monrovia and returned to Atlanta.

Certain facts emerged from Monath's survey and from reports by the CDC hot lab on the animal specimens and the blood samples from villagers in the area. The Zorzor outbreak, like that at Jos, seemed to stop at the termination of the secondary cases. There were other parallels. Only the index case appeared to be wildly contagious. At Jos, there were many people, patients and hospital workers alike, who were exposed in one way or another to Tamalama, the index case. The secondary cases seemed to come out of direct, close family contact with those who had been infected from the index case. The same was true at Zorzor.

A theory began to emerge: maybe the virus mutated when it passed through a human host. This, in fact, is the principle behind the production of vaccines. The virulence of the virus is softened by passing it through several animals, until it no longer has the power to infect but has the ability to produce antibodies. With Lassa, of course, it was still just theory.

The suspicion remained strong that a rodent or bat was the source, in view of the virus' capacity to cross-react slightly with the other rodent-borne viruses of the arenavirus group. But the new reports from the CDC on Monath's bats and rats still showed no virus.

For six months the animal tests continued to prove negative. Meanwhile, precious quotas of immune plasma were distributed to Ibadan, Jos, and Zorzor in case of another emergency—although in any real crisis the supply would be woefully inadequate. It was difficult, if not impossible, to get donors among the villagers. Fear of the disease, plus traditional mores and taboos, made those who had had the virus unwilling to have anything more to do with it.

It had been two years since John Frame had begun his search for recovered Lassa virus cases in Sierra Leone, and the area continued to arouse his curiosity. Situated directly next to Liberia on the west coast of Africa, it seemed ripe for an outbreak of Lassa fever. He did not have to wait long for his suspicions to be confirmed.

Just three months after the terror had died down in Zorzor, late in the summer of 1972, Paul Goff, a Peace Corps doctor in Freetown, Sierra Leone, sent an alert to the CDC in Atlanta that some very suspicious febrile illnesses had been developing in the Panguma Catholic Hospital. The cases were unresponsive to antibiotics. The patients had drifted in slowly, over a period of eight or nine months. A number of deaths had been reported. Panguma was only one hundred air miles from Zorzor, across the Sierra Leone–Liberia border.

There was not much specific data about the illnesses, but the staff at the Panguma Catholic Hospital was becoming worried. The death rate was picking up fast. A laboratory technician at the hospital had died. Goff was particularly concerned because of the danger to Peace Corps volunteers in the area.

Tom Monath cabled back from the CDC that there was a possibility it might be Lassa, although it was not typical for the disease to develop so slowly. The other outbreaks had struck fast and furiously. But Lassa fever seemed to be able to lay down its own laws. He asked Goff for some serum to test.

The situation did not look good to Monath. The development of another crisis so soon after the Liberian outbreak would put a heavy strain on the hot lab. Intense work in the tropics is exhausting and takes its toll. To return to Africa after such a short time was not an appetizing thought. His family was just getting resettled in Atlanta. He had been lucky in the Liberian incident. He was not sure just how long his luck might hold out.

There was also the problem of CDC funds, which were not too easy to come by. If it were a real emergency, something would definitely have to be done. A lot would depend on how the serum checked out. The CDC could not embark on another major expedition without confirmation.

Another piece of news arrived before the specimens. One of the nurses had been evacuated from Sierra Leone earlier—before Lassa had been suspected—to the Hospital for Tropical Diseases in London. She had jammed her finger with an intravenous needle while treating a feverish patient. Monath cabled for a blood specimen from her. Then he met with Bob Kissling, Roy Chamberlain, and heads of other sections of the CDC to set up a contingency plan in the event that the specimens showed up positive for Lassa.

Any such plan would have to be put into effect swiftly if the need arose. There was always the danger of its being too little and too late. It would be necessary to choose a well-balanced team of doctors and scientists who could move in fast and bring relief to the stricken area. Making up the team was another problem. Whoever was chosen would be facing major risks, even with immune plasma available.

Tom Monath was the obvious choice to head the team for the CDC. His experience in Liberia would be invaluable in another rain forest outbreak in Panguma. Monath was not elated. But there was a job to be done, and he agreed to take it on if necessary. If it turned out to be Lassa, he thought, they surely would be able to solve the riddle of the animal reservoir this time. That gave him some consolation, and even incentive.

The rest of the team was picked with equal care. Jordi Casals and Graham Kemp would be borrowed from Yale. They would spell each other, Kemp going first, Casals joining later. They would be backed up by Kent Campbell, a young epidemiologist out of Duke medical school; David Fraser, another epidemiologist, Harvard-trained; and Verne Newhouse, an entomologist from Montana. All had arranged to leave their posts if the Sierra Leone specimens showed Lassa virus.

When the tests were completed, there was no question. The disease was clearly Lassa. The contingency plan went into effect.

One additional precaution was taken. The men literally were going into a battle zone, and there was the very real possibility that one or more might have to be evacuated. CDC officials got in touch with the Air Force to see what help and recommendations it might provide. The Air Force agreed to have emergency flight equipment available at Maguire Air Force Base in New Jersey in the event that one of the team came down with Lassa fever symptoms. A commercial flight, of course, was out of the question now that the dangers of Lassa had been so well documented.

The town of Panguma, population 3,100, lies in Sierra Leone at latitude 8° 10' north and longitude 11° 05' west. The CDC report places it at an altitude of 950 feet, in a zone of cut-over rain forest. The terrain is characterized by rolling hills with patches of primary forest interspersed with clear farmland. Rainfall is between 100 and 125 inches a year. There is diamond mining in the area, in addition to the farming of cocoa and coffee.

The CDC team arrived to find that a total of sixty-four cases had accumulated, with twenty-three deaths. The tension that hung over the town of Panguma and the Catholic hospital was marked. The entire children's ward was converted into an isolation unit.

But in spite of the pall, the Catholic sisters moved about buoyantly and indefatigably in the white concrete building, maintaining their lilting Irish wit. Their faces were covered with masks, their hair bound back by surgical caps, their bodies draped in long hospital robes. There was death everywhere, but they never gave the impression of being depressed or of having any fear for themselves. They were tending the victims who lay prostrate and helpless on the white iron hospital cots. One patient was going into shock at the moment the team arrived.

The first Lassa case that Tom Monath and Kent Campbell encountered was Hawa Foray, the wife of a prominent local villager. She was in the outpatient room and obviously in a moment of desperate crisis when they saw her. They went to work at once. The patient's chest was loaded with fluid, and Monath and Campbell immediately began a thoracentesis to attempt to drain it. They took nearly a quart of fluid from the chest. They did a cutdown on the vein in her arm to introduce further intravenous fluids. As they worked, they could hear the family of the victim through the window of the ward, wailing and screaming for their loved one.

The last-ditch treatment proved to be a lost cause. The patient sank further into shock, and within hours she was dead.

It was urgent, Monath felt, to get fresh tissue specimens from the patient, but the family refused to permit an autopsy. Convinced that the collection of a tissue specimen would do more for the family members and their fellow villagers in the long run than strict observance of their wishes, Monath sent one nurse to move the family from the window and another to bring a large-bore needle and syringe. He jabbed the needle deeply into the liver and extracted a tissue specimen, then scraped away some mucosa from the inner lining of the lip. This brief action was to have more important implications than Monath realized at the time.

As part of the general rodent-trapping program, the home and premises of Hawa Foray were automatically searched. Traps were set out, and during four consecutive days and nights after her death eight specimens were caught. They were of the variety known as *Mastomys natalensis,* a wild rat with a long line of nipples to accommodate a large litter. Brownish-gray and about ten inches long from nose to tail, it is smaller and less aggressive than the ordinary house rat. Other members of this rodent family had been trapped before; more would be trapped later.

Each of the eight rats was carefully labeled with a tag tied securely to the right rear leg. After anesthetizing them, the team would take blood samples, snip pieces of liver, lung, heart, and kidney, and put them in small plastic tubes. These would be placed into a liquid nitrogen tank and brought back to the United States by Graham Kemp when Jordi Casals arrived to replace him. The carcasses would be dropped into a vat of formaldehyde and sent to the Smithsonian Institution for precise identification.

This was standard procedure for all the animals trapped, and at the time the eight specimens held no more promise than hundreds of others.

The researchers worked fourteen to sixteen hours a day, always in cap and gown in the wards, always with the hot, clammy respirators over their mouths when they were in the makeshift laboratory with blood specimens or animals. "The respirators make you feel like you're putting your head inside a basketball," Kemp commented later. "It takes a lot of whiskey to keep you going."

But they were making some progress. Within days the plasma they brought with them began working dramatically on at least three patients. It might well have saved their lives.

Certain evidence began emerging more clearly. The Sierra Leone outbreak was more dangerous than the others in one way: it was not just a hospital-transmitted epidemic. It seemed to be more widespread, with infections passed along out in the villages. But by the same token, a very high antibody rate began showing up in the blood specimens of the villagers, indicating that some people were getting the disease in a milder form and surviving.

Still, the total death rate was running close to 40 percent. Six of the staff at Panguma had been admitted to the hospital. Of these, two had died. The sisters and Sierra Leone nurses were well aware of the risk they were taking. Some refused to volunteer for work in the isolation ward, even though they had antibodies.

Clusters of cases from the same compounds or communities began to show up. The mode of transmission could not be pinned down, although it could be rationally assumed that the accidental pricking of a finger by the first sister stricken was clearly a clinical transmission. The usual surmises of causes of transmission were made but not established: contact with infected urine, saliva, or nasal secretion; the breathing of infected respiratory droplets. Gallons of chlorine solution were used to keep the ward clean. Linens and apparel were disinfected before laundering.

Several probable cases began showing up in other hospitals in the region. Some of these were transferred to the Panguma Catholic Hospital, already groaning under the burden.

The same type of problems that had arisen in Jos and Zorzor plagued the team. The local chiefs were often resistant or indifferent to the bloodletting campaign. Reactions of the villagers differed: some thought the bleeding would do them good; others resisted it. Several members of the team went to one house and found the parents out, but an eight-year-old child was there with a babysitter. They reached for him, and the babysitter leaped over the compound wall and disappeared. One man had a favorite wife, didn't want her blood taken, and hid her.

There were similar problems in getting animals. The village hunters were men of great status, and they were difficult to deal with. But young boys were often persuaded to go out and get rats, especially when a bounty was put on them. A concerted drive brought in over 600 small mammals.

One thing began to draw attention: there were many specimens of the mahogany rat showing up. Here, as in Upper Volta and all across the sub-Sahara belt, the villagers chased the rats out of the bush and ate them. Suspicions began growing about this animal, and a special effort was made to get as many as possible.

The team was soon bolstered by the arrival of Jordi Casals. He was able to move into some areas where the others feared to tread, although there were actually few places they hadn't dared to go. Graham Kemp prepared to fly back to Atlanta with some of the animal specimens. His hopes were high.

At an upcountry airport, Kemp waited for the plane that would take him to Freetown for connection with his transatlantic flight. At the airport was a Lebanese man, very sick. He said he was on his way to Freetown to see a doctor. The more Kemp looked at him the more obvious it became that the traveler had all the classic symptoms of Lassa fever. Kemp talked at length with the man, arguing that instead of going to Freetown he should immediately go to Panguma, where plasma was available. The traveler finally agreed, and later his blood specimen turned out to be packed with Lassa virus.

Kemp continued on his return trip.

The rest of the team stayed on, pulling together the survey, assembling more data. Finally they too prepared to pull out. They presented their preliminary report to the Sierra Leone Ministry of Health. Arrangements were made for the local health authorities to move in and take over the job. Local officials would also continue to ship blood specimens and animals to the CDC in Atlanta. For, unlike the sudden and short outbreaks at Jos and Zorzor, new cases were continuing to pile in.

Immune plasma was painfully short. Equipment and instructions were left, however, for the hospital to prepare its own—providing, of course, that those with antibodies could be convinced to donate their plasma.

Kent Campbell and Dave Fraser took off for London to do some follow-up testing of former African missionary workers. The others returned to the United States. They had spent about a month in Panguma. They were tired. Only the thought that the mystery of the source might be resolved by the animal tests buoyed their spirits.

Before they could settle in, however, they were disturbed by the news that Kent Campbell was seriously ill. He had been felled by a violent fever shortly after his arrival in London. Lassa was suspected, and the emergency evacuation plan was put into effect. Dramatically, the Apollo moonshot isolation capsule, originally designed to prevent contact with any strange virus from space, was loaded into an Air Force transport jet and rushed to London. Campbell was put aboard and flown back inside the module for treatment at Columbia Presbyterian.

To the relief of all, tests failed to show that Campbell had come down with Lassa. The illness was never specifically diagnosed and he was later discharged fully recovered. But the strain and terror provoked by the incident emphasized the difficulties of fighting a disease that sprang from unknown wells.

With the crisis over, attention turned again to the search for the vector. Speculation focused on the mahogany rat, and the first tests were awaited with considerable suspense. None of the other animals tested to date had shown any evidence of Lassa virus or antibodies. Perhaps these rats would provide the first real clue to where the virus was lurking in nature.

When the first complement-fixation tests on five mahogany rats came through, there was great elation: using a mouse antigen, the tests showed positive for Lassa antibodies. Everyone concerned with the long, grinding search was in the mood for a major celebration. But the tests were not definitive, and further testing would have to be done to confirm them.

There was one problem, however. Some of the rat serum and tissues were beginning to deteriorate under storage conditions. If this continued, it would be serious and the hope of finding clues markedly diminished. The additional tests were scheduled and given high priority. The results were awaited everywhere: from Lassa to Jos, to Zorzor, to Panguma, to Yale, to Columbia Presbyterian—throughout the medical world.

Tom Monath, working in the hollow, sterile lab of the CDC, continued the exhausting probe. He brought each sample, wrapped in a sealed plastic bag, into the work area through a dunk tank—a tank filled with chlorine bleach, half inside and half outside the hot lab. It was another precaution rigidly adhered to. With his arms punched into the long rubber gloves, he could handle the specimens and examine them through the glass isolators. Brian Henderson, who was the first to work in the lab with the Lassa virus, said: "When you open up a vial of a virus like Lassa inside those glass isolators, no matter what anybody tells you, it still makes you nervous. We really had no idea how to handle Lassa, it was so unusual. When you start from scratch under those conditions, every day is tense."

The tension mounted as Tom Monath continued with the confirmation tests on the mahogany rats. The slow, awkward, almost clumsy procedures demanded by the hot lab routine were taxing to both the nerves and patience. Finally, he was ready to announce his findings. They were clear, direct, and disappointing: it was not the mahogany rat. It was not any animal so far tested.

Monath was discouraged but determined to keep going. The hot lab could handle only about fifty specimens a week at best, and there were hundreds still to be tested. He would have to be selective.

His mind went back to the harrowing case of Hawa Foray, the Sierra Leone housewife who had died tragically within hours after Monath had arrived at the Panguma mission station. Hers had been a classic Lassa virus case, confirmed by both her blood specimen and the liver cells he had extracted by large-bore needle from her body after she had died. He remembered the eight wild rats of the *Mastomys natalensis* species that had been trapped in her house after death. The rodent was common and widely distributed in West Africa, but it usually stayed in the bush. Only when the larger and more ferocious house rat abandoned the premises did it venture into the houses and granaries of the villages.

It was now June 1973, months after the Sierra Leone outbreak. Monath and his technicians put the mahogany rat out of their minds and turned to the eight *Mastomys natalensis* specimens that had been waiting, with others, in storage. Once again they took the snips of tissue, ground them with mortar and pestle in a diluent fluid, inoculated the rows of tissue cultures, and waited for the telltale spots of the cytopathic effects to show up.

To their delight, the new batch of tissue cultures was riddled with cell damage. There was no damage to the control group. Despite the danger of another false lead, they worked with fresh enthusiasm. Harvesting the fluids and cells and freezing them so that the cells would be broken up by the formation of ice crystals, they put them through the usual complement-fixation tests. Monath did not want to admit it even to himself, but for some reason he felt confident that they had at last reached the end of their search. Perversely, he bet one of his technicians $10 that the first isolate of the complement-fixation tests would *not* turn out to be Lassa.

Again there was anticipation, but an anticipation tempered by experience and an inbred scientific skepticism. This time, however, there was not disappointment. Tom Monath couldn't have been happier when he lost his bet. Not only was the first isolate unmistakably Lassa, but seven of the eight *Mastomys natalensis* specimens found in Hawa Foray's house showed the same results.

There was no longer any doubt about the animal reservoir of the Lassa virus. That vicious, malignant speck with its spiky, polka-dotted overcoat that had eluded the virus hunters for so long had at last been bearded in its den.

There was still much to be done, but at least there would be no more blind stumbling. The problem would now shift to intelligent control of this new rodent reservoir and the long, involved process of developing a vaccine.

None of this would be easy. It would require the cooperation and facilities of the UN World Health Organization, Atlanta's CDC, the Rockefeller Foundation virologists, eradication and control teams, and the health ministries of many West African countries.

But as the news of the breakthrough flashed across the medical world, those who had been working so long and so hard with the disease were confident that progress could be made. There was a feeling of immense relief, coupled with a desire to get on with the job of combatting any new or threatening agent that might spring up in the virus universe, just as Lassa had done.

Afterword

I first learned of the Lassa virus when I picked up *The New York Times* early in 1970 to read Lawrence Altman's headline: "New Fever Virus So Deadly That Research Halts." It was not a story that led to calm nerves. I set it aside after reading it, preferring to put it out of my mind.

I gave no more thought to it until a year later, when I happened to be producing and directing a documentary film in Africa involving, of all things, a tour of two of America's leading basketball players: Kareem Abdul-Jabbar, formerly Lew Alcindor, and Oscar Robertson, the "Big O," as he is labeled by sports fans. The American stars were conducting a clinic for African players, and we were moving through eight different countries. Nigeria was one of them.

Workouts for basketball at the University of Lagos, in Nigeria's capital, begin at six in the morning because of the blistering heat. The university has outdoor courts, and by 8 A.M. the sun is merciless. During the filming, I struck up a conversation with a woman, an American professor at the university, who liked basketball so much she had thrust herself out on the courts at that unseasonable time of morning to watch.

She asked if we had heard about the Lassa fever outbreaks

in the United States. I had almost forgotten the news story. It came back all too vividly when she reminded me of it. She mentioned the research that was going on at the University of Ibadan and indicated that it was extremely dramatic. I told her it was interesting but that, being one of the world's worst hypochondriacs, I would just as soon forget it.

As we went on with the tour of Africa, for some reason the story kept popping back in my mind. It haunted me. What type of courage did it take to face a situation like this? What was the current status of the disease? Had it just faded into the woodwork, or what? My curiosity began to get the best of my hypochondria, and I talked with my publishers, who agreed that it might have good possibilities as a book.

I called Wil Downs at New Haven, and he filled me in on some of the background. The story in Zorzor, as a matter of fact, had only recently broken. The situation was far from closed. He invited me up to Yale to chat further. Within a few days I arrived at the impressive new building of the Department of Epidemiology on College Street.

I have to confess I felt squeamish. The recollection of the two men who had been stricken with the disease there punctuated the feeling. It was further intensified by a sign on the first floor of the building, prominently posted inside the elevator: "Warning: Unauthorized Persons Are Not Permitted Above the Fourth Floor." Wil Downs' office was on the sixth floor, and I was not sure I *wanted* to go there.

Wil Downs was cordial and articulate. He took me through the various laboratories, all bright and spotless and not at all ominous—even the Horsfall isolators for the mice. I confess I breathed lightly, and only through the nose. I kept my hands away from everything. But what Downs had to say was of absorbing interest and incredible drama.

As a result, I started a long series of interviews with Jordi Casals, Sonja Buckley, Bob Shope, Graham Kemp, Don Carey, and others. I began to try to learn the intricacies of complement fixation, neutralization, plaques in Vero cell cultures, and other tests carried out at the Yale lab. It was fascinating, and the scientists were all very patient in explaining the processes.

They also were tolerant when I asked them to go over and over each scene from memory, reconstructing it in the most minute detail. All through my various visits to the arbovirus lab, however, I could never overcome my feeling of fear. I tried to keep it to myself, but finally I simply gave in to it and told everyone that I was scared stiff.

Sonja Buckley laughed and said: "Don't worry about that. I am too." We were outside a door with a sign that read: "Rabies: Do Not Enter." But she assured me that she had been around the viruses and rickettsia for thirty-some years and had no intention whatever of getting sick from them. When I reminded her of what she had told me about sucking up fluid from a bottle with a short pipette, she laughed again and said: "That *was* pretty stupid."

At lunch at Kaysey's Restaurant in New Haven, Graham Kemp filled me in on the details of his long odyssey through Nigeria. He made it sound so exciting and interesting that I actually found myself looking forward to going to Nigeria again to follow his corkscrew trails.

In the meantime, I visited Tom Monath at the CDC hot lab in Atlanta, which *did* have an ominous atmosphere to it. Monath took it all as a matter of course, but it was somewhat spooky to look through the glass compartments and see Lassa virus cultures growing and mice scampering in a chamber riddled with death—only inches away.

Monath told me he was just in the process of making up the team to go to Sierra Leone. He felt fairly confident that he would crack the riddle of the source of the Lassa virus. Weeks later, after I had returned from Nigeria, he told me of his disappointment when the mahogany rat had failed to come through with the evidence. "It was a big hangup," he said. "We were so hopeful at first."

My visa for Nigeria came through in mid-December, just before Christmas 1972. I had myself riddled like a punchboard with every conceivable kind of shot or booster: cholera, plague, yellow fever, typhoid, paratyphoid, typhus, tetanus, smallpox booster, and gamma globulin. I carried a large supply of chloroquine. Graham Kemp assured me there would be Lassa-immune serum available at both Jos and Ibadan—within a few hours' flight of any place I'd be in Nigeria. "Don't worry about it," he said. "You'll either be dead in ten days or alive and well." I managed a forced laugh.

I was going to make the trip at almost the same time of year that the previous plateau outbreaks had occurred, in the dry harmattan season. The thought bothered me, but I would at least have the advantage of seeing the country as it was during the time span I was writing about.

I knew roughly what I wanted to cover: the Lassa mission station at the foot of the Cameroon highlands; Garkida, the remote headquarters of the Church of the Brethren Mission; Jos and the Sudan Interior Mission; Miango, the tiny village where Charlotte Shaw and Dr. Jeanette were buried; Ibadan and the virus laboratory there; Lagos, where the Pest House was and where the King of the Motor Park lived; and all the routes covered by Graham Kemp in his peripatetic wanderings. It is nearly 1,200 road miles from Lagos to Lassa. A round trip takes over eight days of hard driving.

Even though I have an international driving license, it was not honored in Nigeria, and I had to hire a driver along with a car. David, who would take me from Lagos to Jos, was a pleasant, smiling Yoruba who dressed in a starch-clean yellow shirt and spoke practically no English. The first day's drive on the way to Jos by way of Bida took twelve grueling hours, and the carnage on the road was incredible. Every blind curve, every hill was a major crisis. I had to constantly remind David to pull over to the right on the precipitous shoulders of the road and slow down. Apparently, in years past Nigerian drivers knew that a truck or car was approaching by the plume of dust that would rise over the hill or around the curve. But with the progress being made in macadamizing the roads, this trick no longer sufficed. The result was evident in the twisted wrecks that lined the route.

I was traveling on a tourist visa, since it would have taken too long to get a journalist visa, and necessarily had to keep a low profile. The missionaries were not aware of the ruse, and I carefully avoided making them partners in the deception. Ostensibly, I was on vacation, although it became increasingly difficult to explain to officials just why I was traveling the baked and dusty savanna alone during the holiday season.

Nigerians are among the most friendly and cordial people in the world. Their smiles are genuine, their curiosity about America intense, their warmth and sincerity obvious. It is only when officialdom creeps in that the situation becomes difficult.

The Nigerians were understandably sensitive, however, about the Lassa virus, even though its territory extended throughout West Africa, if not beyond. I did not particularly emphasize the Lassa aspect of the research, although of course I would have to collect massive information on it from the lonely mission stations.

I spent the first night in the Government Catering Rest House at Bida. The group assembled at the boarding-house-type table was intriguing and fascinating—as cosmopolitan a collection of travelers as you could find anywhere in the world. There was a common bond: travelers far away from home in a strange, exotic, and isolated place at Christmas, sharing a certain loneliness. I sat waiting for dinner in a wicker chair on the veranda, the big paddle fans on the ceiling rotating slowly. I could not help imagining that Sidney Greenstreet or Humphrey Bogart might suddenly walk out of one of the bungalows and ask gruffly what was on the menu for dinner.

I have never felt very cordial toward scorpions or spiders, but only the latter showed up in my room. I did however, leave a sweet cookie on the top of the dresser, and by morning two columns of ants had blackened the wall, one moving up to it and the other down from it. The anthills along the bush roads were impressive, some of them as high as fifteen feet.

The trip from Bida to Jos was grueling. The roads were worse than ever, but the accidents were fewer because the rough surface cut down speed. David was uncommunicative, and I spent most of the time talking into my tape recorder, making audio notes for my journal. Darkness fell long before we reached Jos, and the curtain of blackness that descends over the savanna is heavy. The most startling things were the bush fires in the distance, glowing from miles away like the illusion of a distant city. Some of them are set for the great rat hunts. Others ignite spontaneously in the tinder-dry bush. At night they are awesome.

At the top of the plateau, Jos town is actually a lovely place. The Hill Station Rest House had just been remodeled and was a welcome sight after the fourteen-hour drive from Bida.

At the bar were a cluster of Britishers: several former colonial officers and a young agronomist and his wife. They were cordial but quite curious as to what I was doing up on the plateau. Because of the visa situation, I had to dodge their questions, and it was rather difficult to do. I tried to explain my presence by talking about my interest in the Nok culture of the area, the Benin bronzes (we were nowhere near Benin, however), and my compulsion to travel—which I don't really have. The only way I like to travel is by low-altitude sedan chair or very slow canal barge in clear weather. Planes terrify me. Driving on the Nigerian roads left me limp. With my intense hypochondria, I began to wonder just why I was there, deep in the heart of Africa and still planning to move on to Lassa, which was about as deep as you could get. I had nothing but admiration for the missionaries or anyone else who had ever moved out in the area.

The Church of the Brethren and Sudan Interior Mission people were cordial and generous. In the low-slung buildings of the Evangel Hospital, Hal White, Dolores Rohe, Joan Potter, Dorothy Davis, and the other members of the staff moved about quietly and efficiently, and it was easy to picture them at work during the crises of 1969 and 1970.

When White talked about his experiences, it was with a quiet, objective calm. He recalled every detail of the fight against the virus. He was disarming and frank, analyzing his own strengths and weaknesses, offering no excuses or apologies, and serenely confident in his religious faith. There was no conflict between his profession and his theology; they were part of the same tapestry.

The same was true of the nurses. They were professional but with a quality of burning faith that buttressed, rather than interfered with, their clinical objectivity. Their adoration of Dr. Jeanette was intense and unfeigned. They worshipped her along with Penny Pinneo. The loss they felt when Dr. Jeanette died still clung to them. Their recollections of the incident were prodigious, down to exact phrases and long stretches of dialog.

Penny Pinneo was not in Jos at the time. She was back in the States on furlough for additional study. I had interviewed her before I left, in a missionary rest house in Ventnor, New Jersey, next to Atlantic City.

She was buoyant and articulate and had gained back much of her strength. Her hearing sometimes bothered her, especially the buzzing in her ears. But she was anxious to get back again to Nigeria. Whatever physical energy she lacked she made up for with psychological drive. Her recollection of the crises was extremely detailed, and we talked for nearly six hours without her showing any fatigue.

Ivy Hanna, the dietician at the Jos hospital, was most helpful in shedding light on why the terror of the second wave of Lassa in 1970 did not change into panic. "There I was in the kitchen," she said, "handling all the dishes of the patients and no more upset than you are right now." I didn't mention to her that my hypochondria was working overtime, and that as I walked through the wards and watched the nurses and doctors taking care of the patients, I was dead sure I was going to come down with Lassa any moment. She continued:

> Sometimes I wonder why we weren't more upset, now that I think about it. Half the people were dying. Three out of four of our own people were dead. This is not the most elaborately equipped hospital in the world. We have no facilities for sterilizing the dishes.
>
> I guess we had a sense of God being in control. I know the doctors felt terrible, helpless, I guess. But there was this underburning of truth—our Heavenly Father there. In His will there is peace.

Then she paused a moment, looked at me, and said: "We could do worse than convert *you*."

I explained that I was too far gone, and she laughed. It was the only time any of the missionaries tried to proselytize, which rather surprised me. They were all most restrained, including Ivy Hanna, in trying to impose their beliefs.

By the Church of the Brethren's Land Rover, I moved on toward Lassa and the Cameroon highlands, a two-day drive beyond Jos, down from the plateau and on to the flat savanna where the heat and the harmattan and the dust become most uncharitable. I had a two-quart canteen of halazone-ridden water, and the metal lip of the canteen got so hot that it burned my lips. The choice between keeping the windows rolled up and burning to death or leaving them open to be crusted in dust was often hard to make.

I was worried about that dust, I unhaled so much of it. I was sure that there must be one small Lassa virus lurking somewhere in it. And if there were, I would be the one to pick it up. Up to this point I had not had one bad day, although I was careful not to eat any raw vegetables or salads, drank beer instead of water whenever possible, and made sure the mosquito netting was tucked in securely on going to bed each night. Antimalaria pills are not always effective, and malaria-carrying mosquitoes are plentiful. If you forget to take your regular quota of chloroquine just once, it is not *likely* you will come down with malaria. You *will* come down with it.

By the time we reached Garkida, a little more than halfway to Lassa, I felt as if I had saddle sores. At the Church of the Brethren mission station I was given a round hut with a thatched roof, which was not without charm.

There were double-decker bunks, each with its own mosquito netting, a wardrobe, a table, and a screened crib. It was the designated guest house of the station, small but comfortable. A single light bulb hung down from the ceiling and burned from six in the evening to exactly ten, when the generator was shut off. When it dimmed, very slowly, it created a very spooky feeling.

I had packed a bottle of scotch in my rucksack. At ten each night, when the lights went out, I poured myself a double just before going to sleep. I hoped that I would not be offending any of the missionaries, most of whom were rather uptight about this sort of thing. There was, of course, never a cocktail before dinner—nor wine nor beer—in any of the mission homes. I began feeling a little guilty about my secret vice, but never so guilty as to stop having that nightcap. I figured they were big enough to forgive me if they knew.

Lying in bed, I would inevitably hear the sound of the village drums in the distance. They were fascinating but persistent, recalling the clichés in African novels where the protagonist has to say at least once: "If they would only stop beating those infernal drums!" I would also hear the rustle of bat wings, which I found a little chilling.

The viper situation was no joke. It simply did not pay to step outside your hut after dark without a flashlight and a sturdy staff. I had always thought that "viper" was a generic term for snakes, but soon learned differently. The African vipers have large overhanging fangs, and their venom works with incredible speed. Heavy boots are a must. A victim who does not get specific viper antivenom within a couple of hours is doomed. He will bleed from every part of his body. Vipers sometimes invade the mission houses. One missionary almost stepped on three of them just outside his door early one morning.

Spitting cobras are another menace that the missionaries take coolly in their stride. The cobras appear suddenly in the vegetable gardens, slithering in from the high grass. Their methods are different from those of the vipers: they spit their venom with uncanny accuracy toward the eyes, blinding the victim. For small animals, the blindness means death. The cobra closes in for the kill at his leisure.

There is little fear of pythons. They are so large that they can be easily seen and avoided. Sometimes they are captured for their meat, which is quite tasty.

The eating of rats, according to the missionaries, is not as distasteful as it sounds. If the rats are properly and thoroughly cooked, any virus in them will be destroyed. It is the handling and eating of raw meat that can be dangerous. They are also a valuable source of protein, and the villagers get precious little of that. Missionary children often join the rat hunts, and they have learned to eat rat meat as a matter of course with their Nigerian peers.

The Church of the Brethren mission installation at Garkida is impressive, and its schools and hospitals throughout the scallop of land known as the Tchad depression in the ancient Sudanese empire of Bornu are monuments to the skill and persistence of both early and later missionaries. The mission schools are now being turned over to the Nigerian government, but at one time nearly all the educational institutions were exclusively in the hands of the missionaries.

After a brief stay at Garkida, where Laura Wine was buried, I moved on to Lassa with Von Hall and his Land Rover. Hall is a rugged, practical man whose gruff energy and force cover a genuine sensitivity and deep concern for helping the Nigerian communities lift themselves by their bootstraps. When we turned off the main highway at Michika, I was struck by the isolation of the village of Lassa, more than ten miles away on the dusty ruts. All through the area even the main roads are unpredictable in the rainy season. There are frequent, major road closings when all communication is cut off. A compromise is sometimes reached, with one-way traffic permitted on alternate days. As we approached Lassa, however, we were lucky; both rivers that we had to ford in the Land Rover were manageable.

Lassa is a place of contrasts. As remote as it is, the mission houses, with their brick veneer surfaces, look amazingly civilized. Although the hospital buildings are more than twenty years old and in need of repair, they look strangely modern in the setting, where the village huts dominate the scene.

I walked through the village, the focus of many stares. Strangers are not frequent there. The butchers were at their outdoor stand—two inverted boxes—hacking away at a goat literally covered with flies. They were cheerful and cordial. Walls of rectangular gray mud bricks hid most of the compounds, although it was possible to peek over at times and look inside. The compound walls are a symbol of status. The greater the circumference, the more prosperous the family. They were constructed by what is known as a "Bonee man" or "Gimme man." He would stand on top of the wall as it was constructed, calling down to his helpers: "Gimme! Gimme!" They would in turn hand up the balls of mud, and he would shape them into bricks and place them neatly in line.

I passed one compound where burial rites were being chanted. The man had died of pneumonia at the Lassa hospital the night before. The drums had been beating since early morning. The body had been washed and shrouded and placed in a hammock-like bed inside the compound. The friends and relatives, some with spears, were chanting and dancing to the beat of the drums; nearly all of them appeared to be in a trance. Feeling like the intruder I was, I could not help stopping to look. They paid no attention and kept on with the ceremony. In the heat of the savanna, burials must be quick.

At the time I arrived at Lassa, it was manned only by the Halls and Dr. Daryl Parker and his wife. The Parkers had been missionaries in China and now lived most of the time in the Midwest, where Dr. Parker continued to practice ophthalmology, although he was well past retirement age. For four to six months a year, however, he volunteered to come to Lassa. At the time, he was filling in partially for the Hamers, who were in Fort Wayne, Indiana. The Lassa mission was anxiously expecting a new full-time doctor, but he had not yet arrived.

I stayed at the house the Hamers had lived in when Miss Wine first came down with her tragic symptoms. The house was empty and musty. The furniture was for the most part covered with cloth, and it seemed almost like a ghost house. After the lights had dimmed and gone out, I lay in bed and tried to picture the lives the Hamers had led there: the endless labor in the hospital, the persistent routine of fighting disease that often grew to overwhelming proportions.

The prayer meeting at 6 A.M. in the small hospital storeroom was most touching. Ngamariju Mamza, the supervisor of the nursing staff at the Lassa hospital, led the service in Hausa, and eight or ten of the Nigerian staff joined in, singing their hallelujahs lustily and fervently. The dark cement room reverberated with their rich voices. Dr. Parker and I were the only outsiders there. They made us seem welcome.

The tiny Heathkit radio in the hospital office loomed far larger than its size, as the only link with the outside world. It was fascinating to hear the lonely voices of the various missions come in from all over the Sudan each morning—first with the morning prayer, then with the simple, pragmatic messages of the day's routine.

I had already interviewed Dr. John Hamer and his wife in Fort Wayne, before leaving for Africa. Their memory of the trip in the Land Rover and mission plane was sharp and detailed. They were still puzzled as to why neither of them had come down with the fever—their contact had been so close and constant.

When I left Lassa, the harmattan almost obscured the saw-toothed Cameroon mountains, but their outline could be seen like a ghost image. The tribes that lived halfway up their slopes still remained in retreat, still came down to the flatlands infrequently if at all, still harbored fear of the slave raiders. Other tribes in the area continued to put lip disks in their women. Originally, the duck-billed lips were supposed to make the women less attractive to the raiders.

With a new driver from the Church of the Brethren named Ibrahim, a warm and cheerful young man who handled the Land Rover with less flamboyance than David, we headed back to Jos, stopping at the Government Catering Rest House at Yankari. Here all cars were required to stop at a station along the road to be sprayed against the tse-tse fly. Here also were animals roaming freely. We saw many: hippos, baboons, water-bucks, antelopes, crocodiles, wart hogs, wild buffalo—but no elephants, which were reported to be in the area.

I woke up the following morning realizing it was Christmas, having almost forgotten about it in the strain of the research. It was strange to be in the sweltering heat and so far away from home. Getting out of bed, I noticed that my throat was quite sore and that I could not speak at all. With several long interviews scheduled on my arrival back at Jos, I was upset and frustrated. Then it suddenly occurred to me: Sore throat? Wasn't that the first symptom of Lassa? I gargled long and hard and jumped back into bed. I was worried.

When the steward came to clean up the room, he was most solicitous. He brought me some aspirin, a jug full of water, and fruit. "I am very mad that a cold catch my master," he said. The vestiges of colonialism were still hanging on.

Since I didn't have a fever, I got up in a couple of hours, and we pushed on toward Jos. I desperately wanted to interview some of the nurses that evening, because time was short and I was on a tight schedule. As we drove back over the road from Bauchi to Jos, I made out a series of 3″ × 5″ cards with questions on them for the interviews, which I would use as flashcards. I also wrote out some for general information: "Have laryngitis—Can't talk"; "Please bring me the regular menu"; "One scotch and soda please." The loss of voice was absolutely total. I wrote out one for Ibrahim: "Drive slower." This was a constant reminder that had to be used with any Nigerian driver.

I immediately went to Hal White when I arrived in Jos. He reassured me that it was simply laryngitis, a very common symptom resulting from many days of inhaling the thick dust. I wasn't sure that I believed him. In fact, I was paranoid enough to think he was just trying to comfort me before he ordered me to the hospital. I went through with the interviews, took more aspirin, and woke up the next morning without sore throat, laryngitis, or fever.

The air arm of the Sudan Interior Mission is impressive. The planes are kept in mint condition by the pilot-mechanics. On one trip to a remote mission, I have to confess I was startled when the pilot went into a short prayer just before takeoff. I was further impressed when he buzzed a herd of cattle away from an airstrip before landing. They are an unusual bunch, the missionary pilots, steeped in that strange combination of piloting, navigation, mechanics, and Bible study.

At the University of Ibadan, all the Rockefeller Foundation men had left. Dr. Akinyele Fabiyi was there, a quiet, soft-spoken, perceptive Nigerian who received a Ph.D. in virology from the University of Pennsylvania. While keeping an eye out for Lassa, he was concentrating on a disease called Kata, which was creating havoc among the sheep population of the country. He was determined to make inroads into the virus problems of the nation and was gaining government support in doing so.

Returning to Lagos somewhat behind schedule, I went over my notes, tapes, medical reports, and other research data to see what I might need to complete the story. Actually, the forward progress of the story stopped at the second outbreak in Jos in 1970. The Liberian and Sierra Leone outbreaks were nearly carbon copies of the Jos pattern, but they were important parts to note in the portrait of this monstrous virus.

I checked my schedule and research budget and told myself that I would have neither the time nor the money to investigate directly the fresh Sierra Leone outbreak at Panguma. The virologists working there had generously offered to lend me their notes and observations, and all their medical reports on the crisis.

Because of this, I decided I could cover that part of the story adequately without going to Panguma personally to research it. I satisfied myself that this was the real reason for not including that stopover in my itinerary.

Naturally, it was a complete rationalization. It wasn't the reason at all, and deep down I knew it wasn't.

I didn't want to press my luck any further. I was afraid to go there.

Bibliography

Abdou, I. A., et al. 1952. Plasma protein equilibrium between blood and lymph protein. *Journal of Biological Chemistry* 194:15.

Agramonte, A. 1924. Yellow fever prophylaxis. *Journal of Tropical Medicine* 27:285–87.

Anderson, C. R., and Gast-Galvis, A. 1947. Immunity to yellow fever five years after vaccination. *American Journal of Hygiene* 45:302–04.

Anifinsen, C. 1959. *The molecular basis of evolution*. New York: John Wiley.

Antunes, W. S. 1948. Field control in yellow fever. *Proceedings of the International Congress of Tropical Medicine and Malaria* 1:498–505.

Asimov, I. 1954. *The chemicals of life*. New York: New American Library. Signet Science Library.

———. 1964. *A short history of biology*. Garden City, N.Y.: Natural History Press.

Balfour, A. 1914. Wild monkey as reservoir for virus of yellow fever. *Lancet* 1:1176–78.

Bard, P. 1956. *Medical physiology*. St. Louis: C. V. Mosby.

Barer, R. 1953. *Lecture notes on the use of the microscope*. Oxford: Blackwell Scientific Publications.

Bauer, J. H. 1931. Some characteristics of yellow fever virus. *American Journal of Tropical Medicine* 11:337–53.

———, and Hudson, N. P. 1930. Duration of immunity in human yellow fever as shown by protective power of serum. *Journal of Preventive Medicine* 4:177–78.

Baum, J. J., and Mertens, P. E. Unpublished observations.

Beadle, G., and Beadle, M. 1965. *The language of life*. Garden City, N.Y.: Doubleday.

Beeuwkes, H.; Bauer, J. H.; and Mahaffy, A. F. 1930. Yellow fever endemicity in West Africa, with special reference to protection tests. *American Journal of Tropical Medicine* 10:305–33.

————, et al. 1934. Yellow fever protection test surveys in French Cameroons, French Equatorial Africa, Belgian Congo, and Angola. *Transactions of the Royal Society of Tropical Medicine and Hygiene* 28:233–58.

Bell, G. H., et al. 1956. *Textbook of physiology and biochemistry*. Baltimore: Williams and Wilkins.

Bhamarapravati, N.; Boonyapaknavik, V.; and Nimsomburna, P. 1964. Pathology of Thai haemorrhagic fever. World Health Organization seminar on mosquito-borne haemorrhagic fevers in Southeast Asia and Western Pacific regions.

Biggs, R., and MacFarlane, R. G. 1953. *Blood coagulation*. Oxford: Basil Blackwell and Mott.

Black, B. 1953. *Hyperparathyroidism*. Springfield, Ill.: Charles C. Thomas.

Bloom, W., and Fawcett, D. W. 1962. *Textbook of histology*. 8th ed. Philadelphia: W. B. Saunders.

Borek, E. 1961. *The atoms within us*. New York: Columbia University Press.

————. 1965. *The code of life*. New York: Columbia University Press.

Boyer, P. D.; Lardy, H. A.; and Myrback, K.; eds. 1963. *The Enzymes*. 2nd ed. 8 vols. New York: Academic Press.

Brachet, J. 1957. *Biochemical cytology*. New York: Academic Press.

————, and Mirsky, A. E. 1959–1961. *The cell: biochemistry, physiology, morphology*. 5 vols. New York: Academic Press.

Buckley, S. M. 1962. *Proceedings of the XIth International Congress on Entomology* 2:763.

————. 1969. Susceptibility of the *Aedes albopictus* and *A. aegypti* cell lines to infection with arboviruses. *Proceedings of the Society for Experimental Biology and Medicine* 131:625–30.

————, and Casals, J. 1970. *American Journal of Tropical Medicine and Hygiene* 19:680.

————, and Downs, W. G. 1970. *Nature* 227:174.

————, and Shope, R. E. 1961. *American Journal of Tropical Medicine and Hygiene* 10:53.

————, and Srihongse, S. 1963. *Proceedings of the Society of Experimental Biology and Medicine* 113:284.

Butler, J. A. V. 1959. *Inside the living cell*. London: Allen and Unwin.

Carey, D. E., et al. 1972. *Transactions of the Royal Society of Tropical Medicine and Hygiene* 66:402.

Carpenter, B. H., ed. 1967. *Molecular and cell biology*. Belmont, Cal.: Dickenson.

Casals, J. 1967. Immunological techniques for animal viruses. In *Methods in Virology*, vol. 3, ed. K. Maramorosch and H. Koprowski. New York: Academic Press.

————. 1968 Filtration of arboviruses through "millipore" membranes. *Nature* 217:648–49.

————, and Palacios, R. 1941. Complement-fixation test in diagnosis of virus infections of central nervous system. *Journal of Experimental Medicine* 74:409–26.

Clarke, D. H., and Casals, J. 1958. Techniques for hemagglutination and hemagglutination-inhibition with arthropod-borne viruses. *American Journal of Tropical Medicine and Hygiene* 7:561–73.

Conant, J. B., ed. 1952. *Pasteur's study of fermentation.* Harvard Case Histories in Experimental Science, no. 6. Cambridge, Mass.: Harvard University Press.

Courtney, K. O. 1950. Report on recent outbreak of jungle yellow fever in Panama. *American Journal of Public Health* 40:417–26.

Davenport, H. W. 1950. *The A.B.C. of acid base chemistry.* Chicago: University of Chicago Press.

Davis, G. E. 1931. Complement fixation in yellow fever in monkey and man. *American Journal of Hygiene* 13:79–128.

Davis, W. A. 1940. Study of birds and mosquitoes as hosts for virus of Eastern equine encephalomyelitis." *American Journal of Hygiene* 32:45–59.

Dunker, C. K., and Yoffey, J. M. 1941. *Lymphatics, lymph, and lymphoid tissue.* Cambridge, Mass.: Harvard University Press.

Eagle, H. 1955. The minimum vitamin requirements of the L and HeLa cells in tissue culture, the production of specific vitamin deficiencies, and their cure. *Journal of Experimental Medicine* 102:595–600.

Ebert, J. D. 1965. *Interacting systems in development.* New York: Holt, Rinehart and Winston.

Edington, G. M., and White, H. A. 1972. The pathology of Lassa fever. *Transactions of the Royal Society of Tropical Medicine and Hygiene* 66:381–89.

Forder, L. L., et al. 1952. Circulation of plasma proteins, their transport to lymph. *Journal of Biological Chemistry* 197:625.

Frame, J. D., et al. 1970. Lassa fever, a new virus disease of man from West Africa. I. Clinical description and pathological findings. *American Journal of Tropical Medicine and Hygiene* 19:670–76.

Gardiner-Hill, H. 1961. *Modern trends in endocrinology.* New York: Paul B. Hoeber.

Gay, H. 1960. Nuclear control of the cell. *Scientific American* (January).

Gerard, R. W. 1940. *Unresting cells.* New York: Harper & Row.

Goodman, L. S., and Gilman, A., eds. 1965. *The pharmacological basis of therapeutics.* 3rd ed. New York: Macmillan.

Grollman, A. 1947. *Essentials of endocrinology.* Philadelphia: J. B. Lippincott.

Guyton, A. 1961. *Textbook of medical physiology.* Philadelphia: W. B. Saunders.

Haldane, J. B. S. 1960. "Dex" or "order of magnitude"? *Nature* 187:879.

Ham, A. W. 1957. *Histology*. 3rd ed. London: Pitman.

Hardin, G. 1961. *Biology, its principles and implications*. San Francisco: W. H. Freeman.

Henderson, B. E., et al. 1972. *Transactions of the Royal Society of Tropical Medicine and Hygiene* 66:409.

Horsfall, F. L., and Tamm, L. 1965. *Viral and rickettsial infections of man*. 4th ed. London: Pitman.

Hudson, N. P.; Bauer, J. H.; and Philip, C. B. 1929. Protection tests with serum of persons recovered from yellow fever in Western Hemisphere and West Africa. *American Journal of Tropical Medicine* 9:1–16.

Ihde, A. J. 1964. *The development of modern chemistry*. New York: Harper & Row.

Ingram, V. M. 1963. *The hemoglobins in genetics and evolution*. New York: Columbia University Press.

Kabat, E. A. 1956. *Blood group substances*. New York: Interscience Publishers.

Kendrew, J. C. 1966. *The thread of life*. Cambridge, Mass.: Harvard University Press.

Klotz, O. 1927. Yellow fever in West Africa, *De Lamar Lectures, 1927–1928*. Baltimore: Williams and Wilkins.

Koprowski, H. 1946. Occurrence of nonspecific virus-neutralizing properties in sera of some neotropic mammals. *Journal of Immunology* 54:387–94.

Liefer, E.; Gocke, D. J.; and Bourne, H. 1970. Lassa fever, a new virus disease of man from West Africa. II. Report of a laboratory-acquired infection treated with plasma from a person recently recovered from the disease. *American Journal of Tropical Medicine and Hygiene* 19:677–79.

Loewy, A., and Siekevitz, P. 1965. *Cell structure and function*. New York: Holt, Rinehart and Winston.

MacFarlane, R. G., and Robb-Smith, A. 1961. *Functions of the Blood*. New York: Academic Press.

Marshall, A. H. E. 1956. *An outline of the cytology and pathology of the reticular tissue*. Springfield, Ill.: Charles C. Thomas.

McLeish, J., and Snoad, B. 1959. *Looking at chromosomes*. London: Macmillan.

Mercer, E. H., and Birbeck, M. S. C. 1961. *Electron microscopy: a handbook for biologists*. Oxford: Blackwell Scientific Publications.

Mettler, N.; Buckley, S. M.; and Casals, J. 1961. Propagation of Junin virus, the etiological agent of Argentinean hemorrhagic fever, in HeLa cell cultures. *Proceedings of the Society of Experimental Biology and Medicine* 107:684–88.

Monath, T., and Casals, J. 1970–1973. Unpublished observations.

Moore, J. A., ed. 1966. *Ideas in modern biology*. New York: Natural History Press.

New York Academy of Medicine. 1954. *Hormones in health and disease.* New York: Macmillan.

Nirenberg, M. W. 1963. The genetic code: II. *Scientific American* (March).

Perutz, M. F. 1959. The molecular basis of inheritance. *New Scientist* 5:1192.

Picken, L. E. R. 1955. *The School Science Review,* nos. 129, 130, and 131.

Pincus, G., and Thimann, K. 1948–1955. *The hormones.* Vols. 1–3. New York: Academic Press.

Putman, F. W. 1960. *The plasma proteins.* Vols. 1 and 2. New York: Interscience Publishers.

Rich, A. 1963. Polyribosomes. *Scientific American* (December).

Roughton, F. L. W., and Kendrew, J. C. 1949. *Haemoglobin.* New York: Interscience Publishers.

Schiff, F., and Boyd, W. C. 1942. *Blood grouping technic.* New York: Interscience Publishers.

Scientific American. 1961. The living cell. 205: entire issue.

Selye, H., and Stone, H. 1950. *Experimental morphology of the adrenal cortex.* Springfield, Ill.: Charles C. Thomas.

Simizu, B.; Rhim, J. S.; and Wiebenga, N. H. 1967. Characterization of the Tacaribe group of arboviruses. I. Propagation and plaque assay of Tacaribe virus in a line of African green monkey kidney cells (Vero). *Proceedings of the Society for Experimental Biology and Medicine* 125:119–23.

Smith, C. E. G., et al. 1967. Fatal human disease from vervet monkeys. *Lancet* 2:1119–21.

Smith, C. U. M. 1964. *The architecture of the body.* London: Faber & Faber.

Smith, E. T. 1959. *Exploring biology.* 5th ed. New York: Harcourt Brace Jovanovich.

Speir, R. W., et al. 1970. *American Journal of Tropical Medicine and Hygiene* 19:692.

Swanson, C. P. 1960. *The cell.* Englewood Cliffs, N.J.: Prentice-Hall.

Troup, J. M., et al. 1970. *American Journal of Tropical Medicine and Hygiene* 19:695.

Tullis, J. L. 1953. *Blood cells and plasma proteins.* New York: Academic Press.

Turner, C. D. 1960. *General endocrinology.* Philadelphia: W. B. Saunders.

Varley, H. 1958. *Practical clinical biochemistry.* New York: Interscience Publishers.

Waddington, C. H. 1957. *The strategy of the genes.* London: Allen and Unwin.

Wallace, B. 1966. *Chromosomes, giant molecules, and evolution.* New York: W. W. Norton.

Watson, J. D. 1965. *The molecular biology of the gene.* New York: W. A. Benjamin.

Webb, P. A., et al. 1967. Some characteristics of Machupo virus, causative agent of Bolivian hemorrhagic fever. *American Journal of Tropical Medicine and Hygiene* 16:531–38.

Werner, S. C. 1962. *The thyroid.* New York: Paul B. Hoeber.

Whitby, L. E. H., and Britton, C. J. C. 1953. *Disorders of the blood.* London: Churchill.

White, H. A. 1972. Lassa fever, a study of 23 hospital cases. *Transactions of the Royal Society of Tropical Medicine and Hygiene* 66:390–98.

Wintrobe, M. M. 1956. *Clinical hematology.* Philadelphia: Lea & Febiger.

Zimmerman, B. 1952. *Endocrine functions of the pancreas.* Springfield, Ill.: Charles C. Thomas.

Index

ABOUT THE AUTHOR

JOHN G. FULLER is the author of the best sellers *Incident at Exeter, The Interrupted Journey,* and *The Day of St. Anthony's Fire,* as well as the more recent and highly acclaimed *200,000,000 Guinea Pigs.* He is also a playwright, has written, directed, and produced a number of TV documentaries, and has won an Emmy Award as producer of one of the *Great American Dream Machine* series. He lives in Weston, Connecticut.